Reflections
on Biblical Themes
by an Octogenarian

Reflections
on Biblical Themes
by an Octogenarian

REUBEN J. SWANSON

Wipf & Stock
PUBLISHERS
Eugene, Oregon

REFLECTIONS ON BIBLICAL THEMES BY AN OCTOGENARIAN

Copyright © 2007 Reuben J. Swanson. All rights reserved. Except for brief quotations in critical publications or reviews, no part of this book may be reproduced in any manner without prior written permission from the publisher. Write: Permissions, Wipf & Stock, 199 W. 8th Ave., Eugene, OR 97401.

ISBN 10: 1-59752-877-3
ISBN 13: 978-1-59752-877-1

Manufactured in the U.S.A.

Dedicated to

My Students

Who over the Years

Stimulated My Thought

and Enlarged my Growth

Spiritually and

Intellectually

Contents

Foreword · ix
In the Beginning · 1
The Conception and Birth of Jesus · 17
Genealogies in Matthew and Luke · 29
The Baptism of Jesus · 35
Signs and Wonder Stories in the Gospels · 43
The Gospel of Matthew as an Anti-Pauline Polemic · 69
Textual Criticism · 91
The Composition of the Gospels · 121

Foreword

❧ This series of essays represents my personal reflections upon a few Biblical themes that are relevant for my own faith and life. They do not, of course, exhaust my own thoughts and reflections upon these and other Biblical themes, but are indicators of the direction I take in my understanding and interpretation of Scripture. My insights and understanding of these themes have grown out of a lifetime in the ministry, in the classroom, and from my research into the text of the Greek New Testament. My analysis and viewpoint may not be acceptable to all readers, but how can we grow and expand our minds and spirits unless we consider points of view that seem at first to be inimical to our own faith and life?

My personal observations have led to the conclusion that there is much Biblical illiteracy manifested among people who have been life-long members of the church. I do not mean this to be ignorance of detail and general information of the Bible, but rather a lack of understanding of the deeper meaning of Scripture and its implications for our daily life. This lack of spiritual insight and understanding was well characterized by Bishop Hans Lilje in a speech delivered as long ago as 1948, who said, "The American people are hollow inside." He was speaking out of his own personal experiences as an anti-Nazi who was delivered fortuitously from death at the hands of Adolf Hitler. His observation, as a matter of fact, appropriately describes the universal condition of most Christians. What is even more dreadful to me is that we are not really very disturbed about our lack of spiritual depth. We most often avoid or are upset by difficult spiritual problems and questions. We are satisfied with a rather naive and childlike faith and understanding.

I am reminded of a Charles Schultz "Peanuts" cartoon of the '60s. Charlie Brown said to Linus, "You don't mean to tell me you bring that blanket to school with you? Don't all the kids laugh at you?" Linus replied, "Nobody laughs at a straight A average." Many of us look upon the Bible and our understanding of it as a security blanket. The possession of a Bible and our knowledge of it is our salvation. We have emptied the cross of

Foreword

Christ of its meaning and purpose. Knowledge has become our salvation, rather than a dying and rising experience with Christ as the Apostle Paul sets forth so succinctly in Galatians 2.19-20, "I have been crucified with Christ; and it is no longer I who live, but Christ who lives in me. And the life I now live in the flesh I live by faith in the Son of God, who loved me and gave himself for me."

It is my hope and prayer that these "Reflections" will stimulate thought and discussion, so that we together may attain to the full stature of the man or the woman in Christ. If this be the end result of my thoughts and reflections, I will give thanks to God who has created me and all that exists, to God who has redeemed me and made me to be a partaker of his gracious gift of life in heaven on earth.

In the Beginning

❧ How did our universe come into existence? Was it created? Or did it just happen in a great bang that occurred approximately fifteen billion years ago? Can we speak definitively about time periods of such magnitude? Or must we be silent and only let the affirmation of faith speak for us? Without question creation is a most nebulous subject for most of us. There are specialists who probe the vast expanses of the universe with powerful telescopes, who measure radiation in outer space emitted by that initial gigantic blast, as well as the radial velocity of distant objects that demonstrate to them that we live in an expanding universe with great distant galaxies larger than our Milky Way traveling in space at almost the speed of light. The topography of our planet Earth has been shaped by the inexorable forces of nature—wind, water, heat and cold—over more than four billions of years. In contrast, there are religious enthusiasts with very modest estimates of the age of the universe, who depict it as created in six of our working days only a few thousand years ago by the word of God. All the features of outer and inner space—galaxies, stars, planets, oceans, mountains, plains, minerals, fossils, living creatures—were brought into being and shaped into their present forms instantaneously by the word of the living and powerful God.

Is it possible to reconcile these two disparate views? To affirm that the picture of our universe painted by the scientist is largely authentic and at the same time to hold with the religious enthusiast that all has been created by God but over a tremendous span of time? Is there an irreconcilable conflict between a modern scientific understanding of the beginnings and of the evolution of our universe and a religious faith that attributes the existence of all that was, all that is, and all that will be to God?

My own point of view is that there is no conflict except in the minds of those who hold dogmatically to one view to the exclusion of the other. A dogmatic point of view cannot be attributed to one side only, for there are scientific as well as religious bigots, scientists and religionists who subscribe to very circumscribed and narrow opinions upon the subject under discussion. The principle that I would advance is that *the God of our religion and the God of our science are one and the same God.* That is to say, the God who has created me and all that exists is the God who created the faith in me to believe this. There are many, many mysteries still unsolved in matters scientific and religious, but the answers we have as to the origins and the actualities of our existence and of the meaning of our existence originate from the one source—the Creator God.

The Biblical Accounts of Creation

The substance of this discussion will focus upon the biblical accounts of creation as these are reported in the Book of Genesis, chapters one and two. The reference to plural accounts may even come as a surprise to some readers, since the emphasis in the discussion of creation has mostly been upon the more familiar narrative in chapter one. There is a second, an older and more primitive account, in chapter two that has not often received the attention it deserves in our discussions. The later account in chapter one portrays creation as an orderly progression from the origins of light to the origins of man in a series of events over a six day period; day after day God brings into existence higher and higher forms of material and physical existence until finally the ultimate is reached with the creation of man in the image of God himself.

This account of an orderly progression compares favorably in many aspects to the scientific understanding of the origins and development of life as set forth in the theory of evolution. The use of the term "theory" should not prejudice us against any particular viewpoint, scientific or religious, since there are no evidences to prove conclusively a case for either point of view. Ultimately, we must admit that whether we approach our subject from a scientific or from a religious point of view, we rely upon the premise of faith and not upon fact. That we have observed "things" to work in a certain way does not at all demonstrate that we know all there is to know upon the subject. We must acknowledge in all humility that what we think we know we know in part and always from a particular and subjective point of view. The scientist approaches the subject matter in a subjective way because he or she has been conditioned by a subjective system or society to observe and to examine the subject matter according to certain preconceived presuppositions in the same degree that the religious philosopher approaches his or her task. If there is any difference in degree of subjectivity, it is only the difference from observer to observer, whether scientist or religious philosopher, each of us being in bondage to a greater or lesser degree to our previous conditioning. We are never completely free from our past and from our conditioning. We are subjective in our observations and in our conclusions just because we are human. Our growth towards objectivity is always the struggle of a lifetime and wherever we are on the time scale of life the horizon before us is always growing and enlarging with new and exciting possibilities. Even what has just been said is only a possibility and not at all a probability, depending entirely upon our openness to the future.

The big-bang theory of the origins of the universe or the theory of evolution are neither the answer nor the obstacle in the way of our holding to a concept of creation. Rather they are working hypotheses that offer plausible explanations for some aspects of existence but not for all. This writer has no quarrel with these working hypotheses except to qualify some points with reference to the theory of evolution. The pattern of development set forth in the model of a tree with the beginning of the first one-celled plant or creature and the proliferation of all higher and more complex forms of life in a great series of mutations from that one beginning seem to this writer to be too narrowly circumscribed. If it was possible for carbon dioxide, methane, nitrogen, and steam to spontaneously evolve into life once, why not a number of times and in different places? And why not in different mixes, so that the resulting life forms were more or less complex and thus the bases for the resultant genera? Inasmuch as the basic building blocks of life, the amino acids and nucleotides, only differ qualitatively in all forms of life, there is a high probability that this goes back to their very beginnings. This possibility has greater plausibility to this writer than the explanation customarily offered. There are areas of the universe and of our existence that have not yet been explored, in part because of our ignorance of their existence and in part because we lack the tools for investigating many of the deep recesses of the universe and of human life. We forge ahead into the unknown both in our scientific and in our religious investigations with expectation and hope, always aware that the last word has not been said and that there are new concepts and new possibilities awaiting the intrepid and the open-minded.

The Biblical accounts of creation in the Book of Genesis are not to be taken as literal and factual descriptions of how and in what order things came into being. They are expressions of the faith of the community that identified itself as the people of God. The existence of the community as an historical entity was comparatively young when these accounts or confessions of faith were made. They reflect the cosmology, the world view, of the time in which they were composed and are not to be interpreted as appropriate for a twenty-first century understanding of the genesis or of the evolution of the universe and of life. The twenty-first century reader must see them against the backdrop of the time in which they were composed and the purpose for which they were intended. For example, the unusual feature of the author's account of creation in chapter one of Genesis is the affirmation that God created light on day one and only placed the sun, moon, and stars in the heavens on day four. Obviously, this cannot be the true order, for there could not have been vegetation and fruit-bearing trees on day three without the sun in its place. This order of the author results not from any observations of the way in which things happened, but is an expression of his religious intuition. If we are to understand the intention of the writer, we must divest ourselves of our twenty-first century presuppositions and enter into the historical and religious milieu of the sixth century before Christ.

The Creation Stories as a Confession of Faith

The most meaningful understanding of the cosmology and religious presuppositions reflected in chapter one of Genesis is to assume that this story of creation received its final formulation in the time of the Babylonian exile when the community of God's people had been uprooted from their land and taken as captives into a foreign country. In Babylon they were exposed to a high level culture and to a highly developed and sophisticated religion. The Babylonian empire was one of the greatest and most powerful of ancient times and its capital and religious center at Babylon on the Euphrates River was one of the wonders of the ancient world. The attractiveness of Babylonian culture and religion severely tested the faith of the captives, diluting and threatening their loyalty to their own religious and cultural tradition. The land of Judah was devastated, the temple at Jerusalem in ruins, the royal family and the leading citizens in captivity. The pathos, the tragedy, of the people is reflected in one of their hymns: "By the waters of Babylon, there we sat down and wept, when we remembered Zion. On the willows there we hung up our lyres. How shall we sing the Lord's song in a foreign land?" (Psalm 137.1–2, 4). Moreover, Marduk, god of Babylon, had overcome Yahweh, God of Israel, in his own land. In ancient times the gods were closely identified with the land and with the success or failure of a people in warfare. Natural disasters too were expressions of the anger of the god who ruled the land. Thus the exiles were sorely tempted to reject their ancestral faith, their religious heritage, even their God who had failed them in their time of crisis, and to adopt a new and more powerful god, Marduk. The great temple tower of Babylon towering high into the heavens was a far more impressive building than their own modest temple in Jerusalem that was now in ruins. The author of this creation story perceived the threat to Israel's future and formulated a confession of faith as an expression of the historic faith of Israel and also as a critique of the Babylonian religion.

Such an occasion for a confession of faith is not unusual. A parallel example would be the formulation of the Nicene Creed, one of the major confessions of the Christian community that was shaped and molded in a time when the community was under severe attack from within as to the verities of the faith. The great principle set forth in the confession of faith shaped and molded by the forces unleashed from without against the very existence of Israel as the people of God was that Elohim, the God of Israel, is the Creator and Lord of all. This is the firm conclusion of the author pronounced with assurance and certainty, in spite of the very fragile nature of the existence of the people of God.

A comment upon the name of God, Elohim, used in this confession of faith is in order here. This is a plural form of the god name, El, meaning "mighty one," common in ancient Mesopotamia and in Canaan before the coming of the Israelites from Egypt. The common use of the plural form, Elohim, does not refer to a plurality of gods, but rather to the divine power taken as a whole as it is revealed without any idea of a clearly defined divine person. Although we have said that the setting for this confession is Babylon in the sixth century before our era, the author gives to the confession the imprimatur of antiquity by using the earliest name for God from before the time of the patriarchs.

The name of God introduced to Israel in the time of Moses, Yahweh, meaning "he who causes to be," is reserved by this author for the Mosaic time period and thereafter when its use is historically correct. The god of Babylon, Marduk, who was now competing with Yahweh for the allegiance and loyalty of the Israelites, was the sun, that heavenly body worshipped most frequently in ancient and primitive cultures as the source of being. Nebuchadnezzar, king of Babylon, ruled by divine election, chosen and appointed by Marduk for his exalted position as ruler of Marduk's land. Marduk is supreme among the gods, the author and source of light and life, the very sun in the heavens. The author of our confession reduces Marduk to a lesser status, however, by the simple expedient of declaring that the sun, the moon, and the remaining heavenly bodies were created by Elohim, the one true God, and only on the fourth day of his creative acts. Light, the very essence and radiance of light, came to be in the very beginning as a result of the powerful word of Israel's God. The order of the creative acts is not only a defense of the God of Israel, but an attack upon the Babylonian premise that the sun is god. How can the sun be preeminent if it was placed in the heavens long after many other and more significant events had already occurred? The God of Israel is the source of light, not the sun, nor the moon, nor the stars.

The Place of Man in the Cosmos

Another significant feature of this confession of faith is the place of man, that is, the true Israelite, in the cosmos. Man, in Hebrew the word is Adam, is created in the image of God. This does not mean for the writer that man resembles God in any way physically, mentally, or spiritually. Rather man is given dominion, that is, authority, in the earth. He is to administer and exercise God's rule in the sphere of creation. God has created all that is and it is "very good." Man's calling is to use all of the created world for his own comfort and well-being and yet preserve the earth and all that is in it for the generations to come. His rule is not to be self-serving, destructive, or wasteful. He does not own the earth or the land; it is God's own possession. Man is God's steward. His vocation is to exercise careful and judicious stewardship over the earth to assure that future generations are blessed and served by him. The writer did not anticipate the problems of pollution, the waste of natural resources, the threat to man's environment so characteristic of our modern age and yet in a sense he did. He was aware that the wrong and destructive use of the resources of the earth would be detrimental and dangerous to the future of mankind.

We note also that man is male and female. Man is a generic term that encompasses both sexes. There is nothing of superiority here, male over female; rather there is equality of personhood and differences only in function. Man and woman together are to populate the earth and through concerted effort bring order out of chaos. Creation is not complete and finished with God's final word on day six. Rather creation is in a primitive and unfinished state, so that man's task is to develop, to cultivate, and to renew all that has been placed in his charge. This task male and female are to do together in partnership under the dominion of the God who had created them.

The Setting for "in the Beginning"

The setting for the author is "in the beginning," yet the beginning had no observers. The confession is marvelously descriptive of a sequence of events that are shrouded in the distant past, how distant the author could not know. If he composed in the sixth century before our era as we have surmised, he has reached back into a past that is lost to us and given an account that is true in essence but not in detail. Did he borrow from antiquity? Perhaps, since there are points of kinship between his description of cosmology, that is, his understanding of the universe, to that which is common in the Mesopotamian world from a much earlier time.

The universe is a three-tiered structure with the heavens above, the earth beneath, and the water under the earth. But evidently his basic motifs and content were more consonant with those concepts and practices that had developed in the worshipping community of Israel over many centuries of worship in the temple at Jerusalem. How much of the organization and arrangement of the material into the pattern in which it now appears in this confession of faith, or how much of the content has been provided by the author we cannot know, but it is not improbable that some of the arrangement and some of the content are his own contributions. The composer is never limited to the language or to the concepts of the past, but is always creative in the arrangement, the word choice, and especially in the meaning he indelibly imprints upon his composition. The references to the days of creation are vague and indistinct. It would be fortuitous if we could equate them with geological periods of time designed by specialists of this discipline in our twenty-first century, but such is not the case. This would be a kind of *eisegesis*, reading into the text our own presuppositions and subjective assumptions. This is the real problem of hermeneutics, or interpretation, that too often we have done just that. We have approached our biblical subject or our biblical study with our own agenda, looking for support and verification for a theology that has little rapport with scripture and more kinship with philosophy or sociology. Our text is suggestive and we are to be imaginative, but the rules of interpretation demand that our solutions be grounded in a knowledge of the language, the history, the sociology, the literature, and the religion of our source and in the times of which it speaks and the time in which it was composed. There is nothing basically contradictory in this confession of faith to a modern scientific view of "the beginning," but at the same time we cannot promulgate this text as a true and definitive account of "the beginning" superseding any of the findings or conclusions reached through a modern scientific approach. It is more proper in the opinion of this writer to view the two approaches, the religious or biblical and the scientific, as complementary and not mutually exclusive.

The Sabbath as the Setting for the Confession of Faith

The primary intention of the confession of faith is to provide the ground and the basis for the observance of a Sabbath day, a day of rest, by the worshipping community. On the seventh day, Elohim rested from all the creative work that he had done. In a similar way, man is to rest periodically and regularly from his normal activities as steward of the earth in order to set aside a time for response to and communion with his Creator God. Total attention to his own concerns can only result in a self-centered and self-indulgent creature. The center of the universe is not man but God. God the Creator is not a part of creation, but is totally independent and apart from it. He is above and beyond all that he has made; yet he is intimately involved in all that occurs within it. The universe, that is, earth and man, is his concern and his continuing activity is to guide and direct the course of history to the conclusion that he has appointed for it.

The origins of the Sabbath, the concept of a regular day of rest for worship and for a time of special attention to the concerns of the Creator God, are lost in antiquity. The writer's purpose here is to anticipate the establishment of such a day for the observance of the things of God in the Mosaic period, for there it is specifically stated in one of the primary commandments of the Mosaic code that man is to "remember the Sabbath day to keep it holy." Its observance became fixed very early in the life of the community of God's people and therefore was of prime importance to distinguish the believing Israelite from the people of the land of Babylon. In summary, the keeping of the Sabbath was an important witness to the commitment of the Israelite to the God of Israel and a confession of his faith to the unbelieving Babylonians among whom he lived. Thus the Sabbath is to be seen as the culmination of the writer's account of the creation of the universe by Elohim in six days and his declaration that God rested on the seventh day from all his work. The normative activities of God are set aside regularly and periodically for the renewal of his being. How necessary then for man created in the image of God to set aside a day from his normal activities in order that he might be renewed and re-created by his Creator for the vocation that has been entrusted to him.

The Second Account of Creation

When we turn to chapter two of Genesis, we enter a new and strange world. This account of creation is earlier in time by several centuries and is much more ancient and primitive in some of its detail. The earth and the heavens are made by God without reference to time, not even to "in the beginning." There is no vegetation, no rainfall, only a mist watering the face of the ground. In this barren setting God acts to create man. The setting for this act of God has no reference to probability, or even to possibility. Nevertheless the description of the creation of man is striking in its theological insight and perception. The Lord God formed man of dust from the ground, and breathed into his nostrils the breath of life; and man became a living being. It is Yahweh Elohim who acts in this account of the creation of man. The divine name revealed first to Moses and then through Moses to the people of God is used in this account of creation, the name Yahweh, meaning "he who causes to be." It is used in tandem with the older name for God already encountered in the later account of creation, Elohim, as discussed above. It is Yahweh Elohim who acts decisively to create. The life work of Moses is usually placed by critics in the thirteenth century before our era. This would translate into a date approximately B.C.E. 1250 according to our calendar. Therefore the use of the divine name Yahweh in the account of creation calls for an explanation.

The author of this second and earlier account of creation is usually identified by critics as the Yahwist, since he prefers to use the divine name Yahweh in his account of events even from the very beginning. Why does he do this, since obviously this is historically inaccurate? The earlier name, Elohim, by which God was addressed, and even the singular form El, is well documented in the traditions reaching back to early times. The author is not so concerned with historical accuracy as with another and more compelling concern. There is only one true God. Whatever he may have been called, he was and is Yahweh forever. Therefore it is theologically correct to address him by the unique and singular name Yahweh. The earlier divine name, Elohim, was probably not in his account, but was added by editors who joined the various strands of tradition together into a consecutive and orderly account sometime during the Babylonian exile, perhaps in the fifth century before our era.

The Yahwist wrote at a time when the Kingdom of Israel was at its zenith politically, that is, during the David—Solomon era. Saul, the first king of Israel, laid the foundations for a monarchy, but it was David who united the Israelite tribes and through a series of smashing military successes over neighboring states molded the conquered area into a kingdom that became the dominant power in the area east of the Mediterranean Sea in the tenth century before our era. The kingdoms of Egypt and Mesopotamia had all suffered declines and the vacuum was filled by this new and astute empire builder. His son and successor, Solomon, did not add new territory but carried forward the process of inner development and exploitation of the resources, including a massive program of building that included the temple at Jerusalem.

A New Threat to the Faith

A new threat to the faith of Israel emerged at this time, resulting in part from the many alliances with neighboring kingdoms sealed by marriage between the royal houses and in part from the trade and commerce with

In the Beginning

these kingdoms. Foreign ideas, customs, and even religious practices were introduced that, along with the growing emphasis upon wealth, luxury, the enslavement of captive peoples, and particularly nationalism, threatened the religious basis of the community. The Yahwist composed his epic account as a challenge to the alien religious ideas and practices that were infiltrating the community of God's people and weakening their loyalty to the one true God. His intention is to focus attention upon the purpose for which Yahweh has called Israel out of slavery in Egypt and established her in the land of promise. Israel is called to be a blessing to the nations. It is a perversion of her calling to become like the nations, to set priorities and goals that are basically materialistic and self-seeking. The author's theological perspective is unbounded and universal. What Israel has received as blessing from the one true God, Yahweh, is to be shared with all nations and all peoples. His insights and perceptions at such an early date in the history of mankind, or even in the history of the community of God's people, are unique and exceptional. He anticipates the great eighth century prophets and their universal viewpoint that mankind is one family created by the one true God and called to live together for the mutual good of all.

The Meaning of "Man"

Who is man? Yahweh Elohim formed man (*'adam*) of dust from the ground (*'adamah*), and breathed into his nostrils the breath of life; and man became a living being. Man is creature, created of dust, of the basic elements of which the universe is composed. Therefore man is related to earth out of which he came and to all life that springs from the dust of the earth. How prophetic of our twenty-first century image of man, for we and all life, whether plant or animal, are shaped out of the same basic building blocks, the amino acids and nucleotides, common to the simplest forms of one-celled plants and animals and to man, the most complex of all creatures. The thread of unity and harmony runs through the entire constituency of the universe, whether we study a speck of dust from our planet's surface or probe the farthest reaches of outer space with powerful telescopes.

We are dust, but we are more than dust and this is the genius of the Yahwist to have perceived a dimension to our being that transcends the dust out of which we have come. Yahweh Elohim formed man of dust from the ground, and breathed into his nostrils the breath of life. The distinctive element that sets man apart from all plant life, from all creatures, is the inbreathing by God. It must be more than a happy coincidence that the word for wind or breath and the word for spirit are one and the same in the Hebrew and Greek languages. The Hebrew word, *ruach*, and the Greek word, *pneuma*, fulfill this dual capacity. Thus when God breathes into man, a creature of dust, that lump of dirt is inspirited and comes alive, a living being.

What is the Yahwist telling us by his description of man as a lump of dirt transformed into a living being? There is something so profound here that it boggles the imagination. It is incredible that an unknown thinker four thousand years ago could have arrived at such a profound concept of being. On the one hand, man is creature shaped of the same material as all creatures with physical capacities inferior to some and superior to other creatures. On the other hand, man is creature endowed with mental capacities that distinguish and set him apart from all living beings. All this was without doubt readily apparent to the Yahwist. But the quality of being that he perceived in man alone, a quality not found in other creatures except perhaps to a minimal degree, is the potential for man to be spiritual. The inbreathing, the inspiriting of God, gives to man a dimension, a quality, which sets him apart from all life. Without that inbreathing man is creature with physical and mental traits marking him as superior to some and inferior to others. But inbreathed by the breath, the spirit of God, man comes alive. He becomes aware of the Creator God who has made him and of his potential for life on a new and higher level, a life lived in trusting relationship with God and in loving relationship with man. He becomes aware that it is his glory to be preeminent among the creatures and that his preeminence is a gift and an opportunity to tend the earth and keep it.

The Highest Level for Human Attainment

Life can be lived on more than one level. The genius of the Yahwist was to perceive that the highest level for human attainment is possible only through the inbreathing of God. Only in and through the divine inbreathing is it possible for the potential within creature man to be stimulated and set free, so that he might attain to the highest levels of spiritual understanding and expression. Man alone of all created beings has the possibility and the potential to realize a three dimensional life in which body, mind, and spirit achieve the highest attainments, but only through the inbreathing, the inspiriting of God. Man is unique but his uniqueness is only latent and unrealized until he is in a true knowing, trusting, and responsive relationship with his Creator. Without that inbreathing he is creature; he is born, he lives, he dies, he returns to the dust out of which he came. But inbreathed by God and responsive to that inbreathing his life is unending. His future is forever.

Since we have acknowledged in our discussion that the scientific dating of the beginnings of our universe is intrinsically acceptable to a religious understanding of creation, that is to say, that this event took place some fifteen billions of years ago, the question rises as to the beginnings of human life. When did human beings first appear on this great time scale? The anthropologist searching for clues and evaluating the evidence has come to the conclusion that the emergence of man as a distinct genus came approximately three million years ago. Where then are we to place the Yahwist's Adam on this time scale? There is no suggestion as to a date or an historic time in our biblical account. The event of creation and the advent of man belong to prehistory. It would not be correct in the view of this writer to equate or identify biblical man with the precursors of *Homo Sapiens* identified by the anthropologist. What then? Who is our biblical Adam?

The Biblical Adam

Adam represents the breakthrough in the history of man from bondage to creature hood, from finitude to authentic life, to the life of spirit. Through billions of years from the first beginnings of the universe, through millions of years from the first beginnings of the emergence of man, there has been forward movement through countless mutations to higher and more complex forms of material existence. And, finally, the culmination is reached with the unleashing of man the creature from bondage to his focus only upon satisfying the needs and appetites of his body and mind to realize authentic being as man who is the handiwork of God, inbreathed and inspirited by the Creator to realize his full potential as spiritual being. There have been numerous breakthroughs in the history of mankind that have been all-important and decisive for his future, but none to compare to this breakthrough into self-realization and self-awareness as to his place and role in the total design and purpose of the universe. Man alone is singularly blessed with this knowledge and understanding. With this gift given through the breath of God comes man's calling to live up to his potential, to fulfill his role as caretaker and steward of the earth, of all plants and creatures in it, and even of the universe itself.

A New Concept of Community

The first Adam, a member of the genus *Homo Sapiens* that had developed and burgeoned over eons of time, was already deeply rooted in the community of family. The revelation that came to him in this moment of inbreathing by God distinguished and set him apart from all members of the community and at the same time opened the way to a new concept of community that was no longer narrow and provincial but as inclusive as the universe. There were sharp distinctions and differences between the inbreathed and the not inbreathed. The highest role of the true Adam was to share his insight, his understanding, his perception, his new dimension of personhood with all those around him to the end that his gift from God become the common property of the entire human family.

That process continues to the present day and will continue to the end of time. For this dimension of personhood is not transferred from generation to generation through the genes, that is, through the procreation of the human race. Each individual begins where pre-Adam began as a creature of body, mind, and soul awaiting the inbreathing of God to awaken the life of spirit, the awareness of personhood, the sense of calling and purpose that comes to life when the Creator God breathes into each one the breath of life. Without this inbreathing man is creature living below the level of humanity, striving towards his own goals, sating his appetite for things, and when his last day has come sinking into the abyss of nothingness and oblivion. Inbreathed by God, man knows his highest purpose is to be the intermediary through whom the Creator continues to inbreathe and create the life of the spirit universally.

Conclusions

The two accounts of creation were written at different times in history and under very different circumstances. The one is a classic expression of the "who" of creation; the other a most insightful perception into the nature of personhood. Both affirm unequivocally that the God of Israel is Creator and Lord of all that was, of all that is, and of all that will be. Both affirm that apart from the Creator God there is no authentic existence. To be at one with God is the wellspring of life, for from that relationship of recognition and acknowledgment rises the possibility to be and to do that which is far above and beyond the capacity of creature hood.

The contributions of the ancient biblical writers to our twenty-first century understanding of the universe and of human life are immeasurable. How impoverished we are, how lacking in spirit, when we choose to ignore or discard them. Their reflections, not so much upon the "how" of creation or the order of creation, manifest a profound probing into the meaning of existence, a probing that is most provocative to the mind that still searches for answers today. The Yahwist, for example, who antedated a Plato or an Aristotle by several centuries, had already arrived at germinal ideas of the nature of human existence that are still fresh and stimulating. Unfortunately, these ideas have mostly been lost to us because they were set forth in what are considered by many to be merely sectarian religious writings of little importance for modern man. Our egotism, our sophistication, is often our worst enemy, preventing us from perceiving and learning from the giants of the past just because they are ancient.

Perhaps the most valuable lesson of all that we might learn from a review of their thoughts upon the origin and the meaning of existence is humility. In reality, we know so little of the universe that is our home and so little of man the most complex of all the creatures inhabiting the universe that we ought not disparage those ancients who probed so unerringly into the deepest mysteries and suggested for our consideration possibilities that far exceed in profundity our sophisticated explanations. What does it profit us if we arrive at answers to the deep mysteries of the "how" of our origins and utterly fail to perceive the meaning and the purpose of it all?

The Conception and Birth of Jesus

☙ The conception and birth of Jesus of a virgin is one of those peripheral references in our gospels that has attained a central place in the theology of the church. The word "virgin," *parthenos* in Greek, occurs in only two passages, the first in chapter one of Matthew, a quote from Isaiah 7.14, and the second in chapter one of Luke's gospel. The passages are as follows: "Behold, a virgin shall conceive and bear a son, and his name shall be called Emmanuel" (Matthew 1.23) and "In the sixth month the angel Gabriel was sent from God to a city of Galilee named Nazareth, to a virgin betrothed to a man whose name was Joseph, of the house of David; and the virgin's name was Mary" (Luke 1.26–27). Matthew has prefaced his citation from Isaiah with a reference that implies the virginity of Mary, although this is not precisely stated: "When his mother Mary had been betrothed to Joseph, before they came together she was found to be with child of the Holy Spirit" (Matthew 1.18).

Strangely, there is no reference to the virgin conception and birth elsewhere in our New Testament, not even in the remainders of the gospels of Matthew and Luke. There is no reference in John's gospel, in the writings of Paul, nor in any of the canonical epistles. Even more striking is the absence of any suggestion in the main bodies of the gospels of Matthew and Luke that their reference to the conception and birth from a virgin has in any way influenced their image of Jesus as they portray his life and ministry throughout the course of their gospels. Immediately it becomes apparent that the scriptural support for this highly regarded teaching is very minimal. Only two references and one of these a quotation of a highly questionable passage found in Old Testament Isaiah. Why then has this teaching attained such preeminence in the theology of the church that a denial of its validity has been cause for persecution and even banishment as a heretic? My purpose is to examine the passages cited and the theology that has grown from them, and to suggest an alternative interpretation of the passages that have given birth to this theology.

The Problem of Legitimacy

The suggestion is made in the essay on "Genealogies" that the conception and birth of Jesus had created problems for the Christian community. Evidently there was a question about his legitimacy. Matthew in particular suggests this when he writes, "When his mother Mary had been betrothed to Joseph, before they came together she was found to be with child of the Holy Spirit." Evidently there was no refuting the reality of Mary's pregnancy prior to her marriage to Joseph, but the assumption is made that this pregnancy is of the Holy Spirit and not of human origins. This assumption, of course, is a very untenable conclusion from a rational point of view. Later Jewish sources refer to an illicit relationship between Mary and a Roman soldier resulting in the conception and birth of Jesus. Thus the references in Matthew and Luke to Jesus' conception and birth from a virgin appear to be an apology, that is, a defense or a response to these charges. Since Jesus was recognized and adored in the community as Savior and Lord and since there was a question as to the propriety of his conception and birth or at least a lack of knowledge of the attendant circumstances with which to refute the slanderous charges, one solution was to formulate stories that attest to his miraculous conception and birth of a virgin. His conception and birth was not as other men or as an ordinary man. God intervened in a unique and supernatural way, and Mary was with child of the Holy Spirit. Such a claim raises the question above the level of criticism and controversy.

Matthew documents the validity of the claim of the community by an appeal to scripture. This is in character with his method of finding proof texts from the scriptures to support his thesis that Jesus is the fulfillment of scripture and of God's plan of redemption. The validity of this method is open to question as will be pointed up in other references in our essays. Furthermore, there is a problem with the citation of Isaiah 7.14, since the author of Matthew cites the Septuagint, the Greek translation of the Jewish scriptures that were composed in Hebrew. The Hebrew text that reads, "an *'amah* (young woman) shall conceive and bear a son," is translated in the Septuagint by the Greek word, *parthenos*, "virgin." *'Amah* has no connotation of virginity, but refers to a young woman, either married or unmarried, and in the context of Isaiah unquestionably refers to a young married woman. The problem for this writer with Matthew's use of scripture is

The Conception and Birth of Jesus

precisely this: he searches scripture to find passages that he believes support his thesis concerning Jesus, takes them out of context, and embodies them with a meaning inappropriate to their original context and intention. Perhaps his use of this particular passage from Isaiah and its application to the birth of Jesus is excusable, since the Septuagint translation of *'amah* by *parthenos* is so appropriate for what he is attempting to do. But the question rises whether it is ever necessary or appropriate to defend or rationalize the acts of God. The Apostle Paul, citing Isaiah 40.13 "Who has known the mind of the Lord, or who has been his counselor?", properly rejects this approach. There is always a flaw in the method of using proof texts to demonstrate a particular thesis, even though this particular example has resulted in a veritable superstructure supporting the supernatural birth of Jesus and his divinity as well. The question remains whether such proof can be found or whether the proof offered is authentic and necessary.

The Role of Dreams in Matthew

According to the author of Matthew, the information about the conception by the Holy Spirit is communicated to Joseph by an angel of the Lord who appears in a dream. It is apparent that the central figure in the birth stories in this gospel is Joseph, not Mary. This is only one of four revelations to Joseph communicated to him by an angel through a dream. The angel of the Lord directs him to flee to Egypt to save the young child from the attempt of Herod to take his life (2.12), informs him of the death of Herod and bids him return to the land of Israel (2.19), and sends him to Galilee to circumvent the threat from Archelaus (2.22). In addition, the wise men are warned in a dream not to return to Herod (2.12). These references point up the mythological character of the birth narratives in this gospel. Myth does not denote that these stories are untrue. Myth is a way of portraying historical events according to the world view of the people and of the time. Just as the world view of the Yahwist was mythological—his three tiered universe with the heavens above, the earth beneath, and the water under the earth, so the world view of the gospel writers is mythological with their references to angels and divine guidance through dreams.

But there is something more here that needs to be noted. Why do dreams play such a prominent role in this account? Immediately it becomes apparent that the writer is steeped in the ancient religious traditions of

19

Israel. Who is Joseph, referred to as the father of Jesus in verse 16, "Jacob the father of Joseph the husband of Mary, of whom Jesus was born"? Does not this call to mind the patriarch Joseph? Was not the distinguishing feature of the patriarch his dreams and his ability to interpret them? Is it not probable then that the name Joseph, known as the husband of Mary and father of Jesus, stimulated the author of our gospel to create by analogy a similar pattern of divine guidance for his leading character in these stories?

The Use of Mythology

There is no supporting documentation for the visit by the wise men, the murder of the children at Bethlehem by Herod, or the sojourn in Egypt of the child Jesus. The visit by the wise men, or magi, is particularly instructive as to the use of mythology and burgeoning of tradition in the early community. The three become Oriental kings identified as Gaspar, Melchior, and Balthasar by a later generation. The appearance of the star in the east was the signal to the three, members of a hereditary priestly class among the ancient Medes and Persians, of the birth of a king. The connection is not made, but it should be remembered that the Jews had been ruled by the Persians from approximately B.C.E. 539 when Cyrus the Great conquered Babylon to their overthrow by Alexander the Great, the founder of the vast Macedonian Empire, in B.C.E. 331. Perhaps there were bits of Jewish lore concerning a coming king that had filtered down to Persian society and to this priestly class of magi during this long period of association. Astrology, initiated and practiced in ancient Mesopotamia from the time of the Assyrians who emerged approximately at the time of David's kingdom, had developed into a system of beliefs that the heavenly bodies exercised a strong influence over the lives and affairs of the human family.

The appeal of astrology is still strong in our twenty-first century in the lives of the many who religiously consult their astrological tables, although there is not an iota of evidence to support the claims made by practitioners. We are so mesmerized and awed by Matthew's account of the appearance of the star in the east to guide the magi that we have lost our critical acumen to evaluate the myth. There have been numerous efforts by modern astronomers to equate the star in the east with a conjunction of planets that supposedly occurred at the time of or soon after the birth of Jesus. The problem is that we have no fixed date for his birth, inasmuch as our gospel records are incomplete and our present calendar that identifies the year C.E. 1 as the year of his birth is evidently in error, as noted elsewhere. But a larger problem is the account that says the magi sighted the star in the east and traveled west, or more correctly southwest, to Jerusalem. Evidently the star disappeared for a time, for they had to make inquiries as to the place of the birth of the king of the Jews. When they resumed their journey, "the star that they had seen in the east went before them, till it came to rest over the place where the child was. . . . and going into the house they saw the child. . . ." (Matt. 2.9, 11). Modern astronomy would find it difficult indeed to verify such phenomena, for the movement of stars and/or planets has never been known from observation to be so precise a directive.

Other Motifs in the Matthean Account

There are a number of motifs that play a role in this formulation of the birth narratives by our author in addition to the "Joseph motif" and the "angel and dream motif" referred to above. There is the motif of the wicked king who seeks to destroy the infant Jesus who is destined to be the deliverer of his people from oppression just as the wicked Pharaoh sought to destroy the infant Moses who was born to deliver his people from Egypt. There is the motif of the descent into and the coming forth from Egypt of the infant Jesus, essentially a recapitulation of the history of God's people in Egypt and the history of salvation. There is the motif of the continuing threat in the land of promise, so that the child Jesus as Israel of old must take refuge in an isolated locale until he comes of age. The reader must judge whether these are authentic accounts of historical events or whether the author has set forth in these constructions his faith that the inscrutable purpose of God will come to fulfillment despite the peril and threat that constantly confronts the young and endangered Christian community. These are themes and motifs created and developed by a highly fertile and imaginative mind. They become prosaic and dull when subjected to our proclivity to read them as factual and literal accounts of reality. They are expressions of the worshipping community and to be cherished not as history but as interpretation of the event of salvation, an event so marvelous that it is impossible to depict the reality and the fullness of it in human language.

The Lukan Account

Luke's account is to be read in a similar fashion. When compared to Matthew's account, the narratives in Matthew and Luke are mostly divergent and conflicting in their detail. The points of agreement are limited to the reference to the conception and birth of a virgin, the names of the principal characters—Joseph, Mary, and Jesus—a birth in Bethlehem but under quite different and irreconcilable circumstances, and a growing up in Nazareth. To sharpen the contrast between the two accounts, let it be noted that according to Matthew Joseph and Mary are residents of Bethlehem and it may be presumed that Jesus is born in their home, whereas in Luke's account their residence is in Nazareth and they only come to Bethlehem to fulfill the conditions of a census that has been appointed by Caesar Augustus. Thus it is only by chance or by divine guidance that Jesus is born in a stable in Bethlehem, which in itself is an assumption since the only reference is that the newborn baby was "laid in a manger." If these stories were not side by side in our scripture, it might even create a problem of identity; are the two authors speaking of the conception and birth of the same person?

Luke is the liturgist with his hymns and liturgical settings. There is no scriptural documentation as in Matthew to demonstrate the authenticity of the claim that Jesus is born of a virgin. The angel Gabriel appeared in Nazareth "to a virgin betrothed to a man whose name was Joseph, of the house of David" (Luke 1.26–27). There is the same link that Joseph is the father of Jesus in Luke's genealogy as in Matthew's, but he has placed the genealogy after the baptism of Jesus rather than prior to his birth as in Matthew. But this link conflicts with the references in the conception and birth accounts that state that Mary was a virgin and refer to Joseph only as a surrogate father. Why list genealogies at all and why trace them through Joseph, since he was not the father of Jesus? Luke suggests that Mary was of the tribe of Levi (1.36) and not of Judah, the tribe from which David was descended. The key, as we have noted, is that a link must be forged with David, since the Messiah was to descend from that great king.

Two Supernatural Births in Luke

Luke even outdoes Matthew in his zeal for the miraculous, for he tells of two supernatural births, prefacing the birth of Jesus of a virgin with the birth of John to the aged couple, Zechariah and Elizabeth. Elizabeth, as Sarah of old, is beyond the age for child bearing; yet she who was barren conceives in her womb and bears a son who becomes the forerunner and announcer of the Messiah. A second unusual, if not supernatural birth, that of Samuel, may also be in the background, especially since there are clear points of reference between Hannah's prayer in First Samuel 2.1–10 and Mary's "Magnificat" in Luke 1.46–55. Again it is probable that this author has taken motifs from scripture and formulated a story to enhance the marvel of the event of salvation.

Mary Plays the Leading Role in Luke

Luke's narrative also differs from Matthew's account by focusing attention upon Mary, the mother of Jesus, rather than upon Joseph. The revelation of the impending birth of this child is given by the angel Gabriel to Mary, not to Joseph. Mary formulates the great hymn we entitle "The Magnificat," although some Old Latin texts attribute this to Elizabeth. Joseph is more of a prop in the narrative of the birth at Bethlehem, a kind of onlooker rather than an active participant, since it is Mary who does the wrapping of the child and also keeps and ponders in her heart all that is told them by the shepherds. Simeon addresses his prophecy concerning the future of the child to Mary and she is a leading actor in the account of the second visit to the temple when the boy Jesus is twelve years of age. This is in character with the tendency of this author to emphasize the role of women throughout his gospel narrative in contrast to Matthew and the other evangelists. Elizabeth, Anna the prophetess, and especially Mary are all in the forefront, whereas the male characters only play supporting roles or even fade into the background.

The Problem with a Virgin Conception and Birth

How did the idea of a virgin conception and birth originate? Is it true in a literal sense? Or was it created by the early Christians to defend their beloved Jesus from slander and to give to him a more than proper birth certificate? The question of virgin conception and birth is a live issue from a scientific point of view, since conception and birth within the human family without insemination by a male is to this time impossible. There must always be appended this qualification to such a statement, since we must acknowledge that there is much that we do not know and perhaps can never know in spite of the great progress of scientific investigation. For the present we must acknowledge from a scientific point of view that virgin conception and birth is an improbability, if not even an impossibility. There is no problem from a religious point of view for those who interpret the scripture literally, for Luke the Evangelist says through the angel Gabriel, "with God nothing will be impossible" (Luke 1.37). How are these two points of view to be reconciled? How can the sophisticate of the twenty-first century hold to both conclusions that are in fact contradictory?

Virgin conception and birth is not a real option for a twenty-first century scientist. Conception and birth in the human family normally results from the joining of the male sperm with the female ovum in the womb of the mother, although there are some differentiation from the norm in our twenty-first century laboratories. But the point remains that the conception of Jesus in the womb of Mary either was the result of a union with an unknown male or with Joseph. The alternative is to accept the conclusion of the religious believer that God intervened directly in this one birth and that the conception of Jesus was the result of Mary's impregnation by the Holy Spirit. If the latter is our conclusion, then the question rises, Does God ever act in that way? Is it consistent with the nature of God whom we know through scripture and through faith to violate the laws of nature that govern the universe that he has made? If the universe is the result of his creative act and if the universe is governed by laws or principles that are expressions of God's will, how is it possible for God who is true and trustworthy in all that he does to violate from time to time in a capricious and inconstant way his own principles or laws? Is it ever safe to maintain even in defense of his divine majesty that the end justifies the means?

The Integrity of God

My mind and heart affirm the integrity of God. God is faithful, God is trustworthy, God is true. This is the cornerstone of my life to affirm with the Apostle Paul, "Let God be true though every man be false" (Romans

3.4). The view that "all things are possible to God" grows out of our human weakness and not out of our strength. Our strength, the only strength for us, is God's strength in us. The image of God that is sealed upon our hearts must be freed from every idol, from every human desire and endeavor to find security in that which is not God.

My own point of view is an integration and an expression of all the knowledge that has come to me from science and from religion. Jesus is born of woman as every human and in the same way that every human is conceived and born. Even our confession that "he was conceived by the Holy Spirit" does not distinguish him from our conception and birth. If God is Creator, as we affirm in another article of our faith, than *each one of us is conceived and born of the Holy Spirit.* Our conception and birth is not simply or merely the result of a natural process of procreation. Each one of us is the handiwork of God who in a unique creative act has brought me and every human into being. God is never aloof or far removed from the universe that he has made. He is not a part of it, but is above and beyond it. But at the same time he is intimately involved in every new life that comes into existence, whether plant or animal or human, because he is always and ever the Creator God. He creates moment by moment in the same dynamic and wise way that he has always created and always will create. There has never been an interruption of his creative work nor a violation of the process that he instituted from the very beginning of time. God is God and it is for us to let him be God, rather than to fashion and shape a creature God in the image of man.

The Pauline View

How then, if Jesus was conceived and born in the same and natural way as we are, can he be distinguished from us to be our Savior and Lord? He is one with us in conception and birth, in life, in nature, in his humanity, but he is called and set apart by the Creator and Redeemer God for his unique role as Savior. The Apostle Paul states the reality in this way, "the gospel concerning his son, who was descended from David according to the flesh and designated Son of God with power according to the Spirit of holiness by his resurrection from the dead, Jesus Christ our Lord" (Romans 1.3–4). There is no reliance upon miraculous conception and birth, no dependence upon a divine human, but only the qualification that he was descended from David according to the flesh. The distinction is in his calling and in his resurrection, a unique creative act of God, a creative act that is not all that different from the rebirth that we see in nature and in the human family constantly. This is what sets Jesus apart, for God has acted through this one man to reconcile the entire creation and especially the entire human family to himself.

What then is the meaning of the "virgin conception and birth theology" that we find in the opening chapters of the gospels of Matthew and Luke? Did they intend their words to be read literally? Did they intend to set up criteria to measure the faith or faithfulness of the members of the community? Is the confession or the acknowledgment that Jesus was actually and literally born from a virgin a *sine qua non* for faith? Is this one of those beliefs that is essential for salvation and for remaining within the good graces of God? I think not and I would propose another and distinctive possibility, a new interpretation of what the evangelists had in view.

A Reinterpretation of the Gospel Accounts

Inasmuch as no canonical New Testament writing other than the opening chapters of the gospels of Matthew and Luke make any reference to a virgin conception and birth and inasmuch as this was not the theology of the earliest Christian believers and inasmuch as the evidence suggests that his origins created problems for the church, it is altogether possible that he was an illegitimate child. Is this the death knell for our faith in Jesus as God's Son and our Savior? Not at all! It is very possible that this is what the Apostle Paul refers to in First Corinthians when he writes, "God chose what is foolish in the world to shame the wise, God chose what is weak in the world to shame the strong, God chose what is low and despised in the world, even things that are not, to bring to nothing things that are, so that no human being might boast in the presence of God" (1.27–29). Was Paul aware of the question of Jesus' illegitimate birth? Probably. How could any believer of the time be unaware. Was it a stumbling block to Paul? Not at all. For God chooses what is low and despised to carry forward his great plan and purpose for the redemption of the entire human family. Who would have been lower or more despised in that generation than a child born out of wedlock? The attitudes of many of us towards such an innocent have hardly changed over the centuries. What could be more damning to the criteria we have set up for God to be God than his choice of an illegitimate child to be raised from such ignominy to his position of lordship over all?

Our Salvation Always and Ever of God

What did the evangelists intend by their references to the virgin conception and birth of Jesus? Is it possible that they were simply enunciating their faith that our salvation is beyond the reach and the capacity of man? Is it possible that they were setting forth in a worshipful and reverent way that the ways of God are beyond our understanding? For who has known the mind of the Lord, and who has been his counselor? There is nothing inconsistent or contradictory in their teaching when understood in this way with the Pauline point of view expressed in the words, "by grace you have been saved through faith; and this is not your own doing, it is the gift of God" (Ephesians 2.8). God alone accomplishes our salvation without any assistance from us; in fact, God works his work of grace in us in spite of our resistance and our efforts to second-guess and improve upon what he has done. Jesus is Jesus without regard to human origins, or manner of coming into the world, or credentials, or legitimacy. He is Jesus, our Lord and Savior, because God has chosen him, God has appointed him, God was in him reconciling us to himself. The marvel of God is just this that he calls those who are unworthy—sinners, unrighteous, those whom he has every right to throw upon the trash heap, and through them accomplishes his work of grace. The evidence is in scripture itself, when we consider the life history of a few of the great personages in the history of salvation—Moses, David, and Saul who became Paul. And he has called *you* and *me* to be his disciples, witnesses to his grace and of our salvation.

The virgin conception theology is one of the most sublime expressions of the human spirit, liberated from the dungeons of ignorance, from bondage to sin and ego, and enlightened by God's Spirit to confess with reverence and awe, "I believe in God the Father, I believe in God the Son, I believe in God the Holy Spirit."

Genealogies in Matthew and Luke

ঞ The genealogies in our two gospels, Matthew and Luke, may seem to be uninteresting topics for discussion. We are mostly bored by a long list of names, many of which are unfamiliar and never referred to in another Biblical passage. Numerous genealogical tables in the Old Testament are never listed as favorite passages for our devotional reading. But these tables are of high importance because they provide the background for an understanding of the need for and the purpose of the genealogical tables in our gospels.

There are numerous examples in the Old Testament of historical crises in the life story of God's people, Israel, when their future, both physically and spiritually, was in jeopardy. One of the most serious of these was the exile to Babylon in B.C.E. 587. The land of Judah was devastated, Jerusalem and the temple in shambles, and their religious heritage threatened by exposure to a superior religious culture. The people of God survived this threat largely because of the devotion and commitment of their religious leaders, the prophets and priests. A new chapter began in their religious development in B.C.E. 540 with the rise to power of the Persian king, Cyrus the Great. He gave them a choice—remain in the land of Babylon or return to Jerusalem. Many chose the second option. Their problems did not abate, however, since they had to rebuild their homes and restore the land to productivity. A first option was the rebuilding of the temple, a very important option since the Mosaic law required worship and sacrificial rituals that could not be observed apart from the temple. There were threats from the inhabitants of the land, especially the descendants of the northern Israelites, whose capital had been Samaria. There had been rivalry and strife between the northern Israelites (Ephraim) and the southern Israelites (Judah) ever since the breakup of David's kingdom after the death of Solomon. The northern kingdom came to an end in B.C.E. 721 when Samaria was destroyed by the Assyrians and the people deported and scattered throughout that vast kingdom. The Assyrians imported exiles into Samaria from many parts of their kingdom and eventually religious practices and ideals changed radically as a result of their influence upon the Samarians. Intermarriage resulted in ethnic differences as well.

Upon their return from Babylon, the Judahites were confronted by the problem of relationships with the inhabitants of the land—Samarians to the north and descendants of their own people who had not gone into exile. The latter had belonged to a lower class of society and the lack of spiritual leadership had resulted in a degeneration of their faithfulness to the Mosaic religion. Intermarriage with Samarians and with people brought into the land by the Assyrians had also weakened their religious loyalties. Their desire to share in the rebuilding of the temple and in the worship of the new community founded by those who came from Babylon led to conflict. Those who had returned from Babylon did not consider the inhabitants of the land to be true Israelites. They excluded them from the congregation of God's people and rejected their overtures for help in rebuilding the temple.

Conditions for Membership in the Community of Israel

When Nehemiah came from Persia to become the head of the new community in Jerusalem, he enacted a number of conditions for membership in Israel. Two of the more important were faithfulness to the Mosaic religion and second, proper birth credentials. Genealogical tables came to be highly important because intermarriages with the inhabitants of the land now made it incumbent upon the member of the community to document his lineage to meet the second of the above criteria. Nehemiah even enacted legislation to forcibly separate intermarriages, since they did not meet the requirements for membership in the community. This episode in history accounts for the preparation and inclusion of genealogical tables in the Old Testament and throws light upon the reason for the preparation of a genealogy for Jesus, two of which are included in the gospels of Matthew and Luke.

Difficult questions were raised for the Christian community by the Jews of the time about the legitimacy of Jesus. They rejected the use of their scripture by the Christians to prove that Jesus was the Messiah and counterattacked by questioning his legitimacy. Jewish sources from the time respond to Christian propaganda by stating that Jesus was born from an illicit union between Mary and a Roman soldier. It was necessary, therefore, for the Christians to refute this slander by demonstrating that Jesus was a true Jew of proper birth and that he was faithful to the Mosaic tradition in his teaching and in his deeds. Since the gospels of Matthew and Luke speak to this issue specifically by presenting a genealogy of Jesus, it is apparent that it was a very live question at the time of their writing.

A Comparison of the Two Genealogies

A comparison of the two genealogies raises new problems, however. Matthew begins his genealogy with Abraham and traces the family tree in a descending line to Jesus through Joseph. Luke begins with Joseph and traces the family tree in an ascending line to Adam the son of God. Matthew's genealogy is more provincial; Luke's more universal. But serious discrepancies appear between the two lists. Matthew's list is constructed in a symmetrical pattern of three groups of fourteen names. A count demonstrates that a name is missing in group three, which was probably the result of a scribal omission very early in the history of the transmission of the text, since there is no textual evidence for the necessary fourteenth name to complete the symmetry. Matthew's forty-two names (actually forty-one in our texts) from Jesus to Abraham become fifty-seven in Luke's list. There are fifteen names, not fourteen, from Abraham to David and forty-two names, not twenty-seven, from David to Jesus in Luke's family tree.

The internal discrepancies are even more serious, since Matthew traces the descent from David through Solomon and Luke from David through Nathan. From that point there is total disagreement between the two lists except for the two names Zerubbabel and Shealtiel during the period of the Babylonian exile. In fact, the grandfathers of Jesus are different in the two genealogies, Joseph being the son of Jacob in Matthew and the son of Heli in Luke. Every effort to reconcile the two lists has ended in failure and there have been some ingenious proposals. For example, it has been suggested that Matthew traces the physical descent of Jesus and Luke his legal descent. This is a remote possibility, since Jewish Levirate marriage required that a younger brother marry the widow of his deceased elder brother whenever that brother died without an heir. This was to assure in perpetuity the family line and the rights of inheritance. This possibility suggests that Nathan, an elder brother of Solomon, died without an heir; Solomon married the widow, and the son born to this union was physically his son, but legally the son of his deceased brother Nathan. This stretches the limits of credulity, however, since the two lists converge again with Zerubbabel during the exile, separate after Shealtiel, and converge once more with Joseph as the father of Jesus. The only possible explanation is that the two lists represent two different traditions that developed in different Christian communities confronted with the same need to legitimize the person of Jesus and provide him with proper birth credentials. This was necessary in order to carry out the mandate of the Lord to witness to all people, both Jews and Greeks (Matthew 28.19–20), that Jesus the Christ was the Savior of all the world.

Sources for the Genealogies

At the time these authors wrote, about C.E. 80–85, it would have been very difficult to gain accurate information for a genealogical tree. The invasion by the Romans in C.E. 66 to put down the rebellion of the Jews and the subsequent destruction of many cities and villages resulted in the destruction of records that might have supplied information for the evangelists. Since there was a widespread tradition among Jews of the time that the Messiah would descend from David, it is evident that both writers are concerned to link Jesus genealogically with King David and also with the patriarchs, Abraham, Isaac, and Jacob. Matthew's genealogy for Jesus fulfills this requirement appropriately, since he simply traces the royal line of kings from David to Joseph. He then extends the link back to the patriarchal fathers—Abraham, Isaac, and Jacob. Thus he has supplied the necessary credentials for Jesus, so that he might be accepted by the Jewish reader as the expected Messiah. The sources for Luke's genealogy are not nearly so evident, since he has traced the descent from David through Nathan. There is only a passing reference without information about this son in 2 Samuel 5.14 (see also Zechariah 12.12). The extension of this genealogy to Adam links the descent of Jesus to God's original creation and demonstrates his relationship to all humanity, whereas Matthew typically places the emphasis upon Jesus' Jewish lineage. The sources for the names in Luke's genealogy from Heli to Zerubbabel are unknown. He has used genealogical lists from Genesis, Ruth and Chronicles for other portions of Jesus' family tree.

It may be that the effort to provide Jesus with proper credentials came about through a kind of syllogistic argument. The three parts of a syllogism are: thesis, antithesis, and synthesis. Accordingly, the thesis with which the Christian community begins is, Jesus is the Messiah; the antithesis, the Messiah descends from David; and the synthesis, since Jesus is Messiah, therefore he descends from David. The genealogical lists are constructed accordingly. Of course, it may be argued that this is true to fact, but the unresolvable problem remains that there are many irreconcilable differences between the two genealogies.

The Importance of the Genealogies

What, if any, is their importance? They are important historically, since they throw light on problems that the Christian community encountered in its proclamation to the Jewish community that Jesus is the Christ. They are important theologically, since they demonstrate the mystery of salvation. Our salvation is not in any way the result of human wisdom or achievement. Salvation is the gift of God, and God's act of redemption transcends human reason and understanding. The circumstances of Jesus' birth and lineage do not result in nor are they the cause of our salvation. God alone is Redeemer and Lord. The testimony of our gospel writers was never intended to be a proof that can logically demonstrate to us the mind and purpose of God, nor to give us the security of knowing that this is how it came about. Problems and questions remain, no matter how sincerely and thoroughly we search for answers. And this drives us back to the basic, fundamental principle of our faith as stated so succinctly by Paul, "By grace you have been saved through faith; and *this is not your own doing, it is the gift of God*" (Ephesians 2.8).

The Baptism of Jesus
Matthew 3.13–17; Mark 1.9–11; Luke 3.21–22

❧ The three accounts of the baptism of Jesus in our gospels provide an opportunity for a critical comparison of the intentions and special concerns of each writer and some conclusions as to how we are to read and interpret their "stories about Jesus."

If we begin with Mark, which according to many critics is the oldest and most primitive account, we have a rather straightforward narration of this event in the experience of Jesus. Let us note first that the time reference is very indefinite—"in those days." It may surprise some readers to learn that one of the unanswered problems for New Testament students is a meaningful chronology for the events in Jesus' life. Our calendar, or method of reckoning time for the Christian era, was designed by Dionysius Exiguus in the sixth century; supposedly he began with the year of Jesus' birth. But there was obviously an error of some magnitude when he designed our calendar, since Jesus, according to Matthew and Luke, was born when Herod the Great was King of the Jews. Yet Herod died in B.C.E. 4 according to known records. We find that time references throughout the gospels are vague and indefinite. The writers did not have precise information for a chronology of Jesus' life and deeds. In fact, we do not even know precisely the year of his crucifixion because of contradictory references to the time of that event in our gospels.

The Role of John the Baptist

Mark relates that Jesus came from Nazareth of Galilee and was baptized by John in the Jordan. John the Baptist plays an important role in all gospel accounts as the forerunner, the one who announces the Coming One. In fact, John is mentioned more often than any other person in our gospels after Jesus himself. References to Peter, the leading disciple, are sparse by comparison. A peculiar feature of Luke's account is that he makes no mention of John in the baptismal account. He has already completed his references to John, since the preceding pericope tells of his death. The author of Luke does refer to John in prison in a later passage (7.19), when he sends disciples to Jesus to inquire whether or not he is the Coming One. Mark and Matthew are more consistent at this point, since they narrate the death of John much later during the ministry of Jesus (Mark 6.14–29; Matthew 14.1–12). This discrepancy in Luke's account should alert us immediately to a peculiar bias on the part of the author of Luke. He, more than the other gospel writes, wants the reader to focus exclusively upon the ministry of Jesus without the intrusion of a ministry by another.

The Markan Account

The baptismal experience, according to Mark, was a unique and radical event in the life of Jesus. He came as many others in response to the preaching of John and was baptized by him. We should be aware that baptism did not belong to the religious rituals practiced customarily by the Jews of the time. John's baptism was a radical departure from Jewish practice and was therefore rejected by upper-class Jews and religious leaders (Mark 11.27–33). Baptism was only for proselytes, Gentiles who converted to the Jewish faith, except among a sectarian group known as Essenes where baptism was an initiation ritual for membership. John's call to baptism was a demand that all Jews become like Gentiles before God. They too must through baptism be washed and cleansed of all sin in preparation for the eschatological judgment that was coming upon the world. The eschatological judgment was the final judgment marking the end of the age and the beginning of the reign of God through his Messiah, according to a current expectation among many Jews of the time. That Jesus accepted baptism by John indicates, according to Mark, that he accepted the premise and the requirements of John's baptism. That is, he acknowledged his sinfulness before God and accepted God's requirements for righteousness.

Baptism was a profound mystical and spiritual experience for Jesus. Mark's statement, "he came up out of the water," may be a recapitulation of the experience of Israel who had been delivered from destruction by God when he parted the waters of the Reed Sea. There may be some relatedness of ideas in this reference from Jesus' baptism in Mark to Paul's reference in First Corinthians, "our fathers were all under the cloud, and all passed through the sea, and all were baptized into Moses in the cloud and in the sea" (10.1–2). Just as the fathers had experienced a baptism of deliverance in preparation for their calling to be the people of God, so Jesus experienced deliverance through baptism from all that oppresses mankind, from all that separates from God, from all that frustrates God's purpose for his creation. His life events—baptism, wilderness, ministry in the land of promise, death—encapsulate the life experience of Israel as the people of God; but with a difference, since God's redemptive purpose that began with the patriarch Abraham and continued through Moses and the prophets is now finalized in this chosen one who came up out of the water to make salvation effective for all mankind.

Our English translation does not do justice to the expression, "the heavens opened." The Greek word is much more dramatic—"the heavens were torn asunder." In this way the author of Mark dramatizes the radical nature of the event for Jesus. It was indeed a most profound awakening, or awareness, for Jesus of God's call to become the Messiah, the anointed of God. The authors of Matthew and Luke tone down the expression, since they have a different understanding of Jesus when compared to the author of Mark. For Mark, Jesus is the strong son of God, a man called by God out of his people Israel to be the deliverer and savior of his people. There are few, if any, overtones of divinity associated with the person of Jesus in this gospel. This is no longer true for the authors of Matthew and Luke. Sometimes Jesus is a man; at other times he is invested with divinity in an anachronistic way that belongs rightfully to the resurrected Jesus, as Paul sets forth in Romans 1.3–4: "the gospel concerning his son, who was descended from David according to the flesh and designated son of God in power according to the Spirit of holiness by his resurrection from the dead." The experience of Jesus at his baptism therefore is perceived differently by these writers, for Jesus, being divine, cannot have had the kind of religious experience suggested by Mark.

The Dove as Symbol

The descent of the Spirit upon Jesus like a dove is symbolic and figurative. There is nothing visible, or audible, for anyone but Jesus. Yet there are profound religious implications in this reference. The author probably had in mind the passage from Genesis where the Spirit of God brooded over the waters in the beginning when the earth was without form and void. God's Spirit is creative, bringing order out of chaos, not only the chaos and disorder of the earth, but also the chaos and disorder of human life. Man is not genuinely man until he is inbreathed by the Spirit of God and comes alive in a life that is oriented totally to the will and purpose of the Creator God. This was the experience of Jesus at his baptism. His life to this point could reflect many religious hopes and aspirations that were common to the people of Israel. But at this moment through a revelation from God, the call of God and his purpose become clear and decisive for Jesus. From this time on all his energies, his total life, were directed exclusively to the will of God. This, no doubt, is what Paul means when he writes, "he became obedient" (Philippians 2.8). Matthew and Luke are not as clear on this point, since in Matthew the Spirit alights on him and in Luke the Spirit descends upon him in bodily form. That is to say, the dove is no longer symbolic for these writers, since it is in some fashion visible even to others.

The Beloved Son

The clearest distinction is to be seen in the words uttered by the voice from heaven. In Mark the words are, "You are my beloved son, with you I am well pleased." Luke agrees with Mark at this point, but Matthew alters them as follows, "This is my beloved son, with whom I am well pleased." What is a personal and private experience for Jesus according to Mark, now becomes a public announcement in Matthew for the benefit of John or for anyone else who happened to be present and especially for the reader. Matthew has surely made the change here, since the words are a composite of two Old Testament passages, Psalm 2.7 and Isaiah 42.1 It is important that we consider these passages in their original context, before we discuss them in the context of Jesus' baptism.

Psalm 2 is identified by critics as an enthronement psalm; that is, a rubric used in the liturgy for the coronation of the king of Israel. God addresses the man to be enthroned at this occasion as his son. There are no implications of divinity in this address, since Israel had rejected the concept of divine kings common in Egypt and Mesopotamia at this period in history. A first rule of interpretation is that we understand New Testament usage according to the Old Testament meaning, unless we have clear indications of a basic change in intention by the writer. There is no valid reason to ascribe to Mark a difference in meaning for this passage. The only point of significance is the Christian interpolation of the word "beloved," which, of course, gives the passage a Christological connotation. This should be viewed as an addition by Christian theologians and not part of the original citation. This was probably done during the period of oral transmission of the tradition and not an addition by Mark. The problem is why the entire passage was not quoted from the Psalm. The full address to the king in our Psalm is, "You are my son; today I have begotten you." This may have been the original reading in all the gospels, as we actually find in the Western text (Codex Bezae fifth century) of Luke, but, if so, it was expunged by all scribes and the quotation from Isaiah 42.1 substituted. There arose a teaching among some in the early Christian community at an early date called "the adoption heresy" that Jesus was a man adopted by God to become his son. Since this point of view was declared to be heretical by the orthodox, it could have resulted in the expunging of that part of Psalm 2.7 that was offensive, namely, the phrase "today I have begotten you," and the substitution of Isaiah 42.1 in this passage.

The citation of Isaiah 42.1 is an adaptation of that passage to make it appropriate Christian tradition. This is one of the "suffering servant" passages found in Second Isaiah, the best known of which is Isaiah 53. It is strange that Jesus did not use this concept as descriptive of his own understanding of his mission, since the early Christian community interpreted and applied the title to Jesus, as is amply demonstrated in a number of passages in the Book of the Acts of the Apostles (compare Acts 3.13; 4.27; 8.30–35) and in numerous references by Paul to the death of Jesus as a vicarious and atoning sacrifice (Romans 4.25; 5.8; 1 Corinthians 15.3 *et al.*). Mark and the other gospel writers either borrowed this concept from the prophet and applied it to Jesus as the seal of God's approval upon him at his baptism, or they are simply reporting an interpretation and application that was already widely used in the early Christian community; or, if our comments on Psalm 2.7 above are to the point, scribes expunged the offending portion of the passage from the Psalm that may have been the original text in gospel accounts of the baptism and replaced it with this citation from the prophet Isaiah. However the process by which this passage from Isaiah comes to be used in the baptism pericope, it is now interpreted and applied to Jesus as the one who is chosen and commissioned by God to be the Messiah.

Jesus' Understanding of Messiahship

The concept of Messiah, according to Jesus' understanding of his mission and the current view embraced by his contemporaries, was radically different. The current view was of an exalted figure modeled after the great King David and descending from the one who would bring victory to Israel over all her enemies and establish an earthly and worldwide kingdom. At the opposite pole from this secular and political view was Jesus' self-understanding of his mission as a total commitment to God's purpose and will, a life of humiliation and rejection ending in death. His contemporaries, even his disciples, were so conditioned by the former view of the Messiah as this exalted figure of power and majesty that they either rejected the person of Jesus and his message completely or totally misunderstood him until after his death and resurrection. It should be clear to us that there is a fundamental difference between the two images and that our own understanding or, more correctly, our misunderstanding of Jesus' Messiahship is the result of our failure to make this distinction.

Matthew's Radical Departure

Matthew has radically altered the baptismal account in his introductory remarks. Jesus came to John to be baptized; John protests, since it is more proper for Jesus to be the baptizer. However, Jesus encourages him to proceed, since it is proper that he fulfill all righteousness. It is evident that problems have surfaced about the baptism of Jesus in the early community and the author seeks to address them. A reconstruction of the background suggests that Jews, who were the objects of the community's evangelism effort, had raised questions about the propriety of Jesus' Messiahship. He could not be Messiah because he had been crucified and the scripture says, "Cursed is everyone who is hanged upon a tree" (Deuteronomy 21.22–23). Furthermore, they may have asked, "You say that Jesus was sinless. Why then was he baptized by John, since John's baptism was for the remission of sins?" And again, "Why did Jesus accept baptism from John, since you say he was the greater, the Messiah?" There are similar indicators in non-canonical writings of this same difficulty that the author of Matthew addresses here. For example, in the Gospel to the Hebrews, cited by Jerome in his Against Pelagius, we find this testimony, "The mother of the Lord and

The Baptism of Jesus

his brothers said to him, 'John the Baptist baptizes for the forgiveness of sin; let us go and be baptized by him.' But he said to them, 'In what have I sinned that I should go and be baptized by him? Unless, perhaps, what I have just said is a sin of ignorance'." This effort on the part of the author of Matthew, suggesting that John recognized Jesus to be the Messiah when he came for baptism, is a kind of an apology, a defense of the community's interpretation of Jesus' baptism, and is in contradiction with another passage where John does not know Jesus to be the Coming One (Matthew 11.2–3). As the passage stands in Matthew, John becomes the first professing Christian in a pre-Christian era and reflects therefore an addition either by the author or an outgrowth of tradition from the community of which he was a member.

Lukan Additions

Luke has altered the baptism account by omitting any reference to the Baptist, as noted earlier, and by relating that Jesus' experience is the result of prayer. This is in character with one of the particular interests of this writer, since he always describes Jesus at prayer before the critical and decisive decisions of his ministry (cf. 6.12; 9.18; 22.41). The opening of the heavens and the descent of the Spirit become responses to Jesus' prayer and to his openness to God, rather than a sudden, unexpected and spontaneous inbreaking of the Spirit into his consciousness.

Conclusions

Thus the intentions and concerns of each gospel writer become evident to the reader through a careful and critical examination of the baptism pericope. The most consistent account, in the opinion of this writer, is found in the Gospel of Mark. There is no ambiguity, but rather a clear and incisive depiction of Jesus as a man without any supernatural or divine qualifications who is chosen by God from the community of humanity as represented by Israel, anointed with the Spirit, and commissioned to be the deliverer of God's people and all people from the destructive bondage to sin, death, and evil to which every human being is enslaved. The Markan account is most consonant with the Pauline poetic paean,

"Therefore God also highly exalted him
and gave him the name that is above every name,
so that at the name of Jesus every knee should bend.
in heaven and on earth and under the earth,
and every tongue should confess that Jesus Christ is Lord,
to the glory of God the Father."

Signs and Wonder Stories in the Gospels

 Signs and wonder stories constitute a very large proportion of the tradition preserved by the early Christian community about the ministry of Jesus. These stories fall into a number of categories that include:

1) the healing of physical ailments,
2) exorcisms,
3) the control of natural phenomena,
4) raising the dead, and
5) occasions when numerous healings and exorcisms are lumped together into general accounts.

There are eighteen of these stories in the gospel of Mark with six general references, nineteen in the gospel of Matthew with ten general references, and twenty in the gospel of Luke with ten general references. Eleven of these stories are found in all three gospels. To set our discussion in perspective, the signs and wonder stories in Mark constitute three thousand four words of his total of eleven thousand forty-seven words, approximately twenty-seven per cent of the total; the stories in Matthew constitute two thousand three hundred twenty-three words of his total of eighteen thousand two hundred thirty-nine words, approximately thirteen per cent of his total; and in Luke a total of two thousand six hundred eighty-one words of his total of nineteen thousand three hundred forty-six words, approximately fourteen per cent. The word count is based upon the text of Codex Vaticanus

It is to be noted that the signs and wonder stories form a very large portion of the gospels, especially of the gospel of Mark since almost one-third of this gospel consists of signs and wonder narratives. It seems proper at this point to identify the material that is used as the basis for this analysis, so that there may be no question in the mind of the reader as to the inclusiveness or completeness of the analysis. Therefore the signs and wonder stories are named and listed according to category for future reference in the essay.

First and most numerous are the healings of physical ailments. The three gospels have the following in common:

(1) the healing of Peter's mother-in-law of a fever
(Mark 1.29–31; Matthew 8.14–15; Luke 4.38–39),

(2) the cleansing of a leper
(Mark 1.40–45; Matthew 8.1–4; Luke 5.12–15),

(3) the healing of a paralyzed man
(Mark 2.1–12; Matthew 9.1–8; Luke 5.17–26),

(4) the restoring of a withered hand
(Mark 3.1–6; Matthew 12.9–14; Luke 6.6–11),

(5) the healing of a woman with a hemorrhage
(Mark 5.24b–34; Matthew 9.20–22; Luke 8.42b–48),

(6) and the restoring of sight to Bartimaeus
(Mark 10.46–52; Matthew 20.29–34; Luke 18.35–43).

Two additional healings are reported by Mark,

(7) the healing of a deaf man with a speech impediment
(Mark 7.31–37) and

(8) and the restoring of sight to a blind man at Bethsaida
(Mark 8.22–26).

Matthew and Luke add the account of

(9) the healing of the Roman centurion's servant or slave
(Matthew 8.5–13; Luke 7.1–10).

In addition, Matthew has

(10) the restoring of sight to two blind men (Matthew 9.27–31).

Luke adds

(11) the healing of a woman with an infirmity (Luke 13.10–17),

(12) the healing of a man with dropsy (Luke 14.1–6),

(13) the cleansing of ten lepers (Luke 17.11–19); and

(14) the restoring of the ear of the slave of the high priest (Luke 22.49–51).

A summary indicates that Mark and Matthew each have eight healings, whereas Luke reports eleven.

The next most numerous are the exorcisms. Two are reported in all three gospels:

(15) the demon-possessed Legion
(Mark 5.1–20; Matthew 8.28–34; Luke 8.26–39) and

(16) the epileptic (Mark 9.14–29; Matthew 17.14–21; Luke 9.37–43a).

Mark and Matthew report

(17) the exorcism of the daughter of the Syrophoenician or the Canaanite woman (Mark 7.24–30; Matthew 15.21–28)

Mark and Luke report

(18) the exorcism of an unclean spirit in a synagogue at Capernaum (Mark 1.23–28; Luke 4.33–37).

Matthew and Luke report

(19) the casting out of a demon from a man that was dumb (Matthew adds that he was also blind)
(Matthew 12.22; Luke 11.14).

Matthew alone reports

(20) the exorcism of a dumb demoniac (Matthew 9.32–34).

There are four exorcism stories in Mark, five in Matthew, and four in Luke.

The nature signs and wonder stories cover a variety of events and include two narratives in all three gospels:

(21) the wind and the sea obey Jesus
(Mark 4.35–41; Matthew 8.18–27; Luke 8.22–25) and

(22) the feeding of the five thousand
(Mark 6.30–44; Matthew 14.13–21; Luke 9.10–17).

Mark and Matthew report

(23) Jesus' walking on water (Mark 6.45–52; Matthew 14.22–33),
(24) the feeding of the four thousand (Mark 8.1–10; Matthew 15.32–39), and
(25) the cursing of the fig tree (Mark 11.12–14, 20–26; Matthew 21.18–22).

Luke alone tells of

(26) the great catch of fish (Luke 5.4–7).

There are five nature signs and wonder stories in Mark, five in Matthew, and three in Luke.

There is only one story of the raising of the dead in the three gospels, that is,

(27) the raising of Jairus's daughter (Mark 5.21–24a, 35–43; Matthew 9.18–19, 23–26; Luke 8.40–42a, 49–56).

Luke alone has the additional account of

(28) the raising of the son of the widow at Nain (Luke 7.11–17).

In addition, there are the general references in the three gospels that tell of multiple healings and exorcisms without specific detail:

(29) Mark 1.32–34, Matthew 8.16–17, Luke 4.40–41 and
(30) Mark 3.7–12, Matthew 12.15–21, Luke 6.17–19.

There are three additional references to such general healings in Mark and Matthew:

(31) Mark 1.39, Matthew 4.23,
(32) Mark 6.5, Matthew 13.58, and
(33) Mark 6.53–56, Matthew 14.34–36.

Matthew and Luke refer to

(34) numerous healings and also to the raising of the dead in the report Jesus sends with the messengers of the Baptist (Matthew 11.5; Luke 7.22).

Matthew has additional general references at

(35) 9.35,

(36) 14.14, and

(37) 15.29–31.

Luke includes such references at

(38) 5.15,

(39) 7.21,

(40) 8.2,

(41) 9.11, and

(42) 13.32.

The disciples also accomplished

(43) healings and exorcisms as reported in Mark 6.7, 16; Matthew 10.1, 8, and Luke 9,1, 6; and again by Luke

(44) for the mission of the seventy (Luke 10.17).

The Absence of Signs and Wonders in the Jerusalem Ministry

It should be noted that all of these references, with the exception of the cursing of the fig tree (Mark 11.12–14, 20–26; Matthew 21.18–22) and the healing of the ear of the servant of the high priest (Luke 22.49–51), occur in the ministry of Jesus prior to his arrival in Jerusalem. The question is certainly in order: Why the absence of signs and wonders for this period of Jesus' ministry? Since the signs and wonders form such a large portion of his ministry in Galilee and for his journey to Jerusalem and since the gospels report the phenomenal impression these signs and wonders made upon the people, it is strange that Jesus did not use this medium to create a more receptive attitude to himself and for his message in Jerusalem. Perhaps the sign of the raising of Lazarus in John's Gospel provides the answer for the question, a sign that will be discussed elsewhere in this essay.

The Problem of the Use of the Vernacular "Miracle"

The first problem encountered in our discussion of the signs and wonders is the popular attitude towards and the understanding of this material in our gospels. In our current vocabulary these narratives are most often called "miracle" stories with all the innuendoes and implications that this word carries for popular religion. But the word "miracle" as such is never used in the gospels for the deeds of Jesus. They are referred to as signs, wonders, and mighty works. They are evidences, as in the Old Testament, of the presence and of the activity of God in the world that he has created. The word "miracle" is not appropriate as a reference to or for an understanding of these events and experiences, since it carries overtones and meanings that are improper when applied to the deeds of Jesus. For example, Webster's Unabridged International Dictionary defines the word as follows: "An event or effect in the physical world beyond or out of the ordinary course of things, deviating from the known laws of nature, or transcending our knowledge of these laws; an extraordinary, anomalous, or abnormal event brought about by superhuman agency as a manifestation of its power, or for the purpose of revealing or manifesting spiritual force." Some dictionary definitions add to this explanation that a miracle is a suspension of or an interruption of the natural laws.

Unfortunately, the meaning of deviation from or transcendence of the laws of nature has been the dominant theme in popular religious explanations of the signs and wonder stories in our gospels. Thus God is viewed as acting arbitrarily, impulsively, capriciously, and whimsically. He has the authority and the power to do whatever he wills whenever the spirit moves him. He can act in behalf of his clients or withhold his power arbitrarily and capriciously. But this is to reduce God to the level of human impulse and character. God is no longer the Creator God, Lord of heaven and earth, holy, righteous, just, and loving in all that he does. Only one leper, or ten in Luke's singular account, were cleansed of their leprosy; yet there must have been many, many lepers in Jesus' time left to the ravages of this disease. Why did not God cleanse all the lepers and destroy this scourge of mankind if he had the power to accomplish this since he is the loving God? Jesus must have encountered death among his friends and associates on numerous occasions, but there are only two accounts in our three gospels of the raising of the dead, the twelve year old daughter of Jairus and the young man at Nain, again a story reported only in Luke's gospel.

To refer to these events as miracles with the implication that God interrupted or defied the laws of nature in these instances is to raise the question of the goodness of God. What meaning or power can these stories have for us today as the gospel of God if they only recall that once upon a time God acted arbitrarily in behalf of a few individuals and ignored the great majority of those persons whom he had created? Of what value are these stories to us, if they become the basis for our own image of God, a God who acts in this same selective and exclusive fashion today? It is a parody to interpret the signs and wonder stories of the gospels as miracles, that is, as acts of God in which he deviates from the laws of nature and arbitrarily ignores them in an impulsive and whimsical fashion.

The Biblical Image of God

God is the Creator God who has brought into being the universe and all that is within it. He has fashioned and made it according to his will, and the laws of nature that govern and regulate its functions are expressions of that will. God is true. He is true to himself. He is faithful and trustworthy in all that he does. That means he never acts capriciously, impulsively, or arbitrarily. There is meaning and purpose for all his deeds and all his acts work together toward the realization of his eternal and immutable purpose. We can affirm with the Apostle Paul that "the creation itself will be set free from its bondage to decay and obtain the glorious liberty of the children of God" (Romans 8.21). No part of that creation is arbitrarily excluded from the redemptive purpose and intention of God.

The Intention and Purpose of the Signs and Wonder Stories

What then is the intention and purpose of the signs and wonder stories in the gospels? First, they are not told to overwhelm the hearer or the reader with the almighty power of Jesus or to make him acceptable to us. If these stories were literally true, it is very peculiar that Jesus was rejected and crucified. Is it reasonable to suppose that man would destroy the very one who held out such promise to those who suffered from disease and death? If he had the power to stop the ravages of leprosy and restore the wasted flesh of its victims, or to cure those beset by blindness, or exorcise the demons that plagued many, or to multiply five loaves of bread into food for thousands, or still the tempest at sea, or raise the dead child and restore her to her parents, why did he not use his unique power to put these enemies of mankind to rest forever? And having heard the reports of his prowess and fame, how is it that the religious leaders of Israel could nevertheless withstand him and ultimately bring about his death? These stories are not told for atmosphere in order to create the right impression and open the way for the acceptance of Jesus by everyone.

Second, they were not told to illustrate that Jesus had compassion for suffering mankind. The attitude of compassion by Jesus for people in general and persons in particular is scarcely mentioned in our gospels. He had compassion on the multitudes (Mark 6.34; Matthew 9.36; 14.14 and Mark 8.2; Matthew 15.32), he was moved with pity for the leper (Mark 9.22), for the blind men (Matthew 20.34), and for the widow of Nain (Luke 7.13). We may assume that Jesus acted out of compassion or pity for those with special needs, but this attitude is only infrequently mentioned in our gospels.

The Reason for the Composition of Gospels

To understand the point and the purpose of the signs and wonder stories, it is necessary to focus upon the reason for the composition of the gospels. The gospels are not biographical accounts of the life of Jesus or historical accounts of the times or of the beginnings of the Christian community or of the roots out of which that community grew. The *gospels are gospel*, that is, good news of what God has done in and through Jesus and of what God is doing now through the proclamation of the cross to redeem us from sin, from death, and from the powers of evil and to restore us to a true relationship of trusting dependence upon our Creator. The sayings of Jesus, as well as the stories of his deeds, are gospel, that is, message. The signs and wonder stories are particularly appropriate to proclaim the gospel, since each one is an illustration in capsule form of the good news. First, the gospel uncovers the human situation, our sin, our misery, and our helplessness. Second, the gospel proclaims that God comes in Jesus to deliver us from all those enemies that oppress us, which separate us from him, and that hold us in bondage to the powers of destruction. And, finally, the gospel proclaims the new life of freedom and the new relationship to God and to the family of God's people that results when the powerful word of God has set us free.

The Human Situation and the Divine Solution

In his Letter to the Romans, Paul sets forth in graphic terms the human situation, "There is no distinction; since all have sinned and fall short of the glory of God" (Romans 3.22–23). Without exception we are in bondage to the destructive forces of sin and death (Romans 5.12). We sin because we are slaves to sin. We are dead because we are slaves to death. We are all under the dreadful power of the wrath of God (Romans 1.18). Even the law of God is not an aid or a comfort, for it was given to make sin sinful (Romans 5.20), that is, to make us aware of our helpless and hopeless situation. Even the creation is in bondage to decay and destruction, subject to futility (Romans 8.20–21). All these forces are overthrown by God in Christ, for through his life, his death, and his resurrection he has delivered us from the wrath of God and we have peace with him (Romans 5.1). We have been set free from sin (Romans 6.18), from the law (Romans 7.6), and from the power of death (Romans 8.2). We are delivered from all these destructive powers in order that we might become slaves of righteousness (Romans 6.18). The free gift of God in Christ brings justification (Romans 5.16). Through our baptism into the death of Christ, we are raised with him to a new life (Romans 6.4). We are freed from the dread power of the law to belong to him who was raised from the dead, in order that we might live the new life of the Spirit (Romans 7.4–6). The gift of life has been given to our mortal bodies through the Spirit of Christ that dwells in us (Romans 8.11). Even the entire creation will be set free from its bondage to decay to obtain liberty (Romans 8.21).

The Signs and Wonder Stories are Gospel

This is the gospel in theological terms and this is the message proclaimed through the signs and wonder stories of the gospels. Each of the narratives portrays in a unique and picturesque way the redemption of humanity and of creation from all those powers and forces that separate us from God, which alienate us from one another, and which result in our destruction. Let us examine a few of the signs and wonder stories to demonstrate how appropriately they develop the theological themes of redemption and portray so powerfully our new relationship with God.

The Exorcism of an Unclean Spirit

The first of these stories in the Gospel of Mark is the exorcism of an unclean spirit in a synagogue at Capernaum. The prevailing religious view throughout scripture from the very beginning is that every sickness, every disease, every misfortune, every disaster in human life and in nature is the result of sin. The idyllic picture in the beginning is of an Eden in which there is harmony in nature and in the human family. But all is changed with the advent of sin. Man's disobedience, which is essentially the assertion of his ego in defiance of God, destroys that harmony and results in chaos and disharmony both in the human family and in the world of nature. We may quarrel with that religious and theological perspective, but it is the motive power behind the viewpoint and the proclamation of the early Christian community, whether it be reflected in the signs and wonder stories of the gospels or in the more sophisticated and systematic theological reflections of a Paul. The man with an unclean spirit in our story illustrates the human situation in a unique way, for man in general and man in particular is in bondage to evil, demonic powers that have taken the place of God and rule over the human spirit. Such a man is alienated from God, the source of life, goodness, and love. Such a man is alienated from the human community, so that selfishness, greed, lust, and every base motive are the determinative and driving motivations for every attitude, deed and word. The man with an unclean spirit is helpless and without hope. His future is bleak, since destruction and death are the certain lot of all those who are thus alienated from God and man. Even the religious atmosphere of the synagogue is of no avail. All the promises and hopes of religion, of ceremony and ritual, are vain and empty, for these have not delivered him from the fear and expectation of destruction.

But there is one who comes from God, even the Son of God. He speaks the powerful word of the gospel, and the unclean spirit that has ruled and dominated the life of this child of God until this moment is subdued and brought into subjection. There is a new orientation of life. The life fractured and disoriented by the ego-centered forces is now reoriented and brought into submission to the God of the universe who is working creatively to bring order out of chaos and to restore all creation to him and to his original purpose. Who is the man with the unclean spirit? He is not some lone individual who existed near two thousand years ago. He is every man in every time and in every place. He is you. He is I. For under the scrutiny of the word of God and confronted by the powerful word of the gospel, our inner life of self is laid bare, and we perceive the nature and the dominance of that unclean spirit that has ruled until Christ comes. Unfortunately, we lose the essence, the meaning, of the gospel when we read and interpret this story literally. It becomes a kind of fairy story, a once-upon-a-time tale, of a man who actually was delivered from a mental or emotional state of disorientation by Jesus and restored to sanity. And our hope is that, since it happened once upon a time, perhaps it may happen again if we are fortunate enough to have God look with favor upon us in our day. But the gospel is never exclusive and selective in this way. The gospel speaks directly, inclusively, in every time and in every place wherever it is proclaimed, to real people who are in the grip of an unclean spirit. And the purpose of the gospel is always to confront us with God, the loving, caring God who comes to deliver us from our unclean spirit and to make us whole.

The Exorcism Story is a Unique Way to Proclaim the Gospel

The signs and wonder stories are not fairy tales to entertain. They are gospel and they do the work of the gospel. We are afflicted by disease, suffering, tragedy, and death in this life. No one of us will ever escape our finitude and our mortality. God sent his Son into the world, not to provide an escape hatch from the conditions of our humanity, but to deliver us from those forces of sin, death, and evil that have alienated us from him and from one another and that ultimately negate the reason for our existence. These narratives were preserved and recorded in our gospels by the evangelists precisely because they set forth in such a forceful and descriptive way the message of salvation. The sign itself is not the substance, the reality. That is, the story is not the point of focus; it is not intended to capture our attention and entertain. The purpose of the telling is to be a proclamation of the gospel, of the good news of God. The gospel is always proclaimed in our hearing in order to deliver us from our bondage and to bring us into the joy and the glory of the new life in Christ. When we read and hear the signs and wonder stories in this way, we have arrived at the point of appreciation and understanding of what they are all about.

The Cleansing of a Leper

A second example taken from the healing category, the cleansing of the leper, is especially appropriate for the proclamation of the gospel. Leprosy was a fearsome disease characterized by the formation of nodules and macules that enlarged and spread over the body causing a loss of sensation with eventual paralysis, wasting of muscles, deformity and the mutilation and decay of the flesh. Since it was contaminating and contagious and, since there was no cure, the victims of the disease were ostracized from society and forced to wander alone and forlorn outside the pale of human association and contact. There is a lengthy discussion in Leviticus thirteen and fourteen about the disease and of how those who were diagnosed as having leprosy were banished forever from the community unless they recovered and were pronounced clean by the priest. Leprosy itself was incurable and thus special precautions were taken for any form of skin blemish, so that those with lesions or skin eruptions were isolated from the community until the nature of the disease was determined. We can only imagine the horror and the anguish of those who came under this sentence of death. The leper was unclean, cast out of the community of God's people, excommunicated by God and man, for only within the religious community was there access to God and to his gracious forgiveness and acceptance.

This is the human situation portrayed in this signs and wonder story of the cleansing of the leper. It is particularly appropriate to describe the nature of sin; for sin is a leprosy, an uncleanness, which fractures the community and excludes us from the company of God and of his people. There is no access to God and no fellowship with God's people apart from forgiveness. All who are stricken with this fatal disease, and this is every man, are under the sentence of death and there is no reprieve through anything that we can do. Life is hopeless and we are helpless until God comes in his Son to pronounce the word of the gospel, the good news that offers cleansing and forgiveness, the word that restores us to God and to the fellowship of his people. Who is the leper? He is every man in every time and in every place. He is you. He is I. The gospel of God addresses us at the point of our deepest need, uncovering and laying bare our uncleanness, and proclaiming the healing that God alone can provide. The purpose and the point of the gospel is to confront us with God, the loving, caring God who comes to cleanse us from our uncleanness and to restore us to himself and to one another. What power and what depth of meaning we find in this story that proclaims the gospel in such a perceptive and personal way. The message is universal and inclusive for it speaks to everyone of us without exception.

The Feeding of the Five Thousand

A similar but an even more universal message is proclaimed in one of the signs in nature, the sign of the feeding of the five thousand. In our natural state, individually and collectively, we are lost and without God in this world. What does it mean to be without God? It is the lot of everyone of us to be born into this world in ignorance of the one who has created us, to have within us that intuitive sense that life is more than the sum total of its parts. It is that sense of emptiness, the awareness that we are hollow inside, a deep hunger to find meaning and purpose for our existence, and the knowledge that strive as we may we can never attain to the levels of being to which our spirits aspire. It is that hunger within that drives us to find the fulfillment of life in material things, in wealth, in power, in all those things that are not God. It is a hunger, a thirst, for God, for the living God, which has been perverted in a hundred ways, a hunger that we can only understand and formulate into words when the gospel of God has spoken to our innermost self.

There are two narratives of feedings of multitudes in the gospels: the feeding of the five thousand and the feeding of the four thousand. The first is symbolic of the hunger of the Jews for God, since twelve baskets, symbolic of the twelve tribes of Israel, were gathered after all had eaten and were satisfied (Mark 6.43). The second is symbolic of the hunger of the Gentiles, for seven baskets, symbolic of the seventy nations of the world, were gathered after all had eaten their fill (Mark 8.8). The peoples of the earth, even those who consider themselves to be the people of God, suffer from emptiness, from a deep unabating hunger, until the bread of life is given by God. This is not a story about physical hunger, for physical hunger is only symptomatic and reflective of the emptiness of life, of soul and spirit, which is the portion of all those without the gospel of God.

The gospel is not about feeding those who are physically hungry. The gospel is addressed to those who are spiritually hungry because they are without God and cannot find him. Only as we have eaten of the bread of life and have come into a living and responsive relationship with our Creator and Redeemer are our eyes opened to behold the physical needs, the hunger of those about us who cry out to us for bread. Who are the hungry in this sign and wonder story? Every nation, every people, even every individual. We are a multitude like sheep without a shepherd. Society is fractured into special interest groups of every kind, each with its own agenda. There is no unifying center until God comes in that one who is the bread of life to fill us with himself.

The signs of the feeding of the multitudes are directional, for they point ahead even as it is so clearly delineated in the Fourth Gospel to the eucharistic meal in which we partake of the body and blood that was broken and shed for us and for all people. Here we receive so generously from God the food that alone satisfies the deep, urgent hunger that gnaws unsatiated in our vitals until we partake of that bread of life. And even now the community of God's people is not one as we are called to be, for we have not listened to the good shepherd. We still permit the demons of ego to drive us apart each on our own way, to separate us into cliques and self-interest groups. Yet the sign of the feeding of the multitudes is the model of what the gospel is and what it is to accomplish among us and among all the nations of the world. It is a wonder story, but a wonder of a different kind rising above the mere satisfaction of physical and material wants. It is the satisfaction and fulfillment that only the gospel, the good news of God, brings to every nation and to every individual in the world.

Walking on Water

Another of the nature signs, the walking on water, is instructive in another way of how the gospel speaks to human needs. This sign or wonder story is placed immediately after the feeding of the five thousand and is related to it. For the feeding of the five thousand is the gospel speaking to the community of God's people, creating community out of the fragmented bits and pieces of humanity. Jesus sent the disciples away in the boat while he went up on the mountain to pray. From ancient times the sea has been the

Signs and Wonder Stories in the Gospels

enemy, the hostile force, the source of chaos that must be restrained and brought into subjection by God lest it overwhelm his people.

In the very beginning there was darkness upon the face of the deep and the Spirit of God moved over the face of the waters (Gen. 1.2). And God gathered the waters together into one place and brought forth the dry land as a bulwark against the powerful forces of the seas. The sea is a mysterious and fearsome foe, described so vividly in the words of the Psalm, God "commanded, and raised the stormy wind, which lifted up the waves of the sea. They mounted up to heaven, they went down to the depths; their courage melted away in their evil plight; they reeled and staggered like drunken men, and were at their wits' end. Then they cried to the Lord in their trouble, and he delivered them from their distress; he made the storm be still, and the waves of the sea were hushed. Then they were glad because they had quiet, and he brought them to their desired haven" (Psalms 107.25–30). This and other passages in scripture are the background for the sign of walking on the water, as well as for another sign in nature, the stilling of the storm.

From early times in the history of the church, the boat or ship has been the symbol of the people of God surrounded by a hostile and threatening world. From the very beginning the Christian community was besieged by foes on every side, by the Jews who hated them and who had instigated the death of their Lord and by Romans who sought from time to time and in various ways to stamp out this abominable religious aberration. How often the community was like a boat adrift in a treacherous sea threatened on every side by great and powerful foes. How often they appeared to be alone, forsaken by God, in danger of being overwhelmed by the raging storms. How often he was the distant God, the God who appeared not to hear their cries and their pleadings. Where was their Lord? He was either asleep or far removed in a distant place, unmindful of their need.

But in their darkest moment he was there. He came to them walking upon the water, and he said, "I am; have no fear" (Mark 6.50). This is the gospel of God to the church distressed and troubled, to the church fearful and afraid, "I am! I am with you always to the end of the age." Their comfort and their strength were indelibly inscribed in the pages of their scripture, for their God is the one who stills "the roaring of the seas, the roaring of their waves, the tumult of the peoples" (Psalms 65.7; 89.9). The signs and wonder stories are action symbols of the power of the gospel to address human need, specifically the spiritual needs of the individual and of the community. This they do without removing the mantle of mystery that hides God from profane eyes and hands. God is distant, far removed, yet he is near to his church in every time of peril. He comes in that one who speaks the powerful word that stills the storm, in that one who says "I am," the word of peace and assurance to his people in the midst of threat and peril. He leads his church into a secure haven, for as the writer of John's gospel says, "immediately the boat was at the land to which they were going" (John 6.21).

The Gospel of John

The Fourth Gospel narrates a series of seven signs, some of which are unique to that gospel and others of which are repetitions of signs and wonder stories in the synoptics. Five of the signs are repetitions of or related to synoptic accounts:

1) the healing of the official's son at Capernaum (John 4.46–54; cf. Matthew 8.5–13; Luke 7.1–10),
2) the healing of the paralyzed man at the Bethzatha pool (John 5.2–18; cf. Mark 2.1–12; Matthew 9.1–8; Luke 5.17–26),
3) the feeding of the five thousand (John 6.1–14; cf. Mark 6.30–44; Matthew 14.13–21; Luke 9.10–17),
4) walking on the sea (John 6.16–21; cf. Mark 6.46–52; Matthew 14.22–27), and
5) the restoring of sight to the man blind from birth (John 9.1–44; cf. Mark 8.22–26 and the other stories of giving sight to the blind: Bartimaeus in Mark 10.46–52; Matthew 20.29–34; Luke 18.35–43 and two blind men in Matthew 9.27–31).

This leaves two signs stories unique to the Fourth Gospel—

6) the changing of water to wine (John 2.1–11) and
7) the raising of Lazarus (John 11.1–44).

The Changing of Water to Wine

The first sign, the changing of water to wine at Cana, belongs to the category of the nature signs, although it is found only in the Fourth Gospel and is unique when compared to the nature signs in the synoptics. It is difficult to accept this sign as an account of a literal happening, for the chemical composition of water and wine are very different. Water is one of our most common compounds, a molecule being a combination of two atoms of hydrogen to one atom of oxygen, whereas wine is composed of sugar, both dextrose and fructose, a compound of carbon, hydrogen, and oxygen with a chemical formula of six atoms of carbon, twelve atoms of hydrogen and six atoms of oxygen. In addition, there is tartaric acid with a chemical formula COOH:CHOH:CHOH:COOH, malic acid with a chemical formula COOH:CH2:CHOH:COOH, and tannin with an exceedingly complex chemical formula. If we should say that wine, which is so very complex chemically, was actually formed from water, a rather simple chemical compound, at a word of Jesus, we would have to believe that God is not governed by his own laws according to which he created the universe and all that is in it.

And this is precisely the problem, for it is not a question of the capability of God but rather of the nature of God that comes to light with a literal interpretation of the sign. Let us say that God is able to do far beyond our small capacities to fathom or understand. The universe, the planet earth, life upon our planet earth in all its complexity and variety, attest the mighty power and the ingenious inventiveness of God. Even such a simple compound as water defies our imagination and our ingenuity to fathom how it can be and how it is so basic to life and to the life processes. The question is not what God can do, but what he does. Does he ever violate the order of things that he has established? Does he ever act arbitrarily and capriciously? The answer of faith is, No. God is true to himself. God is trustworthy. God can be trusted to be the same yesterday, today, and forever. Therefore the sign of changing water to wine must be seen as directional; it points to a reality that is very different from the sign that it symbolizes.

The Sign Points to a New Beginning in the History of Salvation

A new beginning has been made in the history of salvation with the advent of Jesus, a beginning as different from what has been under the dispensation of the law of Moses centered in temple and ceremonies as wine is from water. There is not a total discontinuity, however, for basic to wine is water, an inherent ingredient of so much that is in the material universe including our own bodies. Again we have the author of John using teaching material from the synoptic gospels and transforming it in the form of a sign into a lesson pointing up the contrast between the new and the old. Jesus said, "No one puts new wine into old wineskins; if he does, the wine will burst the skins, and the wine is lost and so are the skins; but new wine is for fresh skins" (Mark 2.22). Jesus was not teaching a lesson about how to preserve wine for the benefit of wine makers.

This saying is a metaphor, an implied comparison, which points up the contrast between the religion of the Judaism as it was understood and practiced to this time and what God is now introducing and initiating in the person and message of Jesus. What God is doing is not addition, appending the new to the old, but he is making a radical new beginning that calls for a total transformation. The new wine is for fresh skins. The basic understanding, the basic motivation, the basic relationship between God and man is now grounded in a new and divine act of salvation—the death of God to reunite and reconcile the entire human family to himself and to one another. For Jesus is of God in a new and unique revelation of love, a love that takes priority and precedence over the requirements set forth in the dispensation of law, ceremony, and temple. This is the lesson that the author of the Fourth Gospel enunciates at the very beginning of the ministry of Jesus that is evident not only in the sign of changing water to wine, but also in the cleansing of the temple, which he places at the very beginning of that ministry. If the cleansing of the temple had actually taken place at this point in time, there never would have been a ministry of Jesus. He would have been destroyed immediately without an opportunity to deliver his message, his challenge, and his invitation from God to be reconciled. Thus the cleansing of the temple must have occurred where it is placed in the synoptic gospels, for there it becomes the occasion for his death. It is placed in this new location at the very beginning of Jesus' ministry to enunciate and enforce the message of the sign of the changing of water to wine as the new and radical transformation and change to which God calls with the advent of his son.

Death and Resurrection in Biblical Thought

The two accounts of raising the dead in the synoptic gospels, Jairus's daughter and the widow of Nain's son, proclaim the good news in action parables that the last and greatest enemy of mankind has been overthrown (1 Corinthians 15.26). The raising of the dead narratives are perceptive in their portrayal of the tragedy of death and of its finality; there is tumult, weeping, and loud wailing (Mark 5.38) and the dead man was the only son of his mother who was a widow (Luke 7.12). The author of Luke's gospel portrays in graphic terms the sad lot of the woman in the society of the time without a male, either father, husband, or son, as her support. Death is described in stark and forbidding terms in scripture. The dead descend into Sheol where there is no remembrance of God (Psalms 6.5). The dead are in darkness (Lamentations 3.6); they are shades that will not arise (Isaiah 26.14; cf. Psalms 88.10); the dead know nothing and the memory of them is lost (Ecclesiastes 9.5); they have passed out of mind (Psalms 31.12); they go down into silence (Psalms 115.17); they are cut off from God and remembered by him no more (Psalms 88.5); the dead are beyond the love of God and his saving help (Psalms 88.11–12). No wonder there are signs and wonder stories in our gospels to proclaim the good news of hope and promise that has come to light through the resurrection of Jesus. It is even strange that there are so few of these stories, one in Mark-Matthew-Luke, one in Luke, and one in the Fourth Gospel. Perhaps there is not so great a need for such signs and wonder stories about the raising of the dead, just because the great theme of the gospel centers in the death and resurrection of Jesus that is the very heart of the entire New Testament and apart from which there can be no meaningful signs and wonders.

But the accounts we have should not be confused with the resurrection of the dead, for they only point ahead symbolically to that event that is always in the future. The resurrection of the dead is always represented in two stages, first, the resurrection of Jesus, the first fruits of those who have fallen asleep (1 Corinthians 15.20) and, second, the resurrection at his coming of those who belong to him (1 Corinthians 15.23; cf. also 1 Thessalonians 4.13–17). Thus the raising of the dead in these signs and wonder stories is only a return to this mortal life, since there has only been one resurrection to this time. It is of special interest to note the identity of language found in Mark's description of the death of the young girl and the language of Paul. Jesus said, "The child is not dead but sleeping" (Mark 5.39). Paul speaks of those who have fallen asleep in Christ (1 Corinthians 15.18), Christ is the first fruits of those who have fallen asleep (1 Corinthians 15.20), and again he writes, we shall not all sleep (1 Corinthians 15.51).

That the raising of the dead stories are only a resuscitation and not a true resurrection is evident also in the raising of Lazarus story, a sign unique to the Fourth Gospel, for the chief priests planned to put Lazarus to death because on account of him many of the Jews were believing in Jesus (John 12.10–11). The gospel is not the good news that holds out hope that there might be an extension of life in this age if Jesus should just happen along at the right time. The gospel addresses the basic reality of human existence. We are all dead through trespasses and sins (Ephesians 2.1); that is, we are separated from God our Creator who is the source of life. Death is spiritual and eternal, a reality for us even while we exist physically in the flesh, unless we have been inbreathed and inspirited by the living God. It is a perversion of the gospel to confuse resuscitation with resurrection and to proclaim a message that offers such a hope as the substance of what God is offering through Christ.

The gospel always addresses our spiritual situation first, not our physical needs, although our spiritual health may be of the highest significance for our physical health and wholeness. We are a unity of body, mind, and spirit and the lack of wholeness in our spiritual relationship to God reflects itself in the total pattern of our existence. It is a sickness to be driven by physical appetites that dominate the self and are manifested in materialism, greed, lust, and the love of things. It is a sickness to be driven by intellectual pursuits that dominate the self and are manifested in pride, arrogance, self-sufficiency, and godlessness. The good news of the gospel addresses us totally, for only as we are restored to a true and complete relationship of trusting dependence upon God do we became whole persons, freed from the destructive powers of sin, death, and self-centered ego. The new and resurrected life comes to reality for us through the death and resurrection of Jesus and to reality in us through the proclamation of the good news, even through the signs and wonder stories of the raising of the dead. The stories are gospel, setting forth the universal human situation of bondage to death.

Who is Jairus's daughter? She is every woman. She is you. She is I. Who is the widow of Nain's son? He is every man. He is you. He is I. For the gospel is gospel only as it is good news addressed directly and personally to you and to me. The raising of the dead stories are not stories of random events that just happened to happen. The gospel always bears in its bosom the full power of God to bring about even what is proclaimed. The gospel comes alive as it is heralded in the presence of dead hearers and quickens them to life, to wholeness, and to responsiveness to God.

The Raising of Lazarus

The account of the raising of Lazarus from the dead as reported in the eleventh chapter of the Gospel of John is of special interest because it raises the question so acutely of the actuality of these events. Are the signs and wonder stories, and the author of the Fourth Gospel uses the word "signs" precisely to describe the events, accounts of actual happenings? Or are they entirely symbolic? This question can never be resolved with certainty, for the stories have been transmitted by word of mouth for a generation before they were finally recorded by those who were neither eyewitnesses nor participants in the events. My own conclusion is that Jesus did do signs, wonders, and mighty works, but we can never recover precisely what he did or what happened because of the lapse of time between event and the written accounts. But we can be certain that they became much more than wonder tales in the telling by the authors of our gospels.

The stories are gospel, that is, the proclamation of good news addressed to the human family in desperate straits, oppressed by destructive powers, slaves to forces that are beyond human capacity to contend with and to overthrow. Was there a Lazarus of Bethany whom Jesus raised from the dead? There may not have been, since this sign is reported only by the Fourth Gospel. This was a sign of such magnitude that it becomes incomprehensible to think that it was unknown to the other gospel writers. Lazarus had been dead and in the tomb four days, so that corruption and decay had already begun. Yet at the word of Jesus he came forth from the tomb still wrapped in the grave linens that should have impeded his movement. Why is not this stupendous event reported by Mark, or by Matthew, or by Luke? Of all the signs reported by the authors of our gospels, here is one that more than any other gives credibility to the awesome powers of

Jesus, if that is what the signs and wonder stories were intended to do. But this account, more than any other, demonstrates that this use of the signs and wonder stories is unconvincing, and is a misrepresentation of what the authors intended them to be.

The parallels between the account in the Fourth Gospel of the raising of Lazarus from the dead and the parable of the rich man and Lazarus in the Gospel of Luke cannot be merely accidental (Luke 16.19–31). The point of departure is the name "Lazarus." It appears that the author of the Fourth Gospel has developed a very lengthy description of the death and of the raising of Lazarus in order to illustrate the point of the parable; that is, those who are not convinced through the hearing of the message delivered by Moses and the prophets about the verities of God and of life will not be convinced even if someone should rise from the dead (Luke 16.29–31).

The sign of the raising of Lazarus in the Fourth Gospel is the final and greatest sign from God pointing to the resurrection of Jesus. We have already pointed out that Lazarus had only been restored to an earthly existence and was subject to death once more (John 12.10); thus his return to life is not in any sense the equivalent of the Christian view of the resurrection that issues from the resurrection of Jesus. Resurrection was a moot question among the Jews of the time. The powerful religious leaders represented by the Sadducees rejected even the possibility of a resurrection (Mark 12.18; Acts 23.8); they approved and advocated the traditional view of scripture that a father lives on in his sons. The Pharisees were more liberal, for they believed and taught a future resurrection (Acts 23.8), although it was a resurrection of the flesh, a return to an earthly existence. There is no equivalent to the resurrection of Jesus in the tradition of the Pharisees, nor in the traditions of the early Christian community in any of the narratives reported in the gospels or in the Acts of the Apostles. That event retains its unique and singular character in the writings of the New Testament.

The account of the resurrection of Lazarus in the Fourth Gospel, which is a post-resurrection account in the sense that it was composed many years after the event of the resurrection of Jesus, verifies the experience of the early community that their proclamation of the death and resurrection of Jesus was rejected and denied by large numbers of the Jews. It is a commentary upon the conclusion that the parable of the rich man and Lazarus reaches, "If they do not hear Moses and the prophets, neither will they be convinced if some one should rise from the dead" (Luke 16.31).

Jesus had been raised from the dead, and this had happened in accord with the scriptures. This is the point that the Gospel of Luke makes in his account of the post-resurrection events, first when Jesus appears to the two on the road to Emmaus, "Beginning with Moses and all the prophets, he interpreted to them in all the scriptures the things concerning himself" (Luke 24.27), and again to the disciples in Jerusalem, "Everything written about me in the law of Moses and the prophets and the psalms must be fulfilled" (Luke 24.44).

In spite of the clear testimony of all the scriptures, the religious leaders and the majority of the Jews rejected the gospel of the resurrection of Jesus. Their stubbornness and hardness of heart is portrayed vividly by the author of the Fourth Gospel, "the chief priests planned to put Lazarus also to death, because on account of him many of the Jews were going away and believing in Jesus" (John 12.10–11). They were prepared to commit murder, the murder of Christian believers of whom Lazarus is a symbol, in order to bring an end to the false and apostate interpretation and teaching of their scriptures. A survey of references to the Jews in the Fourth Gospel makes evident that they were Jesus' antagonists from the beginning. They were skeptical of his credentials and of his message (John 1.19; 2.18, 20; 3.25; 6.41, 52; 7.11, 15, 35; 8.22, 57; 9.18; 10.24; 11.37; 19.21); they accused him of being demon possessed (John 8.48, 52; 10.19–20); they tried to kill him early in his ministry (5.10, 16, 18; 7.1 10.31, 33; 11.8, 54; 12.11); those who listened to him were put out of the synagogue (9.22, 34); they arrested him (John 18.14) and were the antagonists who prevailed upon Pilate to crucify him (John 18.31, 36, 38; 19.7, 12, 38; 20.19).

The Lazarus Story Points to the Reality of the Resurrection

The evidence of their attitude towards Jesus from the beginning of his ministry and of their role in his death supports the conclusion that the Lazarus story essentially confirms that even the possession of Moses and the prophets did not convince the Jews of the truth of God when Jesus was raised from the dead. The sign, that is the raising of Lazarus, points to the reality, that is the resurrection of Jesus. The sign is never the reality, but is always directional, pointing to that which is the substance of God's disclosure to us. The substance of the gospel is never a restoration to life and health of the physically sick, not even the raising of a dead man or woman. The substance of the gospel is always the message of the cross. God through the death and resurrection of Jesus has delivered us from the powers of sin, death, and evil that hold us in bondage, which dominate us and claim our allegiance and service, and which destroy us without the entrance of God into the world and into our lives in the person of Jesus.

We miss the point of the sign whenever we convert the sign into the reality and yearn and covet that God will deliver us from our mortality now and make us immune to the physical and material realities of life in this world. This we constantly do and this is always a perversion of the gospel. Our salvation is not from disease, suffering, pain, poverty, persecution, and death, but is always a deliverance from the fear and the anxiety that any of these realities of our mortal existence can separate us from the love of God. We want to be freed from our mortality and from those conditions that make our earthly existence less than Edenic, but these yearnings and desires that have such a high priority in our lives are nothing else than an expression of our deep-seated ego-centeredness and our will to be god. Our deliverance is always a dying to self and to the world in order that Jesus Christ may come alive in us and that he might live in us in the midst of this world so that we rise above our base humanity to pursue righteousness and holiness in every life situation and in every life relationship. We have denigrated the gospel by reading into it our hopes and desires and by ignoring or rejecting the powerful message from God that kills our ego and out of the dust of our mortality creates and raises up within us the new life in Christ. The ego, the self, is the bastion that must come down for God to be God in us and through us.

Conclusions

This is the message of all the signs and wonder stories in the gospels, for each one portrays some facet of our human situation and of our deliverance that is always and totally the work of God. The signs and wonder stories are nothing else than the proclamation of the gospel, the good news of God in Jesus Christ. They are a particularly important and valuable method of communication to all those who lived in the world of symbol and myth. It is doubtful that the earliest hearers of the gospel told in signs and wonder stories would have understood them in a literal and factual sense and found in them their support for a belief that God is ultimately concerned with our physical and material situation in the world. They viewed the human situation in quite different terms from our twenty-first century perception, Therefore the gospel in signs and wonder stories addressed them in a powerful and stimulating way. Our principal need in understanding them and their function is to return to the world of the first century and to hear them against the backdrop of the spiritual yearnings of those whose primary concern was not life in this age, but life for the age to come.

The Gospel of Matthew as an Anti-Pauline Polemic

❧ Matthew's version of the confession of Peter, "You are the Christ," is one of the most controversial passages in the New Testament. The meaning and intention of Jesus by his response, "You are Peter," a passage found only in the Gospel of Matthew, has been subject to different interpretations in the church for centuries and has engendered much debate, especially from the time of the Reformation. The position of the church historically, that Peter was the first pope at Rome and that his primacy and authority have been handed down through apostolic succession to the present, is one of the principal points of division among Roman Catholic, Orthodox, and Protestant churches. The Lutheran response to the claim of the Roman Catholic Church has been that the "rock" is not Peter, but the confession that Peter made, "You are the Christ." This explanation is neither satisfactory nor convincing, since it does not speak directly to the problem. The purpose of this essay is to restudy the passage in the context of the gospel and in the context of the historical time in which it was penned.

The Dating for the Composition of the Gospels

The chronology for the composition of the gospels that is used as a basis for this interpretation is as follows: Mark's Gospel was composed approximately C.E. 65 and the Gospel of Matthew approximately C.E. 80, the Gospel of Mark having been used as one of the principal sources for the composition of the Gospel of Matthew. This dating is based in part upon the internal evidence and in part upon citations from Papias, Bishop of Hierapolis, who lived and wrote about C.E. 140. The writings of Papias are no longer extant, but two quotations pertaining to the composition of the gospels are found in Eusebius' *Ecclesiastical History* from the fourth century of our era. The full quotation from Eusebius for the authorship of the Gospel of Mark is "And the Elder said this also. Mark, having become the interpreter of Peter, wrote down accurately everything that he remembered without, however, recording in order what was either said or done by Christ. For neither did he hear the Lord, nor did he follow him, but afterwards, as I said (attended) Peter who adapted his instructions to the need (of his hearers) but had no design of giving a connected account of the Lord's oracles. So then Mark made no mistake while he thus wrote down some things as he remembered them; for he made it his one care not to omit anything that he heard or to set down any false statement therein." The other quotation speaks of the authorship of the Gospel of Matthew: "So then Matthew composed the logia in the Hebrew dialect, and each one interpreted them as he could."

These quotations have been the subject of dispute among scholars and have been interpreted in various ways. The most compelling explanation for this writer is that Mark was Peter's companion and interpreter during his mission to Rome in the seventh decade of the first century. There is a tradition that both Peter and Paul were martyred in Rome during the persecution by Nero in the year C.E. 64. This seems to be an indisputable tradition, inasmuch as no competing claim has been made elsewhere for the burial tombs of the two apostles. If either of them had come to the end of life elsewhere, surely a church tradition would have arisen with a claim to the distinction of being the site of the tomb of so prominent an apostle. The year C.E. 64 then is the terminal date for the death of Peter and the earliest date for the composition of the Gospel of Mark. This seems to be confirmed by the internal evidence.

One of the great watersheds in both Jewish and Christian history was the rebellion of the Jews against Roman rule in C.E. 66 and the destruction of Jerusalem and the temple in C.E. 70. There is no reference in Mark that suggests that these events were history at the time that he wrote his gospel. The Little Apocalypse, a designation for the discourse by Jesus announcing the signs that precede the end of the age, includes the prediction, "When you see the desolating sacrilege set up where it ought not to be (let the reader understand), then let those who are in Judea flee to the mountains" (Mark 13.14). This reference to an unidentified desecration is indirectly identified by the author of Matthew as the temple at Jerusalem, for he alters and adds to Mark, saying, "Therefore when you see the desolating sacrilege spoken of by the prophet Daniel, standing in the holy place (let the reader understand), then let those who are in Judea flee to the mountains" (Matthew 24.15). Luke makes the identification even more specific, "But when you see Jerusalem surrounded by armies, then know that its desolation has come near" (Luke 21.20). In another passage, when Jesus weeps over Jerusalem, Luke quotes him as saying, "The days shall come upon you, when your enemies will cast up a bank about you and surround you, and hem you in on every side. They shall crush you to the ground, you and your children within you, and they will not leave one stone upon another in you" (Luke 19.43–44). It is not probable that we would correlate what Mark wrote with the Jerusalem temple without these additional commentaries by Matthew and Luke. The point is, there is a suggestion in Matthew and in Luke that the destruction of Jerusalem and the desecration of the temple were history at the time the authors wrote their gospels.

If Mark were the earliest gospel and if Matthew and Luke used Mark as one of their principal sources in the composition of their gospels, the theme of one of the essays in this collection, then the response of Jesus to Peter's confession represents an addition to Mark's text by the author of Matthew, This addition must then be viewed in the light of what can be determined about the author's purpose in composing his gospel. The passage in Mark reads, "And he asked them, 'But who do you say that I am?' Peter answered him, 'You are the Christ.' And he charged them to tell no one about him." The parallel in Matthew reads, "He said to them, 'But who do you say that I am?' Simon Peter replied, 'You are the Christ, the son of the living God.' And Jesus answered him, 'Blessed are you Simon Bar-Jona! For flesh and blood has not revealed this to you, but my Father who is in heaven. And I tell you, you are Peter, and on this rock I will build my church, and the powers of death shall not prevail against it. I will give you the keys of the kingdom, and whatever you bind on earth shall be bound in heaven, and whatever you loose on earth shall be loosed in heaven.' Then he strictly charged the disciples to tell no one that he was the Christ."

"You are Peter"

The "You are Peter" passage is unique to Matthew's gospel. If Matthew were the earliest gospel to have been written and if the author of Luke used Matthew as a source in the composition of his gospel and if the author of Mark used both Matthew and Luke as sources in the composition of his gospel, then it is most strange that there is no hint of this saying of Jesus in either Luke or Mark. This is another of those passages that speaks very strongly for the priority of Mark's gospel. Even the addition to Peter's confession, "the son of the living God," also unique to Matthew, suggests a later composition. Is the saying, "You are Peter," actually a Jesus' saying? Or is it a creation by the community or by the author of this gospel? The latter possibility is a very strong probability in the view of this writer. It is one of the clearest evidences to support the exposition that one of the basic motifs in the gospel of Matthew is an anti-Pauline polemic.

The Author of Matthew's Gospel

A study of the internal evidence in the gospel of Matthew suggests that the author was a leader in a Jewish-Christian community, possibly in Syria, in the third and fourth quarters of the first century. This would locate him in that period immediately following the destruction of Jerusalem and the temple in C.E. 70. He was not an immediate disciple or follower of Jesus, but a second generation believer. His dependence upon written sources to compose his gospel, particularly his dependence upon the gospel of Mark, the author of which was also a second generation believer and not an immediate disciple of Jesus, makes it very improbable that the gospel of Matthew could have been written by the man named Matthew in the list of disciples (Matthew 10.3). Why would a disciple of Jesus rely upon a writing about Jesus composed by a second generation believer if he were actually present and participated in the events that he reports?

All the gospels were composed anonymously, and their authors cannot be identified with certainty. The traditional identifications, for example "The Gospel According to Matthew," appear for the first time in manuscripts from the fourth century of our era. There are only fragments of manuscripts from an earlier time, none of which retain the opening words of a gospel. Thus it is not possible to ascertain when authors' names were first affixed to the gospels. A reference was made above to a statement by Papias in the mid-second century that Matthew composed the logia of Jesus in the Hebrew dialect. Papias cannot have referred to the gospel of Matthew, for that gospel was written in Greek and is much more than a collection of sayings or logia of Jesus. It is much more probable that the apostle Matthew composed a collection of sayings by Jesus in the Aramaic language, a Semitic dialect akin to Hebrew. Papias was a Gentile believer from Hierapolis in what is now Asia Minor and probably did not know the distinction between Hebrew and Aramaic.

This collection of sayings is identified by some scholars as the second source used by the authors of Matthew and Luke in the composition of their gospels. There are a large number, approximately two hundred verses, in Matthew and Luke consisting mostly of teaching materials, or sayings by Jesus, which demonstrate a very close verbal agreement. An illustration of this phenomenon has been cited in the discussion of the John the Baptist pericope in the essay on "The Order of the Composition of the Gospels." If this were the collection of logia to which Papias referred, than one can deduce how the name Matthew came to be associated with an anonymous gospel that made this material such a basic element in the account of the deeds and teachings of Jesus.

The Dark Ages for our Knowledge of Christian History

If we can accept for the sake of discussion what has been said above about the background, the conditioning, and the commitment of the author of Matthew's gospel, then it is possible to introduce another element into the picture. The first three centuries of the Christian era may be compared to the dark ages, for there is little precise information about the history of the development of the community. We are almost entirely dependent upon the internal evidence from the gospels and upon the Book of the Acts of the Apostles for the little knowledge we have about the Twelve and their activities from the time of the death and resurrection of Jesus to their own deaths. We have a little information about a few of the Twelve and none about the majority of them. We cannot even decide whether the disciple in question who is called Matthew the tax collector (Matthew 10.3) or just Matthew (Mark 3.18; Luke 6.15), is the same person identified as Levi the son of Alphaeus who was also a tax collector (Mark 2.14; Luke 5.27) or as Matthew (Matthew 9.9), since all the evangelists identify one of the Twelve as James the son of Alphaeus (Matthew 10.3; Mark 3.18; Luke 6.15). We have even less information about those who must have been leaders and decisive persons in the second generation of believers. It is an exciting but difficult task to fit the bits and pieces of information together that have been painstakingly gathered from every possible source into a meaningful and reasonable facsimile of the internal history of the Christian community in the first century.

Conflict in the Early Christian Community

One certain bit of information is that there was a very sharp and bitter conflict in the early community between the Jewish-Christian branch that had its first center in Jerusalem until the destruction of that city by the Romans and the more Gentile oriented branch of the community whose leader was the Apostle Paul. That conflict is graphically portrayed in Paul's Letter to the Galatians, as well as in a number of references elsewhere in his writings. There is also a watered down version in the Book of Acts chapter fifteen that narrates the author's version of the Jerusalem conference. Paul has several references to the role of Peter, or Cephas as he identifies him, in this conflict. First, let us look at these references to place the roles of Peter and Paul in perspective.

Paul's first introduction to Peter, or Cephas, was a private meeting with the apostle three years after his conversion experience upon his first visit to Jerusalem (Galatians 1.18). The second meeting with Peter is fourteen years later when Paul again visits Jerusalem (Galatians 2.9). The impression created by Paul's references is that the Jerusalem church was the center of the Christian community, although not in the sense of exercising an oversight or supervision over the whole. Paul was there as an equal, but there was some question about his credentials because of his past history as a persecutor of the community. The leading apostle at the time of the first visit was Peter, for Paul identifies him as the primary person with whom he meets. The next principal person was James, the Lord's brother, who is mentioned incidentally. But the positions of leadership have changed in the interim between the first and second visits to Jerusalem. The right hand of fellowship is extended to Paul by James, Cephas, and John, who were "reputed to be pillars" in the church (Galatians 2.9).

The change in the order of the listing of names from the first to the second visit cannot be accidental, but must reflect a change in status within the Jerusalem Christian community. What is to be noted here is that Paul's ministry to the uncircumcised, that is, to the Gentiles, was approved by the leaders of the Jerusalem community. They recognized that God's imprimatur was upon Paul's mission to the Gentiles and Paul acknowledged that this same blessing rested upon Peter's mission to the circumcised.

However, this agreement though approved was not honored by James and Peter, for Paul writes, "When Cephas came to Antioch I opposed him to his face, because he stood condemned. For before certain men came from James, he ate with the Gentiles; but when they came he drew back and separated himself, fearing the circumcision party. And with him the rest of the Jews acted insincerely, so that even Barnabas was carried away by their insincerity" (Galatians 2.11–13). The acceptance of Gentiles into the Christian community without any preconditions was one of the most difficult adjustments the first followers of Jesus had to make. The prohibitions against association, especially table fellowship, go back beyond the time of the patriarchs. When Joseph's brothers came to Egypt, he made a feast for them, but "they served him (Joseph) by himself, and them (the brothers) by themselves, and the Egyptians who ate with him by themselves, because the Egyptians might not eat bread with the Hebrews, for that is an abomination to the Egyptians" (Gen. 43.32).

Conditions for Gentile Membership in the Christian Community

Attitudes of contempt and hatred that had festered for centuries were to be erased immediately within the new community. Not all believers were equal to the challenge. First, there was the question of the conditions to be imposed upon Gentiles who sought entry into the community. The Jerusalem community, or at least some of the members of that community who gave high priority to the requirements of the Torah, insisted that Gentiles must first be circumcised and then must observe some of the dietary and ceremonial laws required by the Mosaic law before they were fully recognized and accepted into fellowship. This was the cause of the conflict in the churches of Galatia. According to Acts fifteen, the requirement of circumcision had been waived, but the observance of certain dietary laws had not. The account in Acts suggests that Paul was a party to this compromise, for he was one of those appointed to circulate the letter of agreement among the Gentile churches.

Paul's own account makes such an agreement not only improbable but impossible. He writes that he did not yield submission for a moment on the question of freedom in Christ and that those who were of repute in the church added nothing to his understanding of the question nor did they change his practice of associating freely with Gentiles, even to eating with them. Peter had broken the barrier of eating with Gentiles at Joppa (Acts 11.3) and had been sharply reprimanded by the circumcision party at Jerusalem, but his explanation was seemingly accepted by the church and this departure from norms previously approved.

Conflict at Antioch over Table Fellowship

The church at Antioch had likewise practiced table fellowship from its first beginnings. But there were irreconcilable opponents to the abating of conditions for membership; opponents who insisted that Gentiles must first become Jews before they became Christians. They are variously described as the circumcision party, representatives from James, or as false brethren by Paul, Christians who never approved the changes and who worked insidiously to return the church to their idea of purity of practice. Peter and even Barnabas were led astray by these fundamentalists who came to Antioch and successfully made a case against table fellowship. They must have been persuasive to have swayed Peter after his experience at Joppa and Barnabas after his lifelong commitment to equality and freedom for all believers. The outcome of the issue was either/or for Paul; either believers were free from circumcision and from the requirements of the law, free to serve righteousness in Christ, or they were in bondage to the law and under obligation to fulfill its every requirement. All who preempt for this point of view were under a curse and were no longer in Christ. But in the new relationship in Christ there is "neither Jew nor Greek, there is neither slave nor free, there is neither male nor female; for you (we) are all one in Christ" (Galatians 3.28). The advocates of the position that categorizes believers by birth, or by conditioning, or by obedience to the law are called "false apostles, deceitful workmen, disguising themselves as apostles of Christ" by the apostle (2 Corinthians 11.13) Paul's description of the conflict attests how hotly the issue was contested.

The conflicting views were finally resolved as the Gentile element of the church became the larger component, and we can be grateful that Paul's inclusive view prevailed. However, an exclusive view of faith and of membership in the community has never lacked for supporters in the church

The Gospel of Matthew as an Anti-Pauline Polemic

and the author of the gospel of Matthew was one of the most compelling advocates of this principle. This is not to denigrate the author of this gospel, but rather to examine objectively his purpose in composing it. No one, not even the apostle Paul, has stated so succinctly the very heart and soul of Christian life in the three words of this author, "Love your enemies" (Matthew 5.44). Nevertheless he is the chief advocate of the exclusive point of view in the New Testament.

The Preeminence of Peter in Matthew's Gospel

Matthew alone gives the preeminence to Peter with his addition to the pericope of the confession, "You are Peter." He alone supplies the name "Peter" in the account of the four fishermen called to be fishers of men (Matthew 4.18) and in the story of the healing of Peter's mother-in-law (Matthew 8.14). He alone has the account of Peter walking on the water (Matthew 14.28). Only in Matthew is Peter the one who asks for the explanation of the parable (Matthew 15.15). The lesson of the shekel in the fish's mouth is unique to Matthew and directed at Peter (Matthew 17.24). Only in Matthew is Peter the disciple who asks how often one is to forgive his brother (Matthew 18.21). No one of the passages, however, is equal to the response of Jesus, "You are Peter." The question must be asked, "Why is Peter singled out and invested with such authority?" His track record during Jesus' ministry was not that distinguished. He was the disciple who rebuked Jesus when he announced his impending rejection, suffering, and death in the words exclusive to Matthew, "God forbid, Lord! This shall never happen to you" (Matthew 16.22). Peter alone committed the sin of denying Jesus, even with a curse (Matthew 26.74). Thus the inclusion of this special dispensation to Peter calls for explanation.

What more logical procedure is there than to view this addition against the backdrop of the controversy over the admission of Gentiles into the community of faith? Supposedly the question was resolved with the decision of the church at the Jerusalem conference according to Acts fifteen. But the chronology of Galatians suggests that it continued to embroil the church and created large problems in the churches of Galatia, Corinth, and Philippi. The many references to circumcision in Romans demonstrate how this issue and the larger issue of the relationship of the Gentile believer to the community continued to exercise the church. The author of

Matthew is a spokesman for the point of view reflected by the men from James who caused schism and controversy in the churches of Galatia. Even though Paul had been dead for a decade to a decade and a half at the time of the writing of the gospel, the author was compelled to attack his point of view and to attack him personally in the subtle way of singling out Peter as the one to whom Jesus had given a special dispensation of authority even to the binding and loosing of sins (Matthew 16.19).

Anti-Pauline References in Matthew's Gospel

If this were the only indication of this point of view in the gospel, it would not be compelling. But, in fact, the gospel is replete with anti-Pauline references. How else are we to explain the charge of Jesus to his disciples, "Go nowhere among the Gentiles, and enter no town of the Samaritans, but go rather to the lost sheep of the house of Israel" (Matthew 10.5–6)? Or the response of Jesus to the Canaanite woman, "I was sent only to the lost sheep of the house of Israel" (Matthew 15.24)? The author actually has Jesus making such a remark in Gentile territory! The mission of the believing community was to Jews first and only after the number of converts was complete was there to be a mission to the Gentiles and Samaritans. These are singular readings in Matthew's gospel. In fact, the author of Luke represents Jesus in quite a different way, for Jesus says in his initial proclamation of the gospel in Nazareth, "There were many widows in Israel in the days of Elijah, when the heaven was shut up three years and six months, when there came a great famine over all the land; and Elijah was sent to none of them but only to Zarephath, in the land of Sidon, to a woman who was a widow. And there were many lepers in Israel in the time of the prophet Elisha; and none of them was cleansed, but only Naaman the Syrian" (Luke 4.25–27). Did Jesus speak with a forked tongue? Was Peter acting contrary to Jesus' instructions when he went to Cornelius the centurion at Joppa (Acts 10.23–24)? Was the author of Acts in error when he reported that the Holy Spirit came upon the Gentiles who heard the word (Acts 10.44; 11.1)? Was Paul wrong in his mission to the Gentiles? Was he acting contrary to the mind of Christ when he understood his calling to mean that he was to preach to the Gentiles (Galatians 1.16; Romans 11.13)? Or why is the term Gentile used pejoratively in the saying of Jesus for the condemnation of that member of the community who does not respond submissively to the disciplining church, "Let him be to you as a Gentile" (Matthew 18.17)? Or again in that saying of Jesus, "in praying do not heap up empty phrases as the Gentiles do" (Matthew 6.7; cf. 5.47; 6.32; 20.25)?

What other explanation resolves the inherent problem of Jesus' prohibition against preaching to Gentiles and Samaritans according to Matthew's gospel than that the author was reflecting the effort of the Jewish Christian community to put a curb on Paul's indiscriminate preaching and to his receiving Gentile converts without imposing any Mosaic or Jewish ceremonial requirements upon them? These prohibitions have meaning only as they are seen against the background of the struggle within the church, especially within the indigenous community growing out of Judaism and with strong ties to the Mosaic past, to come to grips with the Gentile problem. At the same time there is a kind of tension within the gospel, since the author quotes with favor the word of the prophet Isaiah that the servant "shall proclaim justice to the Gentiles. . . . and in his name will the Gentiles hope" (Matthew 12.18–21).

The Jewish Heritage Integral for the Christian Life in Matthew

But there is more. Why does the author of Matthew cultivate the heritage of Judaism so assiduously and place it at the center as an integral expression of the Christian life? For this author uniquely encourages the observance of such Jewish practices as giving alms (Matthew 6.2) and fasting (Matthew 6.16)? He quotes Jesus as saying emphatically, "Think not that I have come to abolish the law and the prophets; I have come not to abolish them but to fulfill them" (Matthew 5.17). Is this too directed against Paul's gospel that announces that the law is annulled? For Paul states emphatically again and again that the believer is no longer under the law (Romans 6.14), is dead to the law (Romans 7.4, 6), is never justified by the works of the law (Galatians 2.16, 19; 3.11), the righteousness of God is manifested apart from the law (Romans 3.21), and those who endeavor to live according to the law are severed from Christ (Galatians 5.4). In addition, Paul writes, "There is no distinction between Jew and Greek" (Romans 10.12) and "to those outside the law I became as one outside the law, that I might win those outside the law" (1 Corinthians 9.21).

To whom does the author refer in the enigmatic saying, "Do not give dogs what is holy; and do not throw your pearls before swine" (Matthew

7.6)? Who are the dogs and the swine? Could these be the Gentiles, the very ones to whom Paul is offering holy things and pearls? None of the explanations that have been given for these strange references have answered the question as satisfactorily as our proposal.

And again, who are the false prophets, "who come in sheep's clothing but inwardly are ravenous wolves" (Matthew 7.15), against whom the author warns so strongly? Or the bad tree that bears evil fruit and that is known by its fruit (Matthew 7.17, 20)? Or to the saying, "Call no one your father on earth, for you have one Father—the one in heaven" (Matthew 23.9). Can this be a repudiation of Paul's word, "Though you might have ten thousand guardians in Christ, you do not have many fathers. Indeed, in Christ Jesus I became your father through the gospel" (1 Corinthians 4.15)?

These references also in the setting of the early church conflict that has been described could well refer to Paul. After all, the two sides would only be exchanging epithets, since Paul referred to his opponents as "false apostles, deceitful workmen, disguising themselves as apostles of Christ" (2 Corinthians 11.13). These strong indictments take on new relevance and meaning as they are viewed against the backdrop of the early church conflict. These were strong-minded leaders equally convinced of the rightness of their viewpoints and of their strategy for the conduct of the early Christian mission. Neither side would yield "submission even for a moment" (Galatians 2.5), and the conflict continued over a considerable period of time and with considerable animosity.

The Law is Central for Faith and Practice in Matthew's Gospel

The author of the gospel affirms that the law is the very center of all faith and practice, for "till heaven and earth pass away, not an iota, not a dot, will pass from the law until all is accomplished" (Matthew 5.18). The law, whether it be written in Greek, represented by the iota, or in Hebrew-Aramaic, represented by the dot, will stand as long as the constituent elements of the universe itself. Whom did the author have in mind as he continues with the following? "Whoever relaxes one of the least of these commandments and teaches men so, shall be called least in the kingdom of heaven; but he who does them and teaches them shall be called great in the kingdom of heaven" (Matthew 5.19). Does not this fit the apostle Paul most appropriately in the eyes of the Jewish-Christian community? Was not he the great relaxer of the law? It is when these words from the sermon on the mount are placed side by side with the "You are Peter" passage, that the intention of the author comes to its clearest focus. Peter is placed at the pinnacle as the great advocate and representative of the view that the Mosaic law has been transformed into a higher ethic and that the unnamed advocate of faith alone by grace alone is the least in the kingdom of heaven, since he not only relaxes the commandment but also teaches men so to do. Here we have a record in the gospels of the very substance of the arguments that were marshalled against Paul by the advocates of a law and obedience oriented salvation.

The teaching of Jesus is an extension of the Mosaic law, not a replacement. Jesus is the successor to Moses and his teaching is a reinterpretation and reapplication of the Mosaic law in the new age. In fact, Jesus is superior to Moses and at the same time the great conserver of all that Moses has given. This is set forth in a very subtle way in the setting for the sermon on the mount. Jesus went up on the mountain (Matthew 5.1) just as Moses of old (Ex. 19.20). But there is a dramatic difference, for whereas God spoke to Moses and Moses delivered the word of God to the people (Ex. 20.1, 22), Jesus opened his mouth and taught the disciples the word and the will of God directly (Matthew 5.2). It may not be merely a coincidence that the five teaching sections in the gospel interpolated into the Markan order for the account of the ministry of Jesus correspond symbolically to the five books of Moses that compose the torah.

The teaching of Jesus is transformed by the author of the gospel into a new law, a requirement, which begins with the Mosaic commandment but reinterprets and applies it in a much more intense and demanding way. The member of the new community must produce a righteousness that exceeds that which has been accomplished by the scribes and Pharisees (Matthew 5.20). It is to be noted that righteousness is not purely gift as in Paul, but is a state of being arrived at through disciplined effort in the relationships of daily life. Jesus himself fulfilled all righteousness by submitting to baptism, even though he had no need for its cleansing (Matthew 13.15). He is the model for all who would attain the kingdom through obedience to the law's demand. The priority for those who follow him is to place the kingdom of heaven and its righteousness above every concern and consideration (Matthew 6.33). The author then illustrates the principle of attaining righteousness by means of a series of examples of obedience to the law within the context of the most fundamental relationships of life within the community.

Obedience to the Law in the Relationships of Life

The basic human emotions, anger, contempt, lust, greed, revenge, and hatred, are to be contained. They are not appropriate responses even in the most trying situations. The seeker for righteousness is to respond in ways that are in character with the new ethic modeled by Jesus. The law of old prohibited killing; the new righteousness prohibits anger and contempt that are the precursors of murder. The law of old prohibited adultery; the new righteousness prohibits lust and those inner desires that eventuate in sexual promiscuity, divorce, and remarriage. The law of old permitted oaths; the new righteousness enjoins them. The integrity of the person is sufficient security for the truthfulness of one's word. The law of old permitted a tooth for a tooth, an equal penalty meted out to the wrongdoer; the new righteousness encourages non-resistance, non-retaliation, even a second mile, the other cheek, and the giving of one's cloak to the one who seeks redress by law. The law of old commands love of neighbor and hate towards the enemy; the new righteousness decrees love for the enemy and the persecutor. The follower of the new righteousness practices this new ethic in order that he may be a son of the Father in heaven. The ultimate goal is perfection, not only in deeds and words, but in the inner thoughts and intentions of the heart. The aspirant of this goal is to be perfect, as perfect as the heavenly Father.

The Pursuit of Perfection

It is difficult to quarrel with the ideal and the challenge of this new righteousness. Every follower of the Jesus' way must be committed to the pursuit of perfection. There must be no equivocation, no compromise with the temptations to live below the level of human conduct exemplified by Jesus. The ideal and the goal are not different as these are portrayed by the writer of this gospel and by the apostle Paul. But the ways advocated by the author of Matthew and Paul to reach the ideal are quite different and even contradictory. The author of Matthew offers a do-it-yourself program based upon one's total commitment to the ideal and unblemished conformity to the requisites set forth in the teaching of Jesus through which one reaches that ideal. This emphasis reflects the Jewish orientation of the author and the commitment of his community to preserve the basic tenets and traditions of Mosaic religion. It is evident that it was essential for this writer and for his community to preserve those basic structures of the Mosaic religion that did not appear to be in contradiction with the new righteousness in order to assure continuity with the past and stability for the future.

Paul's Reliance upon the Immediate Presence of the Spirit

Paul, on the other hand, with impeccable Jewish credentials had been set free from dependence upon every external support in favor of reliance upon the immediate presence and witness of the Holy Spirit of God. He writes, "We are discharged from the law (the Mosaic law), dead to that which held us captive, so that we serve not under the old written code but in the new life of the Spirit" (Romans 7.6). The believer is led by the Spirit (Romans 8.14), the Spirit bears witness with our spirit that we are children of God (Romans 8.16), the Spirit helps us in our weakness (Romans 8.26), our status with God is revealed by the Spirit (1 Corinthians 2.10), we are taught by the Spirit (1 Corinthians 2.13), the Spirit dwells in the community as in the temple of God (1 Corinthians 3.16), we are washed, sanctified, and justified in Jesus Christ and in the Spirit of God (1 Corinthians 6.11), we become one spirit with the Lord (1 Corinthians 6.17), and the gifts for service are through the Spirit (1 Corinthians 12.4). Therefore we are to walk by the Spirit (Galatians 5.16). Since we are led by the Spirit, we are no longer under the law (Galatians 5.18). The fruit of the Spirit is described as love, joy, peace, patience, kindness, goodness, faithfulness, gentleness, self-control (Galatians 5.22–23), the very expressions that the author of Matthew admonishes the members of the community to manifest in human relationships. For Paul these are never an attainment of the human spirit through diligent commitment and effort. They are the gift of God (Ephesians 2.8). For the author of Matthew one seeks and strives to attain to the righteousness that exceeds.

Paul's Objective View of Salvation

The difference may be described in terms of the objective and the subjective views of how man is reconciled to God and attains to the life that is pleasing to him. Paul's is the objective view that all is of God. We can do nothing good; we can do nothing to gain the approval of God and acceptance by him. We are in bondage to the powers of sin, death and evil. All our thoughts, words, and deeds are done in obedience to this unholy trinity. We are helpless to change our ways of life and to do those things that the law of God requires. The law of God, instead of being a help to our attaining the favor of God, is in reality a curse, for "all who rely on works of the law are under a curse" (Galatians 3.10). The law was our pedagog or custodian until Christ came (Galatians 3.24) and through the law comes the knowledge of sin (Romans 3.20). The law is never a guide or an aid for the doing of the good, not even for the believer, except in the one instance that it restrains us from doing evil out of fear of punishment. But this is negative goodness, not requisite and essential goodness.

The law is of God, but only as a necessary preparation for our salvation. The law condemns us and makes us aware that there is no help apart from God. God is our Savior, the God who comes in Jesus the redeemer and deliverer. Through the life and death of Jesus, God has overthrown the powers that hold us in bondage. We are set free, liberated from all those forces that would destroy us. We are baptized into the death of Christ and made one with him in his resurrection (Romans 6.3–4). We have received the Spirit of God (Romans 5.5). We live the new life of the Spirit (Romans 7.6) and those who walk according to the Spirit set their minds on the things of the Spirit (Romans 8.5). The Spirit of God dwells in us and our spirits are alive because of righteousness (Romans 8.9–10). We understand the gifts of God in the Spirit, and spiritual truths are interpreted and taught in and through the Spirit (1 Corinthians 2.12–13). In the Spirit we have the mind of Christ (1 Corinthians 2.16). When we are united to the Lord, we become one spirit with him (1 Corinthians 6.17). Our confession of faith in Jesus as Lord can only be made in the Spirit (1 Corinthians 12.3). All the gifts that build up and edify the community are inspired and empowered by the Spirit for the common good (1 Corinthians 12.7). The body of believers, whether Jew or Greek, whether slave or free, have all drunk of the one Spirit (1 Corinthians 12.13). Only as we are set free from the power of sin, do we become slaves of righteousness (Romans 6.18), free to serve God and do his will. It is impossible to think of any positive and helpful activity of the believer that is not inspired and empowered by the Spirit. God is the living and and active God, who through his Spirit is present in us and through our lives brings about the thoughts, words, and deeds that are expressions of the life of Christ.

The Subjective View According to Matthew's Gospel

The subjective view is the very opposite of what has just been described. The problem is, How shall man the sinner be reconciled to a holy and righteous God? What must we do to receive forgiveness and life from God? There must be and there is something that we can do. The law of God, the Mosaic law, sets forth the requirement of God in terms that are understandable and possible. The interpretation is called subjective, because the focus of attention is upon the requirement and our compliance. The human situation is set forth graphically in terms of anger, contempt, lust, falseness, greed, revenge, and hatred.

The Mosaic law, however, did not get at the root problem, since it spoke only to the outward manifestations and expressions of sin. All this has now changed, for Jesus the teacher and model has set forth by word and example how we are to overcome our sinful attitudes and attain the righteousness that exceeds that of the scribes and Pharisees. The Mosaic law is not abrogated, however; it remains as a sure guide and aid in attaining to the true righteousness. It is of God and it is our reminder to practice piety, prayer, and fasting, not for recognition from men, but to fulfill the conditions of life in the new age. We are to lay up treasure in heaven (Matthew 6.20), serve only one master (Matthew 6.24), renounce anxiety and live in total dependence upon God (Matthew 6.25–34). We are not to judge or take note of the faults of others, but rather be aware of our own (Matthew 7.1–5). We are to ask and seek and knock, for only the persistent will find the way that leads to life (Matthew 7.7–14). Not every one who says, "Lord, Lord," will enter the kingdom, but only those who do the will of the Father (Matthew 7.21). Only those who hear the words of Jesus and do them will survive the storms of life (Matthew 7.24–27). The disciples, as leaders in the new age, are singled out for special instructions for living and for mission (Matthew chapter 10), and only the ones who endure to the end will be saved (Matthew 10.22). Additional precepts to be observed by the disciples are given in Matthew chapter eighteen, including admonitions against despising little ones (Matthew 18.10) or causing them to sin (Matthew 18.6), on reconciling disagreements among members of the community (Matthew 18.15), and on forgiveness (Matthew 18.21–35). Everywhere the emphasis is upon the possibility and the capability of doing whatever is needed to attain the ideal and to fulfill the requirements of the ethic of the new age.

The Objective and Subjective Views not Mutually Exclusive

The objective and the subjective views are not mutually exclusive, for it is evident in the Matthean view that God plays a large role in the event of salvation and it is equally true for the Pauline view that man plays a role, although a rather minor one. But the point of emphasis distinguishes the Matthean as subjective and the Pauline as objective. And it is the contention of this essayist that the author of Matthew has greatly magnified the subjective point of view as a foil against the Pauline view that he considered ill-advised and even dangerous. His love for tradition, his respect for the Mosaic heritage, his conviction that Israel was the chosen people of God was a primary motivation in his interpretation of Jesus as the new and greater Moses and of his teaching as the new law in obedience to which one could attain the higher righteousness and the life of the new age.

The freedom of the believer, as Paul proclaimed it, is very dangerous to those who must have safeguards and securities in life, to those who need directives so that they may know what God requires and how and when these requirements may be fulfilled. Of course, Paul does not actually abrogate the Mosaic law as he was accused of doing. He simply placed it in proper focus. The law remains as the constant accuser and condemner of both believer and unbeliever. The believer is never without sin, and the law of God must always be present as a constant reminder and accuser to drive the sinner to Christ. But the law is never an aid to help us gain salvation, nor an aid or guide to the saved to help them fulfill righteousness.

The Value of the Matthean Interpretation

The value of the Matthean interpretation is that it serves as a corrective to all those who do not take the teaching of Jesus seriously. He deepens and interiorizes the application of the teaching, so that we are led to see that the mere outward or external observance of the requirements of God are a far cry from what God seeks from us. It is not the word or the deed that necessarily condemns us, but the absence of the proper motivation and attitude that excludes us from the grace and favor of God. Though the author rejects and seeks to correct what he considers to be the error of the Pauline point of view, a Christian life structured without law, he nevertheless establishes impossible criteria for the new righteousness of the new age. Who is able out of his or her own resources and even with the help of God to renounce or refrain from anger, contempt, lust, dishonesty, greed, or hatred? The spirit indeed is willing, but the flesh is weak.

A Strange Mixture in the Matthean Viewpoint

There is a strange mixture in this gospel of the provincial and of the universal, of the exclusive and of the inclusive. The problem of Jewish nationalism has not been resolved. Whereas Paul uses the expression, "to the Jew first and also to the Greek" (Romans 1.16; 2.9–10; 3.9; 10.12; 1 Corinthians 1.22, 24; 10.32; 12.13; Galatians 3.28), in an inclusive sense, the author of Matthew uses the term "Gentile" in an exclusive and even a pejorative sense. There is a universal and inclusive element in the gospel, for in the very beginning of the gospel Gentiles in the persons of the magi from the east come to do homage to the king who is born. In the announcement of the signs that precede the end of the age, the author says that the gospel is to be "preached throughout the whole world, as a testimony to all nations; and then the end will come" (Matthew 24.14). But this sounds more like a concession than a mission to include Gentiles in the gift of salvation. And the consistency of the attitude of the author is to be noted in the command that concludes his gospel, "Go and make disciples of all nations, baptizing them . . . , *teaching them to observe all that I have commanded you*" (Matthew 28.19–20). The teaching of Jesus consists of commands that are to be observed or obeyed and this is the substance of the gospel for this writer. There is to be a Gentile mission, but the conditions under that Gentiles are to be included are not different from those imposed upon the members of the Jewish Christian community that the author represents. They were to be Jews first and then Christians. The Mosaic law, including ritual and ceremonial elements, are evidently to be required of the Gentiles, and the teaching of Jesus is understood and interpreted as an extension of the law. Thus the writer consistently maintains his understanding of Jesus' teaching in a legalistic way, rather than as gospel to be heard and the life that issues from it as gift from God.

The conflict over the admission of Gentiles into the new community and over the requirements that were to be imposed upon them for membership was much more divisive and extended than some of our sources, namely, the Book of the Acts of the Apostles, suggest. The cumulative evidence from the gospel of Matthew suggests that this gospel is one expression of that conflict and that the author had an ulterior motive in mind when he penned his gospel, namely, an anti-Pauline polemic, in order to attack and counteract what he considered to be a false and perverted interpretation of Jesus' teaching. His attack was not overt and therefore much more compelling. The high respect that this gospel enjoyed in the early church and its wide use in Greek speaking congregations indicate that, though it may not have succeeded in the intention of the author to overthrow the Pauline point of view and establish the priority of the viewpoint of the Jerusalem church, nevertheless it did succeed in establishing a counter point of view to the Pauline conception of salvation.

The Objective and Subjective Views in Christendom Today

These two points of view are represented in Christendom today. The Matthean viewpoint, which gives a much larger role to obedience to the law, to the understanding of the teaching of Jesus as a new law to be observed, and to the human role in salvation, still prevails in many circles and is probably the dominant view of the majority of Christians. The Pauline point of view when it is truly understood, for the prevalent version is most often a watered-down, misunderstood, and misrepresented version, is still feared and rejected by many. It is rejected because it strips the human ego of any capacity and of any role in the event of salvation. Our ego demands that we participate in the event of salvation, at least to the extent of assisting God to accomplish that which we think he is not able to do without us.

It is most depreciating for us to confess with Paul, "I (ego) have been crucified with Christ; it is no longer I (ego) who live, but Christ who lives in me (ego); and the life I (ego) now live in the flesh I (ego) live by faith in the Son of God, who loved me (ego) and gave himself for me (ego)" (Galatians 2.20). The subjection of the ego to Christ, or the death of the ego, in Pauline theology is a most objectionable feature for those who espouse the subjective view of salvation. There are many earnest, sincere Christians who have never understood, or have rejected, the Pauline view as a viable brand of Christianity. How often we hear the subjective view of the gospel in modern preaching and teaching, "You must accept Jesus Christ as your personal Savior," rather than the objective view of Paul, "I have been crucified with Christ."

The great majority of Christians today still prefer a life hedged about with security blankets and safeguards, a life in which we really never have to make the hard choices as to what Christ wants us to be and to do, rather than the freedom to speak and to do as a minority of one under the guidance of and in the power of the Spirit. There is the fear that we will be prone to error and, above all, that the guidance of the Spirit may be, or may be interpreted to be, an ego trip. Life is much simpler when all the options are covered; when all we need to do is to look in the rule book and determine that bit of legislation in the teaching of Jesus that covers the present situation. This is the option that was preferred by the author of the gospel of Matthew. In fact, he was so committed to this point of view that he both confidently attacked the great apostle of freedom and offered an alternative—a safety net or a security blanket that he represented as having the imprimatur of none other than Jesus himself and of Peter the first among the apostles.

When we truly and honestly analyze the human psyche, however, it is apparent that we have a tremendous proclivity to hide our true self from our self. Our ego is the driving, motivating, force that so often decides our choices in life for good or for ill and determines the quality of our relationship with one another. There is unacknowledged greed, lust, envy, hatred, anger, pride, and, above all, self-righteousness in all of us. How impossible it is to control these human feelings and expressions by and through our own self-will, even when we are convinced that we are "in Christ." As the Apostle so rightly said, "The good that I would do, I do not do; and the evil I would not do, I do." The Apostle was uniquely aware of the hidden forces of evil that are always present within our psyche and that come to expression in spite of our best efforts to control or deny them. The solution to our dilemma does not and cannot lie in a rigorous self-discipline, for we have not the power nor the capacity to be other than what we are apart from the grace of God. It is beyond our ability to accept Christ as our personal Savior, for we are not gods but humans. We cannot reach up to the heavens to bring Christ down. But the marvel of God's grace is that he has reached down to deliver us from our bondage to self and to raise us up to the highest heavens. The solution to the human situation is not to live up to the standards imposed from above, but to surrender, to become what the Apostle sets forth so succinctly in the opening words of his letter to the Romans, "Paul, called to be a slave of Jesus Christ, set apart to be an apostle for the gospel of God."

Textual Criticism

❧ Textual Criticism is one of the disciplines of New Testament Studies mostly unfamiliar to the majority of church members, clergy and laity. Yet it is a basic discipline for Biblical studies. The study of the scriptures is limited mostly to our English translations and few of us realize how much research and study has been involved in the production of our translations over the centuries. Textual criticism is an obscure, but most interesting, chapter in the history of the Christian community

A Common Language and Scripture in Greek.

The original writings of the New Testament, for example, the gospels of Matthew, Mark, Luke, and John, the letters of Paul and the epistles, are called autographs. The autograph is what the author actually wrote. Paul's reference in Galatians 6.11, "See with what large letters I am writing to you with my own hand," suggests that the body of the letter was written by an amanuensis, that is, a professional writer who recorded what Paul dictated. Unfortunately no autographs are extant. They disappeared very early in the history of the Christian community through extensive use and perhaps from willful destruction. Persecution of the Christian community by Jews and especially by the Roman government could have resulted in deliberate destruction of Christian writings in order to bring an end to this heretical movement. The autographs were written in Greek, the *lingua franca* (international language) of the time. It is interesting to note that Greek had become the official language in much of the Mediterranean world as a result of the empire building of Alexander the Great in the fourth century B.C.E. He was not merely a conqueror and empire builder, but a missionary for Greek culture that he considered to be the highest expression of the human spirit. This is an evidence to this writer that the Creator God is the Lord of history who determines history's direction and outcome. Paul writes in Galatians 4.4, "But when the time had fully come, God sent forth his son." Centuries before this event the groundwork had been laid by Alexander's cultural revolution in promoting Greek language and thought throughout his vast empire. When the Christian community emerged upon the scene in the first century of our era, there was a common language throughout the known world in which to communicate the gospel, the good news of God's redeeming act in Jesus the Christ. This common language had made such an impact upon the Jewish community that their own scriptures had been translated from Hebrew into Greek in the three centuries before the coming of the Christ. This translation is known to us as the Septuagint, the translation of "the seventy." This translation became the "bible" of the early Christians. Thus when the salvation event, the death and resurrection of Jesus, was a reality, the community that emerged had two vehicles immediately at hand to propagate their message—a common language and a translation of scripture into that language. Is not this indeed an evidence of the providence of God and of his overruling direction of human history? Thus when Christian writers took in hand to record the event of salvation and their interpretation of that event, they naturally recorded their account in Greek.

The Autographs

The earliest Christian writings, the autographs, were written on very fragile material, either papyrus, a paper made from the papyrus plant that was particularly vulnerable to wear, or vellum, the skins of "clean" animals. We recall the Jewish restrictions on the use of certain animals for food. The same restrictions applied to the use of skins for writing purposes, especially for "sacred" writings. The autograph, of course, was written to a local Christian community of which the writer was a part. The intrinsic worth of these writings for telling the gospel and the respect in which their authors were held made it imperative to produce copies to circulate among all the communities. Thus there developed within the community a group of professional copyists known as scribes to produce the copies necessary for a growing community in order that all might share in the good news and that materials might be available for the evangelistic work of the community. Copies for the local churches were also necessary to combat the bizarre and even heretical teachings and interpretations that began to circulate very early. Note the many references to scribes in our gospels. There were scribes of the Pharisees and scribes of the Sadducees. The Christian community was only following a long established custom and practice in the Jewish community from which it emerged.

The Scribes

Though the scribes may have been "professional" in the sense that this was their lifetime vocation, they did not reproduce perfect copies of the autographs or of the exemplar from which they copied. It would be asking too much to expect them to reproduce exactly what was before them. The human being has never lived who could hand copy a perfect replica of the New Testament or any large portion of it. There was also another factor at work, however. The early Christian writings did not have the imprimatur of scripture and scribes were at liberty to make changes when they believed they could correct or improve upon what was before them. The first task of the textual critic is to read the manuscripts and record the variants found therein and they are numerous. There are two types of changes made by the scribes in their copying called the unintentional and the intentional. The first type, the unintentional, is not as significant as the intentional. They include the type of inadvertent errors any copyist makes: misspellings, omission of words or phrases, repeating words or phrases already copied, and similar errors. They are not usually critical for our analysis of the text, since they are often readily recognized. But there are always instances where it is difficult to determine whether a variant resulted from an inadvertent error or was an intentional change by the scribe. Intentional changes are more significant, even though some are simply the correction of misspellings or an improvement of poor grammatical construction in the autograph or exemplar used by the scribe. Some intentional changes are highly significant, however, since the critic must choose between readings, that is, make decisions as to which reading seems to be more in character with the overall thought patterns of the writing. There are readings, for example, in which we find conflicting geographical or historical information, harmonization of the text in parallel passages in the gospels, and even changes that reflect a different theological perspective or understanding of Jesus.

To clarify the above, let us look at a few examples. Differences in spelling may sometimes result in a possible and acceptable reading. In the John the Baptist pericope (Matthew 3.4) we read that the Baptist wore "a garment of camel's hair." The change of an *eta* to an *iota* in the word "camel" in two manuscripts suggests that he wore a garment of "rope." καμήλου] καμίλου 28 565. A humorous example of such variation occurs in the story of the prodigal son (Luke 15.25). When the elder brother returns from a day's work in the field he heard "music and dancing." The addition of an *iota* in the word "dancing" in one text changes the passage to read, "he heard music and little pigs." χορῶν] χοιρῶν A* Such occurrences do not create problems for the critic, but are evidences that we must always be aware that not one of our manuscripts is an accurate and perfect account of what the author wrote or dictated to his amanuensis nor of what God intended us to receive as a basis for faith.

Intentional Changes

The earliest manuscripts (third and fourth century) of Luke 4.44 read, "He was preaching in the synagogues of Judea." A fifth century manuscript omits the offending "of Judea," reading only "he was preaching in the synagogues," and two other fifth century manuscripts read, "He was preaching in the synagogues of Galilee."

ἦν κηρύσσων εἰς τὰς συναγωγὰς τῆς Ἰουδαίας B 𝔓⁷⁵ ℵ
Ἰουδαιας] Γαλιλαιας A D 𝔐 K Θ Λ Π 28 565
omit   C L

There is no other reference to a ministry by Jesus in Judea in the gospels of Matthew, Mark, and Luke prior to his visit to Jerusalem that culminated in his crucifixion. The author of Luke evidently wrote "Judea" in this passage, which was subsequently changed either by omission of Judea or by substitution of Galilee to correct what was thought to be an error in the exemplar and to bring this passage into harmony with the unanimous testimony of the gospels on this point.

Another example is found in Matthew 27.17, which reads in ninth and tenth century Greek manuscripts and in an early Syriac version, "Pilate said to them, 'Whom do you desire that I release to you, Jesus Barabbas or Jesus who is called the Christ'?"

Βαραββᾶν] Ιησουν Βαρραββαν Θ ¦ Ιησουν Βαραββαν 1*.
1582*

The reading, Jesus Barabbas, is not found in our English translations, since the great majority of early manuscripts and versions (early translations into Latin, Syriac, and Coptic) read only "Barabbas." It is probable, even though this would seem to be an incredible coincidence, that the original reading was "Jesus Barabbas" on the following grounds.

Barabbas or Jesus Barabbas?

First, Barabbas is a surname from the Aramaic meaning "son of Abbas." Is it possible that this man's given name was Jesus? The name, Jesus meaning "Savior," was very common in the Jewish community from ancient times. There are many variations of the spelling from Joshua to Hosea to Hoshea in the scriptures. In fact, Hebrews 4.8 reads, "For if Jesus had given them rest, God would not speak later of another day." Our English translations read Joshua for Jesus in this passage, because obviously the author refers to Old Testament Joshua and the names are precisely the same in Greek. A reading of the Book of Joshua in the Septuagint version confirms that the Greek spelling of the Hebrew name, Joshua, becomes Jesus in translation into Greek. Furthermore, a study of ossuary inscriptions (an ossuary is a receptacle for the bones of the dead) indicates the commonality of the name "Jesus" in the Jewish community for the time of Jesus whom we call the Christ. The use of the name begins to abate in the first century of our era with the emergence of the Christian community and their proclamation that Jesus is the Christ, the Lord and Savior of mankind, and soon disappears altogether in the Jewish community. This reflects their abhorrence that a good Biblical name has been corrupted and perverted by the claims of the Christian community with reference to Jesus of Nazareth. Thus it is intrinsically possible that the given name of the criminal, Barabbas, offered by Pilate as a pawn to the Jewish people was indeed Jesus.

Second, it would be natural for the Christian community out of reverence for Jesus the Christ whom they proclaimed as Savior and Lord to expunge this name from the text because of its association in this instance with a notorious robber and insurrectionist. Their reverence for the name Jesus and their respect for his person would bring about an opposite reaction from the use of that name in the Jewish community. Whereas the Jews dropped the offending name from use, the Christians deleted it whenever it was the given name of a *persona non grata*, an unacceptable person. Nevertheless the textual critic must make a decision in this passage whether or not the original reading was Jesus Barabbas. How can this decision be more than subjective, merely an expression of the theological tendency of the critic? There are two principles that are generally applied by the textual critic: first, Bengel's rule named after a pioneer critic that states that the shorter reading is probably the more authentic and, second, the Wordsworth—White rule that says that the more difficult reading is more probably authentic. In our passage the second principle takes precedence, since it is very difficult for twentieth century readers to accept that Barabbas' given name was Jesus, especially since it is supported by only a small number of comparatively late manuscript witnesses.

A rare instance of a singular reading, one that occurs in one source only, which may have been original in the autograph of Matthew's gospel is found in an early church father, Clement of Alexandria, who lived about C.E. 200. His writings antedate all the manuscripts and versions that we possess apart from a few very early papyri fragments, none of which cite the passage in question, namely, Matthew 11.19: "The Son of man came eating and drinking, and they say, 'Behold, a glutton and a drunkard, a friend of tax collectors and sinners'!" Clement reads "a friend of tax collectors and a sinner." The difference is a change of the word "sinner" from a nominative singular (Clement) to a plural genitive (all our extant manuscripts and versions).

> τελωνῶν φίλος καὶ ἁμαρτωλῶν. plural "sinners."
> τελωνῶν φίλος καὶ ἁμαρτωλός singular "a sinner." Clement
> of Alexandria

It would seem at first glance that the evidence is overwhelming to support the reading in our texts that Jesus was called a friend of sinners by his opponents rather than a sinner as Clement cites this passage. But again the rule of Wordsworth—White applies, the more difficult reading has an intrinsic probability, for two reasons. First, Jesus is referred to as a sinner in John 9.16, where some critics say of him, "How can a man who is a sinner do such signs?" and 9.24 where they say of Jesus, "We know that this man is a sinner." So it is not improbable for the critics as cited in Matthew's gospel to have called Jesus a sinner rather than the much weaker charge, "a friend of sinners." Second, the same principle of reverence for the person of Jesus that has been referred to above would apply here. The Christian community's affirmation that Jesus was the sinless son of God would lead them to alter a passage that suggested he was a sinner. For did not the Apostle Paul write, "For our sake he made him to be sin who knew no sin" (2 Corinthians 5.21), and do we not read in the Epistle to the Hebrews (4.15), "For we have not a high priest who is unable to sympathize with our weaknesses, but one who in every respect has been tempted as we are, yet without sin?" The probability is then that very early in the transmission of Matthew's gospel a scribe or scribes altered this text by substituting an *omega nu* (genitive plural) for an original *omicron sigma* (nominative singular) to bring this passage into conformity with the prevailing view that Jesus was the holy and sinless son of God.

But, we may argue, why, if this was the case, did they not alter the passages in John's gospel in which Jesus is spoken of as "a sinner?" The response and defense of this writer would be that the probabilities for such an alteration in the gospel of Matthew are far greater than for a similar change in John's gospel. All the evidence from the early Christian writers confirms that Matthew's gospel was by far the most popular gospel in the early Christian community. Their citations of this gospel far outnumber their quotations from the other gospels. Furthermore, the audience to which Matthew's gospel was addressed, a Jewish—Christian community, would be far more unsophisticated than the community to which the author of John's gospel penned his profound interpretation of Jesus and the salvation event. Therefore Matthew's community would be more apt to bring that author's religious writings into conformity with their own rather conservative and legalistic point of view.

Another unique reading discovered recently in 𝔓²⁵ from the divorce and remarriage pericope in Matthew 19 is the following:

All texts: εἰ οὕτως ἐστὶν ἡ αἰτία τοῦ ἀνθρώπου
𝔓²⁵ ει ουν αιτιος γινεται ανθρωπος

The latter reading gives a very different meaning to the passage. The passage in all texts reads: "If such is the case of a man with his wife, it is better not to marry." 𝔓²⁵ reads: "If therefore a man becomes a cause (i.e., of divorce) with his wife, it is better not to marry." Here, and uniquely, the burden of blame rests upon the man.

Harmonization

There is also much evidence that scribes frequently harmonized the texts of the gospels. They were very familiar with all the gospels, since copying was their profession and their act of copying repeatedly would tend to fixate certain passages into memory. How natural then to improve upon the text of a gospel they were in the process of copying by adding information not in that gospel from the text of another. Sometimes information from another gospel was added in the margin by the scribe only to appear in the text of a later manuscript.

An example of harmonization occurs in the Lord's Prayer found only in the gospels of Matthew (6.9–13) and Luke (11.2–4). A cursory reading reveals that these are actually two versions of a prayer that Jesus shared with his disciples since there are extensive and major differences between them. Matthew opens the prayer with the familiar, "Our Father who art in heaven," whereas Luke simply says, "Father." The majority of Lukan manuscripts from the fifth century and on together with the Old Latin, Syriac, and Coptic versions read with Matthew, "Our Father who art in heaven," whereas the short version, without doubt the original, is supported only by third and fourth century Greek manuscripts, the Vulgate, and one Syriac manuscript. The scribes' intimate knowledge of Matthew led them to assimilate Luke's reading to the more familiar Matthew. In a similar way, the petition, "Deliver us from evil," is absent in Luke's version of the prayer. We find that this petition was added in Luke's version of the prayer in a majority of the manuscripts referred to in the previous example as a harmonization so that the prayer in the two gospels would conform one to the other. It is also interesting to note that the familiar liturgical ending of the prayer commonly used by Protestants but not by Roman Catholics, "For yours is the kingdom and the power and the glory for ever. Amen," is only reported in Greek manuscripts beginning with the fifth century of our era. An interesting addition to this liturgical conclusion is found in a few manuscripts, "For yours is the kingdom and the power and the glory of the Father and of the Son and of the Holy Spirit for ever. Amen." All the above examples illustrate in one way or another the type of intentional changes made by scribes to correct or improve upon the text in the exemplar before them.

Textual Displacement

One of the most peculiar instances of textual displacement is the pericope of the woman taken in adultery (John 7.53–8.11) that is found in our English versions in that location. However, this pericope is not found in our earliest manuscripts from the third and fourth centuries nor in numerous manuscripts of later centuries. It first appears in the above location in John's gospel in the fifth century manuscript, Codex Bezae, and then in a number of ninth to twelfth century manuscripts. Strangely, it is found at the end of John's gospel in a grouping of cursive manuscripts known as Family One, which are dated from the tenth century and later. Again it appears after Luke 21.38 in another grouping of cursive manuscripts known as Family Thirteen, dating from the eleventh century and later and in the margin of another cursive manuscript after Luke 24.53. Finally, it is found after John 7.36 in a twelfth century cursive manuscript.

Although this pericope is generally acknowledged to be the account of an authentic event, it is difficult to explain this strange pattern of occurrence from absence in the earliest manuscripts to insertion at five different points in the gospels of Luke and John. Evidently it was a piece of oral tradition that was not included in the original autographs of these gospels, but which continued to circulate in its oral form throughout the Christian community. There must have been some hesitance about its inclusion in the gospels in the first five centuries of the community's existence, perhaps out of fear that Jesus' lenience towards this woman taken in such a gross act of adultery and his refusal to punish her might result in a moral letdown in the community. Whatever the explanation for this phenomenon, the point is illustrated that the scribes exercised considerable freedom when copying the exemplar. In spite of the fact that the canon of Christian writings had been established centuries earlier, the scribes were at liberty to make extensive changes in the interior content of that canon.

Theological Changes

Theological changes are more difficult to demonstrate, since there is such a wide divergence in theological perspective and understanding within the Christian community. Our theological underpinnings are not the same, and we always carry much theological baggage with us in our interpretation of the text. However, 1 Thessalonians 3.2 is offered as an example of a passage where a difference in theological perspective has wrought a change in the text. Does the passage originally refer to Timothy as "the fellow worker of God," or as "the servant of God?" The Revised Standard Version reads "servant," although the manuscript support suggests strongly that the earlier reading was "fellow worker of God," the reading chosen by the editors of current critical editions of the Greek New Testament. There were some in the early Christian community who believed that they were "fellow workers of God" and that the gospel makes it incumbent upon the follower of Christ to work and cooperate with God to make it possible for him to accomplish his purpose in the world. This view was rejected by others who insisted that God accomplishes his works without any help or cooperation from man. Those who held the former view were called "synergists" by the latter, a term with a less than complimentary connotation. This would explain why it was necessary to change the reading from "fellow worker of God" to "servant of God" in order to avoid any suggestion that we can cooperate with God or assist him in any way in what he does. Some readings with grave theological differences will be cited in a later section of this essay.

The Task of the Critic

The task of the textual critic is to work through the ancient manuscripts, the versions, and other relevant sources to identify and record the variant readings in order to classify and critically analyze them. The end in view is to identify the older and more authentic readings, and then to render judgments upon the basis of the evidence gathered as to what the author wrote or intended to write. Finally, our task is to prepare an edition of the Greek New Testament that represents as nearly as we can determine through objective methodology what was written, or more probably what was intended by the author. The published result then becomes the basis for our exegetical and hermeneutical study of the New Testament and the basis for its translation into English or any other language or dialect.

This task of the textual critic is a monumental one, since there is so much material to research, to analyze and to evaluate. The grist for the mill of the textual critic includes, first of all, the Greek manuscripts. There are some three thousand of these containing various portions of the New

Testament in various conditions of readability and representing different levels of quality. The critic must make judgments as to their usefulness for the project, since they are not all of equal value. Some late manuscripts are more valuable than earlier ones, since they were evidently copied from a better exemplar. Second, there are numerous versions, or translations, into the various languages native to the early Christian communities. Third, there are lectionary editions prepared for use in the churches for the services of worship and celebration; and, finally, there are the writings of the early church fathers, the scholars of the church, who frequently quote scripture in their treatises.

Handwritten copies in Greek were produced into the fifteenth century, until Gutenberg's press made it possible to mass produce copies that were identical. The more than three thousand handwritten copies that we possess are principally of portions of the New Testament, such as a collection of the gospels, of Paul's letters, of the epistles, and even of the Apocalypse. Fragments exist of papyri manuscripts from the second and third centuries, but the first and the earliest complete manuscript of the New Testament dates from the middle of the fourth century. Since the Christian religion was not recognized and approved by the Roman Empire as a proper religion, Christians were the object of fierce persecution on a number of occasions, informally by Jews and other opponents and formally by some of the Roman emperors, notably Nero in the seventh decade of the first century and Domitian in the tenth decade. Christian writings were probably destroyed in the effort to stamp out a religion that was considered to be obnoxious and false. A change in status came in the early fourth century when Emperor Constantine became a Christian and declared Christianity to be *religio licita,* that is, a licensed religion. This accounts in part for the increasing volume of manuscripts that appear after the fourth century. Of course, the growth of the church is a factor in that increase, but the most probable explanation for the paucity of manuscripts from the period prior to the fourth century apart from the normal erosion of use is their destruction by the enemies of the Christian community in an effort to stamp out this hateful religion.

The Versions

The first Christians were ardent and zealous advocates of their faith. They traveled far and wide throughout the Roman Empire and beyond its borders with their proclamation that Jesus was the Christ, the Savior of all mankind. Christian communities sprang up in many lands where the native tongue was neither Greek nor Aramaic. This soon necessitated translations of the gospels and other Christian writings into the language and dialect of these new converts. Although Greek was the dominant language in Rome in the first century of our era, there were other areas of the empire, notably North Africa, where this was not the case and where Latin was preeminent. This led to numerous translations into Latin. There are more than thirty-five different Old Latin versions extant from the fourth century and on. The existence of so many independent translations into Latin attests to the need for copies of the scripture in the native tongue. The same was true in Syria and Egypt where early versions of the New Testament were rendered into Syriac and Coptic at an early date. These translations are important because they shed light upon the text or texts that were in use in the early life of the church. The versions reflect the underlying Greek text from which they were translated and thus at times give decisive support to certain readings under consideration for the preparation of a critical edition. The problem for the text critic becomes one of linguistics, because it is necessary to know both languages well enough to correlate those readings that are in agreement and those that are variant.

Lectionary Editions

Very few Christian communities in the early history of the church were able to secure complete copies of the Old and New Testaments. First, they were not available and, second, it was a very tedious and expensive undertaking to produce handwritten copies that met the criteria of need and accuracy in the church. Yet it was essential that a copy of the scripture be available for the worshipping community, since the reading of portions of the scripture was a vital part of the worship and also was needed for the instruction and preparation of converts for membership. The lectionary edition was an innovation to meet the need of the worshipping community. These editions included those texts from the Old and New Testaments appointed for reading and for the homilies by the worship leaders at the observances on the holy and festival days of the church. These editions are also important for the text critic, since some are very early and therefore reflect fewer scribal emendations and changes than many of our manuscripts and versions.

Grouping of Manuscripts into Families

The writings of the early church scholars are also very valuable, since the writers frequently quoted scripture. Their quotations are highly important for two reasons: first, they are an aid in identifying the type of manuscript or text used by the writer and, second, they help to place geographically and historically where and when this type of text was in use. The first three centuries of our Christian era may be entitled the "dark ages," since so little is known of the history of the Christian community in this period. One facet of this is our lack of knowledge of the history of the transmission of the text. There are only bits and pieces of information that must be juxtaposed much as we put together a jigsaw puzzle in order to bring coherence to our knowledge of history. Our study of the variants found in the manuscripts has led to a grouping of manuscripts according to type or text family. The internal evidence inevitably leads to the conclusion in some instances that there is a familiar pattern of variants in certain manuscripts and thus that there must be a special relationship between or among them. From the evidence it would appear that a particular manuscript or several manuscripts were either copied from the same exemplar or from one another. A study of the quotations from the New Testament in the early non-canonical writings is an aid in pinpointing where and when these text types developed and is therefore of inestimable value to us in unraveling our puzzle.

The problem is compounded, however, because, as we have noted, there are no two manuscripts that are exactly alike. Usually the differences between any two manuscripts run into the hundreds of instances and even thousands. Each scribe made intentional and unintentional changes, so that every copy produced from the autograph of Mark's gospel was different from every other copy and the same can be said for every New Testament writing. Furthermore, copies were made from copies, so that the number of variant readings was multiplied *ad infinitum*. The attempt to group manuscripts into families by similarity of variants has narrowed the field of inquiry to a degree; but ultimately each manuscript must be treated as an individual with a personality of its own, and its unique and peculiar readings evaluated against the total spectrum.

Qualitative Evaluation of Manuscripts

A study of the individual manuscripts leads to the inevitable conclusion that some manuscripts are more valuable than others for qualitative reasons. Age is an important criterion, but not entirely, since an early manuscript may have been copied from a poor exemplar and a late manuscript from a very good exemplar. Each manuscript must be assessed upon the basis of content. The earliest papyri manuscripts from the second and third centuries are probably the most valuable, since they are closer to the autographs, but they consist only of fragments and it is astounding how many and how serious are the differences among them. The earliest complete manuscript of the New Testament is from the fourth century and is entitled Codex Sinaiticus, since it was found in an Orthodox monastery on Mount Sinai in the mid-nineteenth century. It is generally recognized to be of high quality and very valuable for our knowledge of the text, although it has many singular or unique readings and the scribe was rather careless at his workbench. This is particularly true of his spelling and his omission by *homoioteleuton*; that is, the confusion of similar words or of words ending in similar syllables that led to the omission of phrases or even lines of the exemplar. The manuscript generally recognized to be superior to all others qualitatively is Codex Vaticanus, a fourth century manuscript discovered in the Vatican Library that first appeared in a catalog of the library in 1475, but whose previous history is totally unknown. Unfortunately, certain portions of this manuscript are lacking, for example, the latter portion of Hebrews (from 9.14), the Pastoral Epistles, and the Apocalypse. This manuscript, valuable as it is, was not made available for study by the Vatican until late in the nineteenth century, but since then together with Codex Sinaiticus has become the cornerstone of the modern critical editions of the Greek New Testament. Unfortunately, the editions prior to this time, beginning with Erasmus' edition in the sixteenth century, were based upon inferior manuscripts. Current critical editions are largely based upon these early and inferior editions. The method invariably employed by modern critics has been to edit the older editions by substituting readings that are considered to be superior. The result is an eclectic and conglomerate text, since the method has not always been applied consistently and the end result is that there are actually readings (words and even phrases) without manuscript support as they appear in these editions.

The So-Called Western Text

One of the most intriguing questions for the critic is the relationship of a group of manuscripts largely represented by Codex Bezae (fifth century), with the Greek and Latin texts in parallel columns, and many of the Old Latin texts to other early manuscripts, such as Vaticanus and Sinaiticus. The composition, or copying, of the latter is usually assigned to Egypt, an early center for Christian scholarship. Codex Bezae was obtained from the convent of St. Irenaeus at Lyons in southern France by Theodore Beza, hence its title, and brought to Geneva in 1562. Subsequently, he presented this manuscript to the University of Cambridge. This manuscript is most unusual, since there are a large number of unique readings very different from what we find in any other manuscript or family of manuscripts. Support for these readings is found in the Old Latin manuscripts referred to above. A notable example is found in Luke 6.4 where Bezae adds: "The same day, beholding a man working on the Sabbath, he said to him, 'Man, if you know what you are doing, blessed are you; but if you do not know, you are accursed and a transgressor of the law'." Another notable example is an addition to Luke 23.53 where Bezae reads, "and when he (Joseph of Arimathea) had laid him (in the tomb), he placed a great stone upon it that twenty men could hardly roll." The examples are so numerous that these two quotes hardly do justice to the differences, but the point is that they raise the question of the earliest text type in a very acute way. Codex Bezae and its allies have been designated the Western text, since it is presumed that they originated there. But studies have shown that readings designated "Western" because they occur in Bezae and its allies are also to be found in early papyri fragments from Egypt, the home of the so-called Egyptian or Alexandrian text. What this demonstrates is that the early text was not stereotyped in any way, but rather was very fluid in the early period of the Christian community's history.

Modern Technology and Manuscript Study

The availability of the Greek manuscripts and versions for study and research has been greatly advanced in our day by the production of photostatic and microfilm copies of most of them. The fragile nature of many of them and their location in libraries, museums, monasteries, and private collections throughout the world prohibits their examination by individual researchers. Modern technology has been of the highest importance for research into the text of the New Testament. The photostatic and microfilm copies make it possible for scholars to investigate the problem anywhere. In some instances, microfilm copies are an unacceptable substitute, since it is very difficult to read faded and fragmentary passages; and corrections by scribes between the lines and in the margins do not always show clearly on the tape. But study of difficult passages on the microfilm copy and a comparison of that passage with the conclusions of others set forth in critical editions results in a reliable reading of the passage.

Theological Punctuation

It is to be understood that the reading of manuscripts is a tedious and laborious task, since the earliest manuscripts, called uncial, were printed in capital letters without spacing between words and without punctuation. The reader must have some knowledge of Greek vocabulary in order to make word distinctions and must also identify phrasing and sentences. A change in punctuation can sometimes alter the meaning of a passage drastically. For example, in Mark 1.3 our text reads, "The voice of one crying in the wilderness: Prepare the way of the Lord." This is a quotation from the Old Testament prophet, Isaiah, where we read, "A voice cries: 'In the wilderness prepare the way of the Lord'" (40.3). The use of this passage in a different context and with a different application has made it necessary to change the punctuation to make it relevant as a reference to the ministry of John the Baptist. Another example is John 1.3–4: "All things were made through him, and without him was not anything made that was made. In him was life." A change in punctuation that is preferred by some results in the reading: "All things were made through him and without him was not anything made. That which was made was life in him." Even punctuation in some passages becomes an extension of our theology.

Cursive Writing

A new method of writing developed in the Greek speaking world approximately in the sixth century; that is, a form of longhand called cursive in which Greek letters are joined much as in our present English longhand. However, there is still no separation of words and no punctuation and the reader must adjust to a new set of hieroglyphs. A comparison of manuscripts from the Christian community to manuscripts composed in the secular world during the first ten centuries indicates that the former was often more innovative and open to change than the latter. Christian scribes generally adopted the new cursive writing at an earlier date than scribes of the political and economic order, and also adopted the new method of binding their writings in book form; a book form is called a codex or in plural codices, rather than the customary scroll or rolled form that had been in use for many centuries.

A new critical edition of the Greek New Testament is now in preparation by the present writer in which he is seeking to salvage some of the more important contributions made by numerous scholars in the past and at the same time introduce a number of innovative changes to improve this basic tool and make it more utile for all those who are involved in the various disciplines of New Testament study—source, form, literary, redaction, and composition criticism—and also for exegesis and hermeneutics, that is, the interpretation of the text and its application to our own situation in life and to our twenty-first century ways of thought.

Among these innovations is the selection of Codex Vaticanus to be the basic text for this new edition. Codex Vaticanus, a fourth century manuscript, is cited *in toto*, including its obvious errors, as the lead line in a new format of parallel lines. In fact, all sources used are cited completely, so that the reader may follow the text of any manuscript of choice in its entirety. In the view of this writer the parallel line format is a distinct improvement over any other presentation of the information, for the reader is reading texts that were texts at an early time in the history of the Christian community, rather than a text that was never a text except in the minds of a comparatively few modern specialists in the nineteenth and twentieth centuries.

A second innovation is the parallel line format, a new line being given for each variant of every kind for every manuscript source and version used when compared to the reading in Codex Vaticanus or to the other sources. The various kinds of variants consist of five types: additions, omissions, alterations of the word order, substitutions of a different word or words, and itacisms (differences in spelling). The symbols for the manuscripts and versions used are reported at the end of each line, and spacing is used to equate the texts vertically. These symbols are capital letters of our alphabet for the uncial manuscripts, Arabic numbers for the cursives, and abbreviations for the modern textual editions. The spacing of the parallel lines places the agreements in the texts into an alignment vertically. Thus the reader can visualize similarities and differences among the various sources immediately. This is a notable improvement over the practice in all other current textual editions of placing a few select variants in a very compact and condensed set of footnotes at the bottom of the page. It is most difficult to correlate the variants from text to footnote in this outworn format. The new format makes it possible for the reader to key in the variants immediately and to evaluate the relevance of any particular reading.

A third innovation is the reporting of all variants and all significant information from the sources, since each manuscript or version used is reported in its totality and consecutively. Thus all information from every source used is on the table for consideration. No subjective judgments or decisions have been made that some information is irrelevant for study and consideration and can be safely excluded. It may be that even the misspellings or different spellings by the scribes, especially when oft repeated, or their contractions of the divine names and certain other words that occur frequently in the text, or even the use of Greek letters as enumerations in the margins to denote individual pericopes (the Greek letters have numerical value) may give us clues as to the relationships among manuscripts and shed new light upon the history of the transmission of the text. The task is formidable, the work often tedious and time-consuming, demanding a high-level concentration to assure accuracy and consistency. But there is joy and satisfaction in seeing the form take shape of a work that will lift the lowly discipline of textual criticism to new levels of respect and usefulness within the Christian community.

A Critique of Recent Textual Critical Methodology [1]

After many years of labor on this project, and after the publication of seven volumes in the series *New Testament Greek Manuscripts*, Matthew through Romans and Galatians, this writer has come to a new perspective and understanding of the function and purpose of this discipline. He has come to the conclusion that the very purpose and goal undergirding the discipline of textual criticism, that is, to recover the most reliable and earliest text of the ancient New Testament writings, is suspect and subject to revision. Even if this dictum may be debatable, the writer believes that there is a much more significant reason for pursuing the discipline of text criticism. The traditional purpose and goal in recent and in the dominant methodology has been set forth succinctly by one of the giants of the last century, Kirsopp Lake, in *The Text of the New Testament* as follows: "One of the most necessary parts of the investigations of historians is to criticize the documents on which their researches are based, in order to be certain that the text that they are using really represents *the original writing of the author* . . . . The object of all textual criticism is to recover so far as possible *the actual words written by the writer*. . . . The problem, then, which faces the textual critic is to remove from a number of manuscripts of varying date the corruptions that have crept into the text and to assign to each variation its appropriate cause, thus obtaining in the end *the original pure text*.[2] (italics mine).

The Failure of the Traditional Methodology.

The editor of the volumes, *New Testament Greek Manuscripts*, has been a disciple of this school throughout a long career, but has now come to the conclusion that this is not only an impossible task, but far less desirable than a distinctly different goal. Before setting forth this other goal, however, let me very simply review the impossibility of the traditional goal expressed above by Kirsopp Lake. The first continuous and complete texts of the New Testament are from the fourth century of our era, two to three

---

[1] This portion of the essay is reproduced from the "*Introduction*" printed in *New Testament Greek Manuscripts: Romans* (Tyndale House Publishers, Inc., Wheaton, and William Carey International University Press, Pasadena, 2001), pp. xxxv–xxxi.

[2] Kirsopp Lake, *The Text of the New Testament*, (Rivingtons, London, 1949, 6th ed.), pp. 1f.

centuries removed from the time the autographs were penned. The historical period from 50 C.E. to 350 C.E. is a relatively dark age with reference to the transmission of the text. Even our knowledge of the authorship and origins of the writings is problematic, built upon hypothesis and theory. We possess only fragments of copies of the autographs from any period earlier than 350 C.E. Accordingly, they are extremely valuable, but they suggest that the texts were already in a state of flux at this early time with very distinctive differences in nuance and meaning. To illustrate this point, let us look at a passage from Matthew 19.10 as found in 𝔓²⁵, a fourth century papyrus manuscript:

10 λέγουσιν αὐτῷ οἱ μαθηταί,   Εἰ οὕτως ἐστὶν ἡ αἰτία τοῦ
   ανθρώπου B ℵ^c Θ [u]w
10 λέγουσιν   οἱ μαθηταὶ αὐτοῦ, Εἰ οὕτως <u>ἔτιος</u>
   <u>γίνεται</u>   <u>ἄνθρωπος</u> 𝔓²⁵

μετὰ τῆς γυναικός, οὐ συμφέρει γαμῆσαι. B **uwT** rell
μετὰ τῆς γυν···κός, οὐ συμ······ ········· 𝔓²⁵

The translation differences are as follows:
  a) "If such is the case of a man with his wife, it is better not to marry."
  b) "If thus a man becomes a cause (of divorce) with his wife, it is better not to marry."

According to the principle enunciated by K. Lake *et al.*, the first reading, reported in all critical editions (the second reading is not even reported) must be *the original pure text*. This cannot be proven, however, for a final judgment can only be subjective. We know that the view set forth in 𝔓²⁵ was contrary to historical opinion of the society of Jesus' time for a man to be at fault in sexual matters or in causes leading to divorce. Compare, for example, the adultery pericope (John 7.53–8.11) where a woman taken in the very act of adultery is brought to Jesus for judgment. Why was not the man also brought? He must have been taken in the very act also. The point is that the second reading is most unusual and more in character with the radical teaching of Jesus, who often cut against the grain of accepted public opinion with reference to religious and social mores of the time. There will necessarily be strong differences of opinion among current critics as to which of these readings is *the original pure text*, since each of us comes to

Textual Criticism

the task with our own agenda conditioned by our background, training, and theological bent. Or could it be that neither reading is *the original pure text*?

A very interesting corroborating commentary on this very principle has been pointed out to me by Paul Sellin, retired professor of English literature at UCLA and a specialist in John Donne's poetry, in the following quote, "Most of Donne's twentieth century editors have created synthetic or eclectic texts, adopting a seventeenth-century printing of each poem as copy-text and generally following that printing's accidentals, while sometimes emending its substantives toward manuscript readings. There are, however, a number of problems with this approach. A major one, . . . is that the practice involves the highly questionable assumption that any modern editor—even one very sensitive, learned, and wise—can reach back over hundreds of years and somehow ascertain what must have been in Donne's mind, root out instances of corruption, and synthetically reconstruct a text reflecting what he actually wrote.[3]

To believe that we can reconstruct out of fragmentary and late material *"the original pure text"* is thus a delusion. Whatever is so reconstructed can only be fictional; that is, what we desire the text to be. How can we put ourselves back into the time frame and into the mind of the author of the autograph? There can, therefore, be no agreement among critics as to which reading may have been original, There must always be differing viewpoints and understandings about what the author intended and wrote.

"A New and More Excellent Way"

Therefore the principle is set forth here that the role of the critic is to present the material from the manuscripts *in toto*, since each of the manuscripts is a witness to the historical, sociological, religious, and theological situation in one or more Christian communities wherever and whenever that manuscript was penned. Let me illustrate this principle by reference to several examples:

Ro. 14.17 txt	ἀλλὰ δικαιοσύνη καὶ	εἰρήνη καὶ χαρὰ ἐν
	"But righteousness and	peace and joy in the

---

[3] Gary A. Stringer, General Editor, *The Variorum Edition of the Poetry of John Donne*, Vol. 2, *The Elegies*, (Indiana University Press, Bloomington, 2000), p. LII.

	1646	ἀλλὰ δικαιοσύνη καὶ <u>ἄσκησης</u> εἰρήνη καὶ χαρὰ ἐν
		"But righteousness and asceticism, peace and joy in the
Ro. 14.17	txt	πνεύματι ἁγίῳ
		Holy Spirit."
	1646	π̄ν̄ι ἁγίῳ
		Holy Spirit."
Mt. 19.18	txt	ὁ δὲ Ἰησοῦς εἶπεν, Τὸ Οὐ φονεύσεις, Οὐ μοιχεύσεις
	Clem.	Ου φονευσεις, ου μοιχευσεις, <u>ου παιδοφθορησεις</u>. Clement of Alexandria Pr 108.5.
Mt. 19.18	txt	"But Jesus said, 'You shall not murder, you shall not commit adultery, . . .'"
	Clem.	'You shall not murder, you shall not commit adultery, you shall not seduce little boys, . . .'" Clement Pr 108.5.
Ac. 16.33	txt	καὶ ἐβαπτίσθη αὐτὸς καὶ οἱ αὐτοῦ ἅπαντες
	69	καὶ ἐβαπτίσθη αὐτὸς καὶ <u>υἱοὶ</u> αὐτοῦ πάντες
Ac. 16.33	txt	"And he himself was baptized and all of his own."
	69	"And he himself was baptized and all of his sons."

Not one of these variants is reported in any critical edition to which I have had access. Yet each is highly significant, since each reflects a perspective or attitude in a Christian community at an historical time and place. The first introduces *asceticism* into an important Pauline text, giving this widely accepted practice by Christians the imprimatur of scripture. The second introduces an injunction against *pedophilia* into the ten commandments as if it were an authentic Mosaic prohibition. The third reflects an early and long held view in the church of the non-status of women; only *sons* were baptized. These are but a few examples illustrating the importance of manuscripts as sources informing us of significant historical and sociological viewpoints held in some Christian communities. They are chiefly important, then, not because we have arrived at a mythical *original pure text*, but because they are mirrors reflecting what was the current thought and practice in various communities historically and sociologically.

Textual Criticism

Equally important, if not more so, are variants reflecting various theological differences within the communities, revealing extreme, even what we would call heretical, views. There are numerous occurrences in Paul's Letter to the Romans, for example:

1.4   txt   Ἰησοῦ Χριστοῦ τοῦ κυρίου ἡμῶν   [Jesus Christ our Lord]

**   Ἰησοῦ Χριστοῦ τοῦ **θεοῦ** ἡμῶν 323 460 618 1738
[Jesus Christ our **God**]. See also Ro. 2.4; 5.21

Compare also a reading from a fifth century manuscript, Codex Alexandrinus (A), from the Passion account:

Jn. 19.40   ἔλαβον .. τὸ σῶμα τοῦ Ἰησοῦ καὶ ἔδησαν αὐτὸ ἐν ὀθονίοις μετὰ τῶν ἀρωμάτων
[They took the body of Jesus and wrapped it with the spices in linen cloths].

ἔλαβον .. τὸ σῶμα τοῦ **θεοῦ** καὶ ἔδησαν αὐτὸ ἐν ὀθονίοις μετὰ τῶν ἀρωμάτων
[They took the body of **God** and wrapped it with the spices in linen cloths].

1.7   txt   ἀπὸ θεοῦ πατρὸς ἡμῶν καὶ κυρίου Ἰησοῦ Χριστοῦ
[from God our Father and the Lord Jesus Christ]

618   ἀπὸ θεοῦ **π̅ν̅ς̅** ἡμῶν καὶ κυρίου Ἰησοῦ Χριστοῦ
[from God our Spirit and the Lord Jesus Christ]

1.17   txt   δικαιοσύνη γὰρ θεοῦ ἐν αὐτῷ ἀποκαλύπτεται
["For the righteousness of God is revealed in him."]

1506   δικαιοσύνη γὰρ **α̅ν̅ο̅υ̅** θ̅υ̅ ἐν αὐτῷ ἀποκαλύπτεται
["For the righteousness of a man of God is revealed in him."]

6.4   txt   διὰ τῆς δόξης τοῦ πατρός ["through the glory of the Father."]

945   διὰ τῆς δόξης τοῦ **π̅ν̅ς̅** ["through the glory of the Spirit."]

8.11   txt   τὸ πνεῦμα τοῦ ἐγείραντος τὸν Ἰησοῦν ἐκ νεκρῶν οἰκεῖ ἐν ὑμῖν.
["The Spirit of the one who raised Jesus from the dead dwells in you."]

1506   τὸ πνεῦμα τοῦ ἐγείραντος **ἡμᾶς** ἐκ νεκρῶν οἰκεῖ ἐν ὑμῖν
["The Spirit of the one who raised us from the dead dwells in you."]

These examples are surely not merely scribal errors, but must be intentional alterations of the text to set forth the theological intent of the writer. A clear example of the intentional occurs in the following passage from the gospels:

Mt. 11.30 txt   ὁ γὰρ ζυγός μου χρηστός B **uwτ** rell [my yoke is easy]
ὁ γὰρ ζυγός μου χριστός E K L 13 124 2* 579 1071
[13 124 1071 contract x̅s̅][my yoke is Christ]

It is by far more critical in principle to report all evidence, rather than to make subjective and arbitrary judgments as to what is important and what is not in the search for an *original pure text*. It is not possible without miraculous assistance to reconstruct such a text out of our sources, especially in view of our human frailty. In my judgment there is a far more legitimate and useful goal.

Another caveat of a highly respected textual critic, Ernest Cadman Colwell, is "singular readings should not be included in any *apparatus criticus*. They belong to special studies."[4] There is truth in the second part of this statement referring to "special studies." But the statement is misleading and even erroneous, since, as some of the singular reading examples cited above demonstrate, such readings are of the highest importance as a counter foil to the eclectic text given to us by the critics and sometimes even represented as *the original pure text*. If *each manuscript was Scripture in an early Christian community* and the basis for preaching and teaching in that community, then singular readings as a part of that text are highly reflective of the sociological, religious, and theological viewpoints within that community and must be embodied in sermons, dialogs, treatises, and commentaries issuing from that community. Therefore singular readings must be included, since they are essential to complete the record as accurately as humanly possible of the early history of Christian communities.

---

[4] Ernest Cadman Colwell, "*Scribal Habits in Early Papyri: A Study in the Corruption of the Text*," Reprint from *The Bible in Modern Scholarship*, (Abingdon Press, Nashville, 1965), p. 387.

Textual Criticism

If we should eliminate singular readings from the record, a very large number of readings would be stricken from the Appendix in the volume on Romans devoted to a listing of readings not reported in Nestle-Aland²⁷. Even a cursory examination of some of these singular readings demonstrates that they are far and away more significant than many of the readings reported in Nestle-Aland²⁷ that have strong support in numerous manuscripts. Let us suggest how barren the results of our textual studies would be if we eliminated just one type of variant from our consideration: the *omissions*. Here I would refer only to those omissions of multiple words or phrases that are identified in the appendix by the word *omit* and the manuscript or manuscripts lacking the phrase or even a number of phrases. Sometimes lengthy omissions occur in the same passage in more than one manuscript. This suggests that a common exemplar was used by more than one scribe. There are 126 such omissions listed. The list does not include individual words or even the omission of multiple words in many instances. Many of those listed may be identified as *homoioteleuton*, that is, the leap of the same to the same. They are usually, but perhaps not always, unintentional scribal errors. But they do have consequences for the user of the text. And remember that *each manuscript was scripture* for a believing and worshipping community.

A notable example occurs at Ro. 5.12:

txt Διὰ τοῦτο ὥσπερ δι᾽ ἑνὸς ἀνθρώπου ἡ ἁμαρτία εἰς τὸν κόσμον εἰσῆλθεν καὶ διὰ τῆς ἁμαρτίας ὁ θάνατος, καὶ οὕτως εἰς πάντας ἀνθρώπους ὁ θάνατος διῆλθεν, ἐφ᾽ ᾧ πάντες ἥμαρτον· ἄχρι γὰρ νόμου ἁμαρτία ἦν ἐν κόσμῳ, ἁμαρτία δὲ οὐκ ἐλλογεῖται μὴ ὄντος νόμου, ἀλλὰ ἐβασίλευσεν ὁ θάνατος ἀπὸ Ἀδὰμ μέχρι Μωϋσέως καὶ ἐπὶ τοὺς μὴ ἁμαρτήσαντας ἐπὶ τῷ ὁμοιώματι τῆς   omit 2344

Translation: "Therefore, just as sin came into the world through one man, and death came through sin, and so death spread to all because all have sinned—sin was indeed in the world before the law, but sin is not reckoned when there is no law. Yet death exercised dominion from Adam to Moses, even over those whose sins were not like . . ."

There can be no question but that the absence of this passage from manuscript 2344 was an unintentional omission by the scribe, but what does this omission do for the meaning and exegesis of the context by the users of this passage for preaching, teaching, and writing? The point is that manuscript 2344 was used somewhere within a believing community for devotional, homiletical, and theological purposes. Each of these 126 omissions thus reflects a discontinuity in a Pauline text that has serious consequences historically, religiously, and theologically for a community dependent upon a particular manuscript for its spiritual nourishment. We should also recall in this context that manuscripts were very expensive and difficult to reproduce by any individual community. Whatever the quality, good, mediocre, or poor, of the scribal copying, each manuscript was scripture to a particular community, the basis for the spiritual life of individuals and of a corporate group composing a believing community.

Serious consequences are also reflected in passages where the omission or the addition of a word actually negates the Pauline thought in Romans. For example:

4.16   txt   διὰ τοῦτο ἐκ πίστεως [for this reason it does depend on faith]
             διὰ τοῦτο **οὐκ** ἐκ πίστεως 460 618 1738 [for this reason it does **not** depend on faith]

8.11   txt   τὸ πνεῦμα τοῦ ἐγείραντος τὸν Ἰησοῦν ἐκ νεκρῶν οἰκεῖ ἐν ὑμῖν
             [if the Spirit of the one who raised Jesus fom the dead dwells in you]

      6   τὸ πνεῦμα τοῦ ἐγείραντος τὸν ιν̄ **οὐκ** οἰκεῖ ἐν ὑμῖν
             [if the Spirit of the one who raised Jesus **does not** dwell in you]

What consequences did the addition of the **οὐκ** at 4.16 have for the readers of manuscripts 460 618 1738? The accepted text reads, "for this reason it depends on faith," whereas the addition of the **οὐκ** says, "for this reason it does not depend on faith." At 8.11 the text reads, "if the Spirit of the one who raised Jesus from the dead dwells in you," whereas the addition of **οὐκ** says, "if the Spirit of the one who raised Jesus **does not** dwell in you." It is imperative that we are aware of these serious misconstructions in vital passages in scripture, for only then can we be aware of the source of some of the life and thought problems that arose in various communities.

Or again serious consequences may be found in passages from Romans where a word substitution radically changes the meaning of a passage:

Textual Criticism

8.11   txt   τὸ πνεῦμα τοῦ ἐγείραντος τὸν Ἰησοῦν ἐκ νεκρῶν
             οἰκεῖ ἐν ὑμῖν
             [if the Spirit of the one who raised Jesus fom the dead dwells in you]

        6   τὸ πνεῦμα τοῦ ἐγείραντος τὸν ιν̄ **οὐκ** οἰκεῖ ἐν ὑμῖν
             [if the Spirit of the one who raised Jesus **does not** dwell in you]

11.29 txt   ἀμεταμέλητα γὰρ τὰ χαρίσματα καὶ ἡ κλῆσις τοῦ θεοῦ
       𝔓⁴⁶ ἀμεταμέλητα γὰρ τὰ χαρίσματα καὶ ἡ **κτίσις** τοῦ θ̄ῡ
       056* ἀμεταμέλητα γὰρ τὰ χαρίσματα καὶ ἡ **χρῆσις** τοῦ θ̄ῡ
       796 ἀμεταμέλητα γὰρ τὰ χαρίσματα καὶ ἡ **ἐκλόγη** τοῦ θ̄ῡ

["For the gifts and the **calling** of God are irrevocable."]
["For the gifts and the **creation** of God are irrevocable."]
["For the gifts and the **function** of God are irrevocable."]
["For the gifts and the **election** of God are irrevocable."]

The manuscript at Romans 8.11 that reads "**us**" rather than "**Jesus**" translates, "if the Spirit of him who raised **us** from the dead dwells in you." This can have a rich meaning for us spiritually and at the same time not be contrary to what Paul says elsewhere, since we have been raised from death to life already, although we are still in the flesh. But this is surely not the intent of the passage when read contextually. A scribe has made a change, and I would argue intentionally because it reflects his/her theology or the theology of his/her community. The substitution of three different words for κλῆσις ("calling") at 11.29 also reflect a wide divergence in meaning from the accepted text. The text states that "the gifts and the **calling** of God are irrevocable." The alternates read in this order, "the gifts and the **creation** of God are irrevocable," "the gifts and the **function** of God are irrevocable," and "the gifts and the **election** of God are irrevocable." The latter reading may be very comforting to some, but does it reflect what the apostle intended? or is it a reflection of a sharper theological intent by a scribe or of a theological understanding within a particular community? No critic should ever choose to exclude these substitutions as unimportant, for we then lack a vital piece of information for reconstructing, not the original text, but the profile of the historical church. Such aberrant readings are most significant, and without them we lack a very important window into the thought processes and practices within the church in the course of its history. This leads to a suggestion by two different readers of this thesis that variant readings of the kind noted above, or even the entire discipline of textual criticism, ought to be included under the discipline of Church History rather than under New Testament studies.

How can any academic, or any critic, be satisfied intellectually, morally, ethically, and spiritually with a subjective and selective inclusion of only some of the data? or with the inclusion of readings that agree with his/her theological point of view and conditioning to the exclusion of those that are controversial, but that had consequences for an individual or for a community at some time and in some place in the history of the church? It is of the highest importance, therefore, for those who practice this discipline always to hold in perspective that *each manuscript, each source, was scripture in an early Christian community.*

New Testament Greek Manuscripts: Romans includes a complete citation of eighty-five Greek sources. The point is that this is a goodly number of manuscripts for one editor to read and report *in toto* in a little more than a year's time. But it is a very small number when compared to what is available and ought to be included in the final product—Greek manuscripts, versions, church fathers, and lectionary editions that number in the thousands.

This work is, therefore, highly important because it provides a blueprint and a format for future work in the origins of the New Testament text that can be far more comprehensive, and thus far more useful for generations to come as we search for a more comprehensive understanding of the processes at work across the span of history for the reproduction of the text of the New Testament. It is "user friendly," an attribute that is sadly lacking in nearly all, if not all, of the critical editions in print. Furthermore, a complete reporting of the evidence from each source provides us with unusual and unique insights into the internal history of the Christian community from the fourth to the fifteenth centuries. Many significant variant readings from the various sources listed above are recovered when entire manuscripts are reproduced in a comparative format, making evident that these changes reflect major differences in the thought patterns and practices throughout the many believing communities composing the church. We must raise our sights to become as inclusive as possible, or even all-inclusive, so that everyone, not just the elite scholar, has access to all relevant material for an understanding of the ongoing life of the Christian community in history. We will then have accomplished the worthy goal, not of arriving at the end result of *the original pure text*, which is forever beyond our reach, but of adding a very important chapter to our understanding of what was happening historically, sociologically, religiously, and theologically in the church through the ages.

Finally, it has been suggested by two different reviewers of this statement on purpose and methodology that, in view of evidence set forth in the above, this discipline would be more properly pursued in the area of church history. The discipline of textual criticism has not been without its values. The contributions to our understanding of the text and of the message of the New Testament have been enormous. But even if the restoration of the original text were possible, which has been the goal of the majority of the participants in this discipline, we have before us a far more valuable goal, namely, that of understanding the thinking and the practices within the various streams of the Christian communities and, indeed, within much of Christian history even to modern times.

The Composition of the Gospels

❧ It has long been a commonplace among New Testament scholars that there is a unique relationship among the first three gospels, Matthew, Mark, and Luke. The word "Synoptic" has been coined to identify this relationship, a Greek word meaning "to see together." The similarities in content, in arrangement of materials, and even the word by word agreement have led many to conclude that two of the authors used the one as a source when they composed their gospels. On the one hand, the three gospels are distinct from the Fourth Gospel in most particulars, although there are frequent references in the latter gospel that suggest a familiarity with the content of the Synoptics; on the other hand, the similarity of the three to one another has led to the view that the earliest gospel composed became a basic source for the other two.

There are widely divergent views among contemporary scholars, however, as to the order in which the gospels were written. The view held by the majority is as follows: Mark is the primary gospel and the authors of Matthew and Luke used Mark as a source when they composed their gospels. A second view held by a rather vocal minority is that Matthew was the earliest gospel to have been composed, the author of Luke used Matthew as a source, then the author of Mark used both Matthew and Luke as sources when he composed his gospel. This view is known as the "Griesbach Hypothesis," since the earliest formulation of this thesis is attributed to the eighteenth century scholar J. J. Griesbach. Other possibilities, for example, Luke was the earliest gospel and the authors of Matthew and Mark used Luke as a source, have been argued, but the most viable view in the opinion of this writer is the first, that is, the priority of Mark. This essay will attempt to set forth the reasons and the documentation in support of the Markan priority. The foil for the argument will be the Griesbach Hypothesis and a critique of the method that attempts to substantiate the order of Matthean priority and its subsequent conclusion that Luke used Matthew as a primary source and that Mark used Matthew and Luke when composing his gospel.

Omissions of Matthean Pericopes in Mark

Mark is by far the shorter of the three gospels consisting of forty-two pages in a modern critical edition as compared to sixty-nine pages for the gospel of Matthew and seventy-three for Luke. Thus Mark is shorter than Matthew by twenty-seven pages and shorter than Luke by thirty-one pages. If the author of Mark used Matthew and Luke as sources, the conclusion must be that he radically abridged those gospels by omitting large portions of each. It is of interest therefore to note those pericopes that were omitted by the author of Mark. A comparison with Matthew indicates that the following are omitted by the author of Mark:

1) the infancy narratives (chapters 1–2),
2) the so-called "Sermon on the Mount" (chapters 5–7),
3) the opening of the eyes of two blind men (9.27–31),
4) the casting out of a demon from a man who was dumb (9.32–34),
5) the easy yoke and the light burden (11.28–30),
6) the parable of the weeds among the wheat (13.24–30)
7) and its interpretation (13.36–43),
8) the parables of the hidden treasure, the pearl, the net, and the householder's treasure (13.44–53),
9) healings on the mountain (15.29–31),
10) the announcement, "You are Peter" (16.17–19),
11) a midrash on the temple tax (17.24–27),
12) a discourse on forgiveness (18.15–22),
13) the parables of the unmerciful servant (18.23–35),
14) the laborers in the vineyard (20.1–16),
15) and the two sons (21.28–32),
16) a series of woes upon scribes and Pharisees (23.15–36),
17) the parables of the ten virgins (25.1–13)
18) and of the son of man coming in glory as judge (25.31–46),
19) the death of Judas (27.3–10),
20) the guard posted at the tomb (27.62–66),
21) the bribing of the guard at the tomb (28.11–15),
22) and the command to make disciples (28.16–20).

Omissions of Matthean Pericopes in Luke

A comparison to Luke's gospel indicates the omission of the following pericopes by the author of Mark:

1) the infancy narratives (chapters 1–2),
2) the genealogy of Jesus (3.23–38),
3) the rejection at his home town Nazareth (4.16–30)
4) the great catch of fish (5.1–11),
5) the sermon on the plain (6.20–49),
6) a dead man raised at Nain (7.11–17),
7) the women ministering to Jesus (8.1–3),
8) all but a few reminiscences of the long section known as the journey through Perea to Jerusalem (9.51–18.14) that includes such materials as

   a) the seventy-two sent out for mission (10.1–12, 17–20),
   b) a parable on the theme "Who is my neighbor?" (10.30–37),
   c) Jesus visit in the home of Martha and Mary (10.38–42),
   d) the friend at midnight (11.5–8),
   e) a woman blesses Jesus (11.27–28),
   f) a parable on covetousness (12.13–21),
   g) girded loins and burning lamps (12.35–40),
   h) fire upon the earth (12.49–53),
   i) the need for repentance (13.1–4),
   j) the parable of the fruitless fig tree (13.6–9),
   k) a woman freed from an infirmity on the Sabbath (13.10–17),
   l) a Pharisee warns Jesus that Herod seeks to kill him (13.31–33),
   m) a man with dropsy healed on the Sabbath (14.1–6),
   n) a parable on seating oneself at a marriage feast (14.7–14),
   o) parables of a tower builder and a warring king (14.28–33),
   p) parables of the lost coin and the lost son (15.8–32),
   q) the parable of the dishonest steward (16.1–12),
   r) the parable of the rich man and Lazarus (16.19–31),

- s) servants who do their duty cannot expect special favor (17.7–10),
- t) ten lepers cleansed (17.11–19),
- u) the parable of the judge and the importunate widow (18.1–8),
- v) the parable of the Pharisee and the tax collector (18.9–14),

and following this large interpolation,

9) Jesus and the tax collector Zacchaeus (19.1–10),
10) Jesus weeps over Jerusalem (19.41–44),
11) Jesus teaches in the temple daily (21.47–48),
12) the two swords (22.35–38),
13) Jesus before Herod (23.6–12),
14) women lament the condemnation of Jesus (23.27–31),
15) the two travelers to Emmaus (24.13–35),
16) the appearance in Jerusalem and the command to await the coming of the Holy Spirit (24.36–49), and
17) his ascension at Bethany (24.50–53).

In addition, there are pericopes used in common by Matthew and Luke not found in Mark including such well known ones as

1) the healing of the centurion's servant (M 8.5–13) or slave (L 7.1–10),
2) the demands of discipleship (M 8.18–22; L 9.57–62),
3) the plentiful harvest and the need for laborers (M 9.37–38; L 10.2),
4) a comparison of John the Baptist and the "Coming One" (M 11.2–19; L 7.18–35),
5) the woes and thanksgivings (M 11.20–27; L 10.12–15, 21–22),
6) the fruits of the good and of the bad trees (12.33–35; L 6.43–45),
7) the sign of Jonah (M 12.38–42; L 11.29–31),
8) the unclean spirit seeking rest (M 12.43–45; L 11.24–26),
9) the parable of the leaven (M 13.33; L 13.20–21),
10) the parable of the lost sheep (M 18.10–14; L 15.3–7),

11) the parable of the wedding feast (M 22.1–14) or the great banquet (L 14.16–24),
12) Jerusalem foreseen as forsaken and desolate (M 23.37–39; L 13.34–35),
13) the parable of the faithful and wise slave (M 24.45–51; L 12.42–48), and
14) the parable of the talents (M 25.14–30) or the pounds (L 19.11–27).

It must be noted that Mark has pericopes that are not reported in either Matthew or Luke:

1) the parable of the seed growing spontaneously (4.26–29),
2) the healing of a deaf man with a speech impediment (7.31–37),
3) the restoring of sight to a blind man at Bethsaida (8.22–26), and
4) the account of the young man who fled naked when Jesus was arrested (14.51–52).

The Question of Omissions in Mark

The question rises, and it is a serious one, How is it that the author of Mark failed to use any of these materials in his composition of a gospel if indeed he used the gospels of Matthew and Luke as sources? It seems incomprehensible that any or all of such vital materials as are found in the above lists could have been ignored if the author was acquainted with them firsthand. It is not difficult to understand or to explain how the authors of Matthew and Luke omitted the four pericopes from Mark cited in the previous paragraph in view of the wealth of materials they have reported. The absence of such a volume of quality traditions from the teachings and from the signs and wonders that Jesus did is very difficult, if not impossible, to explain if we adopt the thesis that the author of Mark used the gospels of Matthew and Luke as sources. The problem seems readily explicable if one posits that the author of Mark was the earliest composer of a gospel, that he composed his gospel in Rome, and that his principal source of information was the Apostle Peter.

In the view of this writer, Mark was the great and ingenious pioneer who first created the literary form that came to be called an *euaggelion*, or gospel. Accordingly he is the greatest of the gospel writers, the creator and innovator, although we more often than not fail to give him due respect by focusing attention upon the gospels of Matthew and Luke and referring to Mark's gospel only as a last resort. After all they are so rich in content, in the type and quality of material that is useful in our spiritual life and growth, that it is only natural for Mark to come in a poor third in our estimate of what a gospel should be. But the absence of large quantities of material from the earliest gospel is just what is to be expected from a comparative study based upon the history of religions.

The Order of Development for a Major World Religion

A study of the history of any of the great religions of the world is very instructive for an understanding of the development of tradition as reflected in our gospels. The pattern, Mark as a source for Matthew and Luke, is in large agreement with what we find in the development of the tradition in Judaism, Islam, Hinduism, and Buddhism, to mention the most noteworthy examples. Mark reflects a low Christology in comparison to Matthew and Luke; that is, the Jesus portrayed by Mark is a very human figure with few, if any, divine qualities. It should be evident to us that no one of Jesus' contemporaries, not even those closest to him, had any intimation or understanding that he was a divine being. You may say that the so-called miracle stories refute this predication, but such is not the case since the very human disciples are reported in our sources to have had powers to do signs and wonders as well. This question is discussed in greater detail in another essay in these series.

The historic development of all religions follows a basic pattern. First, the decisive figure of the founder; second, the community of devotees who perpetuate the traditions of his life and teaching; third, the growth of the tradition about what the teacher had said and done; and, finally, the expansion of the tradition about the founder himself and the attribution to him of divine and supernatural powers. The lines of demarcation between the periods are never clearly defined; there is more often an overlapping and impinging of the succeeding period upon the previous time.

This is precisely how I would define the development within the early Christian community and the relationship of the gospels to one another. First, the life and teaching of Jesus that culminates in his death and resurrection. Second, the period of the early Christian community that preserves

The Composition of the Gospels

and perpetuates the traditions about his teachings and his deeds. This is that period in the life of the early community narrated in the Book of the Acts of the Apostles, although the account itself was written in period three and already reflects the viewpoints of period four. I would place the composition of the gospel of Mark at the very beginning of period three at a time when the influence of period two still prevails.

At this point in time the figure of the teacher as he appeared in life still dominates the life and the thinking of the community. Some of the original followers may still be alive, although the majority are either dead or at some place in mission where they are not readily consulted. The tradition that Peter is a main source for the information reported about Jesus by the author of Mark is altogether credible. His Jesus is very human, a man of action and deeds rather than a profound teacher or a divine and supernatural being. This is in character with the image of Peter reflected in all our gospels and in the Acts of the Apostles. According to this understanding it becomes clear why the author does not report from the mass of traditions found in the later gospels where the emphasis is more upon Jesus as a teacher rather than a man of action. The author of Mark has no need to report stories about the infancy and early life of the teacher; in fact, he cannot because this belongs to a later stage of tradition as witnessed by every major religious tradition. Compare, for example, the development of the tradition about the Buddha in the history of Buddhism.

The Buddha was a very earthy figure, despised and rejected by the great majority of his contemporaries. He denied for himself the power of accomplishing miracles. His overwhelming concern was to focus upon the essence of true religion, the hopeless and miserable situation of mankind bound to earthly existence and how one can be freed only by a complete denial of self and the practice of those virtues that lead to nirvana, that is, the end of the fated cycle of rebirths. It is very difficult to glean from the traditions that have come down to us that which is historical and that which has been created by the community at a later time to enhance the figure of the founder. But it is evident that the stories of the Buddha's miraculous birth from a virgin, his many supernatural deeds, and, finally, his elevation to deity reflect a growing tradition over a period of time according to the stages enumerated above.

The growth process may not be so clearly delineated in all religions, but it is there nevertheless. How else can we account for the tradition reported in Exodus that when Moses came down from Mount Sinai with the two tables of the law "the skin of his face shone because he had been talking with God" (Ex. 34.29)? We recall how the Apostle Paul refers to this event in Second Corinthians, saying that the Israelites could not look upon Moses' face and it became necessary to put a veil over his face because of its brightness (2 Corinthians 3.7, 13). Is not this a later embellishment upon the tradition reported in Exodus? What is it but a haloizing and a divinizing of the leader, a process that had already begun in an earlier stage of the tradition as in the Book of Exodus? Islam, the strictest of all the monotheistic religions, manifests this same tendency in certain attitudes towards the prophet Muhammad and in the development of mysticism in which the ultimate goal is illumination and the absorption of the individual into its divine object. Needless to say, Christian mysticism and mysticism in every form of religious expression manifest these same tendencies.

Matthew and Luke Belong to a Late Stage Three

The gospels of Matthew and Luke rightly belong to a later time in stage three, although the impact of stage four is already evident. According to Paul, whose writings belong to late stage two in our analysis of the developing community, Jesus "was descended from David according to the flesh and designated Son of God in power according to the Spirit of holiness by his resurrection from the dead" (Romans 1.3–4). There is a clear line of demarcation between the human and the divine. The Jesus of history is clearly distinct from the Christ of faith. It should be kept clearly in mind that Paul proclaims always the crucified and resurrected Jesus as Savior and Lord. That is his total emphasis. He is not concerned with the Jesus of history; that is, the Jesus who was born, who trod the pathways of Galilee, who spoke on some occasions and acted on others. The gospels are distinct from Paul's purpose in this that their authors purport to tell what Jesus said and did while he trod the shores of Galilee and when in Jerusalem. Of course, the resurrected Jesus was as decisive for them as for Paul. How could they narrate a life-like account of their Jesus without permitting the cross and the resurrection to intrude upon and shape their image of Jesus?

That line of demarcation has been removed when we turn from the gospel of Mark to the gospels of Matthew and Luke and then to the later non-canonical writings about Jesus. The infancy narratives that preface the life and teachings of Jesus and which speak of a virgin conception and birth, suggesting a supernatural origin, may have arisen in response to problems that confronted the early community, but in reality their similarity to developments in other religions suggest a later, or what has been identified as a late third, stage in the development of the Christian religion.

Changes in Attitude Towards Jesus

This is to be seen also in changes that have taken place in the attitudes toward Jesus the founder. A striking example of this is to be seen in the account of the storm at sea (Mark 4.35–41; Matthew 8.18–27; Luke 8.22–25). The storm is great, the disciples are in peril, and Jesus is asleep. They awaken him and say, "Teacher, do you not care if we perish!" (Mark 4.38), which becomes, "Master, Master, we are perishing!" (Luke 8.24) and "Save, Lord; we are perishing" (Matthew 8.25). The address in Mark suggests no more than, "Why are you asleep when we are in danger? Arise and bail out the boat," whereas the disciples according to Matthew's version address a divine figure, the Lord himself, who is able to act in such a way as to control the powers of nature that threaten them.

It should be noted that the divine name for the God of Israel, Yahweh, becomes Kyrios in its translation to Greek. It should also be noted that the word Kyrios is ambiguous, since it can be used either as a polite form of address, "Sir" or "Master," as in Matthew 27.63 where the guards address Pilate, "Lord," or as the divine name of the God of Israel, as in Mark 12.30, "You shall love the Lord your God." There is no clear instance where the word Kyrios is used in the gospel of Mark as an address to Jesus with the inference that he is addressed as a divine being. The one passage that may be interpreted by some in this way occurs in the account of the exorcism of the demons from the man of the Gerasenes (Mark 5.19), where Jesus charges the man to tell "how much the Lord has done for you." But it is not at all clear that Jesus is attributing the exorcism to himself; rather God is the one who has acted to bring about the healing. It seems evident that the word is used in the latter sense as a divine title in the Matthean account of the storm at sea, an address that is correctly a post-resurrection address for Jesus.

This is precisely why, if there was use of one gospel source by another evangelist, it most logically is the author of Matthew using Mark, since it is incomprehensible that the author of Mark, if he found the title Kyrios addressed to Jesus in the text and writing at a later stage than Matthew, would have substituted "Teacher." The absence of a clear-cut address of the title Kyrios to Jesus with a divine implication in Mark and the rather frequent occurrence of this phenomenon in both Matthew and Luke supports the conclusion that the latter gospels represent a later stage in the history of composition. For further examples of the same alteration of title from Teacher to Kyrios, the reader is referred to the cleansing of the leper (Mark 1.40 a pronoun with no title; Matthew 8.2; Luke 5.12), Peter's address to Jesus at the transfiguration (Rabbi Mark 9.5; Lord Matthew 17.4; Master Luke 9.32), the healing of the epileptic (Teacher Mark 9.17, Luke 9.38; Lord Matthew 17.15), and the opening the blind eyes at Jericho (Rabbouni Mark 10.51; Lord Matthew 20.33; Luke 18.41).

On other occasions the author of Matthew introduces the title Kyrios into the text where it does not occur in the parallel passage in Mark. Inasmuch as the author uses Kyrios elsewhere as an address to a divine being, as demonstrated above, the use of the title in these passages also should be listed under this category. The opening of the blind eyes at Jericho (cf. Mark 10.47–48 and Luke 18.38–39; Matthew 20.30–31). Judas' address to Jesus (Mark 14.19; Matthew 26.22). The story of the Syrophoenician woman (a Canaanite woman in Matthew). Note that in Mark's account (Mark 7.26) the woman falls down at Jesus' feet but uses no title of address, whereas in Matthew 15.25 the woman worships him and says, "Lord, help me." The Greek word for "worship" is customarily used in contemporary literature for an act of reverence before a person thought to have supernatural powers. And, finally, Peter's address to Jesus on two occasions unique to Matthew (cf. Peter walking on the water Matthew 14, 28, 30; and his rebuke of Jesus, Matthew 16.22).

The Lukan Usage of Kyrios

Luke uses the title Kyrios most frequently of the evangelists and often in contexts where there is no parallel in Mark and Matthew. Although it may be argued in many instances that the inference is simply "Sir" or "Master," the context and the frequency of occurrence suggest that a post-resurrection understanding of Jesus has permeated the author's image of the Jesus

The Composition of the Gospels

of history. The following instances must be read in context for a correct judgment to be made on the question of meaning:

1) a sinful Peter addresses Jesus as Lord (Luke 5:8),
2) the Lord raises the dead man of Nain (7.13),
3) James and John ask, "Lord, do you want us to bid fire come down?" (9.54),
4) the Lord sends the seventy and they report to the Lord (10.1, 17),
5) the disciples ask, "Lord, teach us to pray" (11.1),
6) the Lord said to Pharisees (11.39),
7) Peter said, "Lord," and the Lord said (12.41–42),
8) the Lord answered his detractors (13.15),
9) the apostles said to the Lord and the Lord said (17.5–6),
10) a question concerning the last time when disciples say, "Where, Lord?" (17.37),
11) the Lord said, a commentary upon the parable of the unjust judge (18.6),
12) Zacchaeus said to the Lord (19.8),
13) Peter said, "Lord" (22.33),
14) the disciples said, "Lord" (22.38, 49),
15) the Lord looked at Peter (22.61),
16) they did not find the body of the Lord Jesus (24.3), and
17) the announcement, "the Lord has risen" (24.34).

Though there may be a difference of opinion whether or not there is an allusion to Jesus as the divine Lord in these passages, there is a strong probability that this is the case and that the resurrected Lord, the Christ of faith, has permeated the thinking and the writing of this author at these points. The contextual use of this title and the frequency of occurrence suggest strongly that this gospel belongs to late stage three in the history of the transmission of the tradition.

The Problem of Objectivity in Depicting the Historical Jesus

The problem for the evangelists who composed their gospels long after the death and resurrection of Jesus was to present him, not as the crucified and resurrected Lord, but as that one who had always and everywhere been visualized by his contemporaries as a man of human origins and of human qualifications and character. Was there anyone who looked upon him as divine during his life on earth? Would the Jews consign a god to death? Would the disciples, those who knew him best, always misunderstand, betray, deny, and leave him to die alone? The significance of the risen Lord for the faith and life of the community made it very difficult to be objective in their presentation of the Jesus of history. How was it possible to view Jesus as he had been and as he had been perceived in his time by his contemporaries, even by his disciples? Their perception of him was colored by the cross and especially by the resurrection to such a degree that they tended to interpret the words that he had spoken and the deeds that he had done according to their present faith in him as Lord and Savior. The authors were post-resurrection believers; they had never known Jesus in the flesh. The farther they were removed from the Jesus of history, the stronger became the tendency to invest the entire life of Jesus from the cradle to the grave with divinity. The image of Jesus presented by the author of Mark has been least affected by this process and this fact argues strongly for the earlier composition of this gospel. The presence of infancy narratives and the changed attitude towards the leader reflected in the use of the divine name of God addressed to him manifest an increasing reverence for him, a reverence that is extended beyond the cross to invest and permeate his entire human life.

An Illustration of the Growing Reverence for Jesus

Another illustration of the growing reverence for Jesus that resulted in an editing of Mark's text by the author of Matthew is to be found in the pericope of the man who came to Jesus saying, "Good Teacher, what must I do to inherit eternal life?" Jesus responded, "Why do you call me good? No one is good but God alone" (Mark 10.17–18; Luke 18.18–19). Matthew's version is very different: "Teacher, what good deed must I do, to have eternal life?" Jesus responded, "Why do you ask me about what is good? One there is who is good" (Matthew 19.16–17). The wording of Mark's version implies that Jesus is not good or at least makes no claim to a goodness superior to his fellow men and women. This implication cries out for correction, because it is contradictory to the position of the church as set forth in other Christian writings that Jesus was without sin and that he in a positive sense manifested a goodness in life equal to the goodness of God. Matthew's rather clumsy editing of Mark's version removes that implication by shifting the goodness to the deed and away from the person of Jesus. If the opposite process is true in this instance, then the author of Luke was responsible for editing Matthew's version and Mark preferred Luke's reading over Matthew's, since he had access to both gospels as he composed. But this would be contrary to what has already been noted as a consistent tendency among all religions in the transmission of their traditions to heighten the holiness and the divine qualities of the leader.

A Heightened Respect and Reverence for the Apostles

The same phenomenon of a heightened respect and reverence for the apostles also attests a later stage in the composition of the gospels of Matthew and Luke, especially the gospel of Matthew. This is illustrated by the incident reported by Mark when the disciples James and John, sons of Zebedee, ask Jesus for the chief seats in the coming kingdom (Mark 10.35–45). Luke does not report this incident, but Matthew states that it is the mother of the sons of Zebedee who put this request to Jesus. We have a clear choice in this instance to decide which of the two accounts is the earlier. The decision can only be made on the basis of cogent arguments to support the conclusion that Matthew was the earlier account and Mark subsequently changed the tradition to make the apostles, not their mother, the culprits. Such an argument flies in the face of reason. This writer can think of no rationale that satisfactorily explains the change of Mark's text to Matthew, although the reverse is readily understood and explained on the basis of a growing respect and reverence for Jesus and for the apostles with the passage of time. It is to be noted that the same verb for the worship of a human with supernatural qualities is used in Matthew's version as a preface to the request and that Jesus' response, which should be addressed in the singular to the mother, is addressed in the plural precisely as we find the reading in Mark. The antecedent for the verbs "know" and "ask" in Matthew's version is the mother, but the plural forms of the verbs are used suggesting that the author did not note the inconsistency in his other alterations of Mark's text.

A second example would be Matthew's insertion into Mark's account of the confession of Peter, that is, the singling out of Peter by Jesus for special honor and authority: "You are Peter (Petros), and on this rock (petra) I will build my church." This pericope is significant enough to warrant a separate essay and will not be discussed in detail in this place. Reference is only made to it because it illustrates in a unique way the growing respect and reverence of the community for Peter, a respect and reverence that reflects distance in time from the apostle. The absence of this exoneration of the disciples and of the elevation of Peter to a high position that is consistently maintained in Mark's gospel argues strongly for its early composition, whereas the opposite is true for the gospel of Matthew.

Differences in the Lukan Account of the Passion

As we turn to the closing episodes in the earthly life of Jesus and to his resurrection, we again encounter massive differences in the portrayal of those events from Mark to Matthew and Luke. It should be noted here that scholars who posit a relationship of dependence in the composition of the gospels without reference to any particular theory are agreed that the author of Luke had access to a tradition other than Mark and/or Matthew for his composition of the passion. The differences in content and arrangement are too great to sustain the argument that he relied upon the other gospels for his account of this event. Luke alone reports the following:

1) Peter and John were sent to prepare the Passover meal (22.8),
2) the meal was eaten with apostles not disciples (22.14),
3) Jesus' desire to eat the Passover with his disciples (22.25–16),
4) the two cups in his account of the last meal (22.17, 20),
5) other additions corresponding to the Pauline account (22.19),
6) the dispute about greatness in the midst of the meal (22.24–30),
7) Satan sifting Simon like wheat (22.31–31),
8) the two swords (22.35–38),
9) one prayer only in an unnamed place on the Mount of Olives (22.39–46),
10) among many differences in the account of the arrest only in Luke's account does Jesus heal the ear of the slave (22.51),
11) the different response of Jesus to his accusers who ask if he is the Christ (22.68),
12) the charges against Jesus before Pilate (23.2, 5),

13) Jesus before Herod (23.6–12) and
14) Pilate's verdict of "Not guilty" (23.13–16),
15) the lamenting women on the way to the cross (23.27–31)
16) the two criminals (23.32),
17) the prayer, "Father, forgive them" (23.34),
18) the promise of paradise to the thief (23.40–43),
19) the cry, "Father, into your hands" (23.46),
20) the reaction of the multitude to his death (23.48),
21) the apology for Joseph of Arimathea (23.50–51),
22) rest on the Sabbath (23.56),
23) and the very different post-resurrection appearances of the risen Lord in Judea and Jerusalem rather than Galilee.

Some of the additions in Luke's account listed above reflect a later stage in the development of his tradition; for example, the two references to Satan (22.3, 31), the meal eaten with apostles, a title that belongs to a later stratum of tradition (22.14), the reference to the angel and the bloody sweat in some early manuscripts (22.43–44), the immediate restoration of the ear cut off with a sword (22.51), the prayer, "Father, forgive them," reported in a few but not all of the earlier manuscripts (23.34), the promise of paradise (23.43), the appearance of the risen Lord in a body of flesh and bones who eats broiled fish (24.39–43), and the ascending into heaven (24.51) that is omitted in some early manuscripts.

In all fairness it must be granted that Mark uses the word "apostles" twice, once in the context of the choosing of the twelve (Mark 3.14) and once upon their return from their preaching and healing mission (Mark 6.30), but Luke uses the title additionally in other contexts (Luke 17.5; 22.14; 24.10). It seems probable that the use of this title in all our gospels reflects a post-resurrection addition into a pre-resurrection setting. I am suggesting that multiple usage in different contexts suggests a later intrusion into the tradition and that multiple occurrences in Luke support the thesis that this gospel belongs to a later stage of the composition process.

The account of the cut off ear reminds this reader of a story in the gospel of Thomas where the boy Jesus heals in similar fashion the foot of a boy cut so severely with an ax that he was bleeding to death. This type of wonder story is an indicator of late tradition. The fact that some of the traditions listed above lack full manuscript support is also a warning to the reader that there is uncertainty about what the evangelist's autograph contained originally. The process of editing by scribes in copying the text of each gospel included the addition of traditions that were evidently not a part of the original, even though these additions have the ring of authenticity and have become an important part of our preaching and teaching portfolio.

Additions in the Matthean Account

But the additions in Luke's gospel are rather prosaic when compared to those in Matthew, which are listed as follows:

1) the son of man delivered up to be crucified (26.2),
2) the naming of the high priest Caiaphas (26.3, 57),
3) the thirty pieces of silver (26.15),
4) the identification of Judas as the betrayer (26.25),
5) the forgiveness of sins given through the blood of the covenant (26.28),
6) the falling away of the disciples specifically on account of Jesus (26.31, 33),
7) the warning that all who take the sword will perish by it (26.52),
8) the twelve legions of angels who could deliver Jesus, but scripture must be fulfilled (26.53–54),
9) Judas' return of the silver, his death, and the field of blood (27.3–10),
10) the dream of Pilate's wife (27.19),
11) Pilate washes his hands (27.24),
12) the people accept the responsibility for the blood of Jesus (27.25),
13) the reed in the hand of Jesus (27.29),
14) the mocking of Jesus as Son of God (27.43),
15) the earthquake at his death and the bodies of the saints raised from the tombs to walk in the holy city (27.52–53),
16) the guard at the tomb (27.62–66),
17) the earthquake and the angel of the Lord at the resurrection (28.2–3),

18) the appearance of the risen Jesus to the two Marys and the instruction to go to Galilee (28.8–10), and, finally,
19) the bribing of the guard (28.11–15).

Just as the birth of Jesus is accompanied by unusual natural and religious phenomena, a star in the east, the appearance of angels in dreams, and the magi, so the culminating event in the life of Jesus is accompanied by earthquakes, dreams, angels, and risings from the dead. The mythological character of these references suggests a late third stage in the development of the tradition and even an entry into the fourth stage. There are references to angels in Mark's gospel; for example,

1) angels minister to Jesus in the wilderness (Mark 1.13; Matthew 4.11),
2) the coming of the son of man accompanied by angels (Mark 8.38; Matthew 16.27; Luke 9.26; also Mark 13.27; Matthew 24.31),
3) the resurrected are like angels (Mark 12.25; Matthew 22.30; cf. Luke 20.36), and
4) angels are ignorant of the day of the son of man (Mark 13.31; Matthew 24.36).

It should be noted that in only one instance, in the temptation pericope, do angels play a role in the present in Mark; all the other references are to the future. Thus we can say that mythological elements are not foreign to Mark, but it is the proliferation of such references in Matthew and Luke that suggest a later composition, especially the role that angels play in God's relationship to his people. Compare references in Matthew 1.20, 24; 2.13, 19; 13.39, 41, 49; 18.10; 25.31; the reference to the devil and his angels 25.41; and references in Luke 1.11, 13, 18, 19, 26, 28, 30, 34, 35, 38; 2.2, 9, 10, 13, 15, 21; 12.8, 9; 15.10; 16.22; 24.23. It is remarkable and should be noted here how many of the references to angels occur in the "infancy narratives" in Matthew and Luke. It is the combination of earthquakes, bodies of saints, and angels in Matthew's account of the resurrection when compared to Mark's very chaste and modest account that suggests an expansion by the former rather than a contraction by the latter. Even Luke's account, though approximate in time to the composition of Matthew, does not contain so many bizarre elements.

The Resurrection Accounts

But a more serious obstacle to the priority of Matthew is the account of the resurrection and the women at the tomb. According to Mark they were greeted by a young man dressed in a white robe; in Luke's account there were two men standing by in dazzling apparel; whereas in Matthew there was a great earthquake, an angel of the Lord, in appearance like lightning with garments white as snow, descended, rolled back the stone and sat upon it. All this was visible to the guards as well as to the women. The gospel of John compounds the problem at this point, since two angels dressed in white appeared. It is difficult to understand how it can be that the accounts of this one event that is the very heart and core of Christian faith and life are so varied and even contradictory. Perhaps the answer is that this is an event that is beyond historical investigation and demonstration. Certainly it is not an historical event in the same sense that every other event in the life of Jesus, even his birth, may be termed historical. And this was the very problem that confronted the composers of our gospels and made it so difficult for them to give an account that meets the standards of historical composition.

But the point of discussion is the relationships among the several gospel accounts of the resurrection and it seems evident to this writer that Mark's abbreviated and modest account could hardly have been composed out of a dependence upon either or both of Matthew's and Luke's accounts. The problem of the ending of Mark's gospel at this point without any reference to an appearance of the risen Lord gives us no basis for supposing what might have been there, if indeed there was an ending that is now missing either by accident or by design. The thesis stands that Mark's account, such as it is, reflects an early third stage in the development of the tradition and Matthew's and Luke's accounts a late third stage with Matthew's account replete with fourth stage elements.

Further examples are cited in another essay in this series, that on textual criticism, which illustrate how this process of the growing reverence towards Jesus has also affected the copying of the text by the scribes as they reproduced copies of the scriptures for use in the churches. The process of edification was and is at work throughout the community from the event of the death and resurrection of Jesus and to the present time, a process that is reflected in our own twenty-first century attitudes towards scripture as an inerrant and infallible blueprint from God encompassing every area of human knowledge from geography, history, biology, and geology to sociology, psychology, and theology.

A Fourth Stage of Development

The fourth stage of development is to be found in non-canonical writings, especially *The Infancy Gospel of Thomas*. Here every vestige of humanity is removed. Jesus as a child carries all the attributes of a divine being. He stretched a beam that father Joseph had sawed too short to fit a bed he was carpentering. He caused figures of birds shaped of clay to come to life and fly. He spoke a word and restored to life a playmate who had died from a fall, one of several miracles of raising the dead. He brought withering and death to those who offended him. He accomplished a number of unusual miracles in nature. He confounded and embarrassed the teachers of Israel with his knowledge and understanding that surpassed human capabilities. It is not strange that this writing and other gospels composed at a later time were not approved as canonical by the community, since the person of Jesus is distorted and falsified beyond recognition. The point is that this development is already inherent in our gospels in those narratives and references to Jesus and to the apostles that invest them with divine powers at the expense of their human character and capabilities. There is a measured progression in the development of the image of Jesus in the community from the Jesus of history to the early traditions as they were repeated orally in the first post-resurrection community, to the first recording of these traditions in the gospel of Mark, to an embellishment of Mark's account in the later gospels of Matthew and Luke, and, finally, to a full-fledged supernatural being and wonder worker in the gospel of Thomas.

Mark as an Abridgment of Matthew and Luke

Let us now examine other facets of the problem of relationships; namely, the thesis that Mark is an abridgment of the gospels of Matthew and Luke, since according to this point of view Mark used both gospels as sources for his composition. When we focus upon the parallel, or synoptic, materials in the three gospels and do a word count using the text of Codex Vaticanus as our base, the results are as follows: a comparison of the parallels between Mark and Matthew results in a word total of ten thousand five hundred and seventy words in Mark to a total of ten thousand three hundred and twenty-six words in Matthew and a similar comparison between Mark and Luke results in a word total of nine thousand eight hundred and three words in Mark to a total of eight thousand eight hundred and eighty-six words in Luke. If the thesis is correct, then Mark has expanded upon Matthew by a factor of approximately two per cent and upon Luke a factor of approximately nine per cent. But this is not a true comparison because of the variance among pericopes.

A word count for the parallels in the stories and events in the life of Jesus and of other persons for Mark and Matthew results in a word total of one thousand nine hundred and thirty-four words in Mark to a word total of two thousand one hundred and forty-three words in Matthew and a similar comparison between Mark and Luke results in a word total of one thousand seven hundred and forty-three words in Mark to a word total of two thousand and thirty-five words in Luke. The comparison demonstrates that either Mark has condensed Matthew's account by omitting two hundred and nine words or Matthew has expanded upon Mark's word total by that number and, if Mark used Luke as his source, then he condensed Luke's account by two hundred and ninety-two words or Luke expanded upon Mark's account by that amount. Such a word comparison, of course, does not give a true picture if Mark used both Matthew and Luke as sources, but does indicate that either Mark greatly condensed his sources or Matthew and Luke greatly expanded upon Mark's account.

A different picture emerges in a comparison of the signs and wonder stories. The word count for the parallels in this material for Mark and Matthew results in a word total of two thousand four hundred and ninety words in Mark to a word total of one thousand six hundred and seven words in Matthew and the comparison between Mark and Luke results in a word total of two thousand one hundred and thirty-nine words in Mark to a word total of one thousand six hundred and thirty-six words in Luke. The comparison demonstrates that either Mark has enlarged upon Matthew's account by eight hundred and eighty-three words or Matthew has condensed Mark's account by that number and that either Mark has expanded upon Luke's account by five hundred and three words or Luke has condensed Mark's account by that number.

The Composition of the Gospels

A comparison of the teaching material has another and different result. The word count for Mark's material totals three thousand nine hundred and twenty words as compared to a total of four thousand one hundred and twenty-six words in Matthew and the comparison between Mark and Luke results in a word total of three thousand six hundred and forty-five words in Mark to a total of two thousand seven hundred and fifty-five words in Luke. This comparison demonstrates that either Mark condensed Matthew's material by two hundred and six words or Matthew expands upon Mark by that number and that Mark expands upon Luke's text by a total of eight hundred and ninety words or Luke condenses Mark's material by that number.

A comparison of the passion narrative beginning with Mark chapter fourteen results in a total word count for Mark's material of one thousand nine hundred and eighty-three words, two thousand two hundred and eighteen words in Matthew's account, and two thousand one hundred and thirty-one words in Luke's account. This statistic is not significant for the comparison between Mark and Luke because the two accounts are not truly parallel, but the comparison between Mark and Matthew demonstrates that Mark either shortened Matthew's account by two hundred and thirty-five words or Matthew enlarged upon Mark's account by that number of words.

What do we learn from this survey? In the three types of material, the events, the teaching, and the passion, Mark has either abbreviated Matthew's material extensively, by two hundred and nine words in the narration of events, by two hundred and six words in recounting the teaching tradition, and by two hundred and thirty-five words in the passion material, or Matthew has expanded upon Mark by those numbers, whereas only in the signs and wonder stories has Mark either expanded upon Matthew by eight hundred and eighty-three words or Matthew has abbreviated Mark by that number of words. The results are somewhat ambiguous in the comparison of Mark to Luke, since Mark either abbreviates Luke's account of the events by two hundred and ninety-two words and his account of the passion by one hundred and forty-eight words or Luke has expanded these materials in Mark's account by those numbers; and Mark has expanded upon Luke's accounts of the signs and wonder stories by five hundred and three words and Luke's teaching material by eight hundred and ninety words or Luke has abbreviated Mark's accounts by these numbers.

My conclusion is that this information simply confirms what has been said above in the discussion of the question from a religio-historical point of view. The tendency of the later writer is to expand upon what he has before him. This is done in two ways: one, by expanding his exemplar by adding additional information to that which is found therein and, two, by inserting into the framework of his exemplar materials that are completely new. Matthew has done this in three of the four categories listed and has inserted new materials at appropriate places into the framework of his exemplar; that is, Mark. But at the same time the author of Matthew is selective, since he edits extensively when it suits his purpose to remove information that is repetitive and unnecessary.

A few illustrations are cited to confirm the methodology and to demonstrate how the conclusions were reached. The reader is invited to compare for himself/herself the following pericopes from the events category:

1) the John the Baptist tradition (Mark 1.2–8; Matthew 3.1–2; Luke 3.1–18),
2) the baptism of Jesus (Mark 1.9–11; Mt 3.1–17; Luke 3.21–22),
3) the temptation (Mark 1.12–13; Matthew 4.1–11; Luke 4.1–13),
4) the transfiguration (Mk 9.2–8; Matthew 17.1–8; Luke 9.28–36),
5) and the temple cleansing (Mark 11.15–19; Matthew 21.12–17; Luke 19.45–46).

The pericope of the beheading of John (Mark 6.14–29; Matthew 14.1–12; Luke 3.19–20; 9.7–9) does not conform to the principle, since Mark's account is longer than Matthew's by one hundred and thirty words and longer than Luke's by two hundred and thirteen. A reason will be suggested later for this discrepancy.

Examples from the teaching category are the following:

6) harvesting on the sabbath (Mark 2.23–28; Matthew 12.1–8; Luke 6.1–5),
7) the Beelzebul controversy (Mark 3.20–27; Matthew 12.22–30; Luke 11.14–23),
8) the secrets of the kingdom (Mark 4.10–13; Matthew 13.10–18; Luke 8.9–11a),
9) the mission of the Twelve (Mark 6.7–13; Matthew 10.5–15; Luke 9.1–6),

The Composition of the Gospels

10) divorce and remarriage (Mark 10.1–12; Matthew 19.16–30; Luke 16.18),
11) the parable of the wicked tenants (Mark 12.1–12; Matthew 21.33–46; Luke 20.9–19),
12) and the son of David question (Mark 12.35–37; Matthew 22.41–46; Luke 20.41–44).

Examples of exceptions to the general rule that Matthew expands upon the teaching material are as follows:

13) a controversy about tradition (Mark 7.1–23; Matthew 15.1–20; Luke 11.37–39),
14) causing a little one to sin (Mark 9.42–48; Matthew 18.6–9); Luke 17.1–2), and
15) the love command (Mark 12. 28–34; Matthew 22.34–40; Luke 10.25–28).

Examples from the passion narrative are the following:

16) the plot (Mark 14.1–2; Matthew 26.2–5; Luke 22.1–2),
17) the bread and cup (Mark 14.22–25; Matthew 26.26–29; Luke 22.15–18),
18) the garden (Mark 14.32–42; Matthew 26.36–46; Luke 27.39–46),
19) betrayed and arrested (Mark 14.43–50; Matthew 26.47–56; Luke 22.47–53),
20) Barabbas and condemnation (Mark 15.6–15; Matthew 27.15–26; Luke 23.17–25),
21) crucifixion and death (Mark 15.21–41; Matthew 27.32–56; Luke 23.32–49), and
22) the empty tomb (Mark 16.1–8; Matthew 28.1–10; Luke 24.1–10).

Examples of exceptions to the general rule that Matthew expands upon the passion tradition include:

23) a woman anoints Jesus (Mark 14.3–9; Matthew 26.6–14; cf. Luke 7.36–50),
24) Jesus celebrates the Passover (Mark 14.12–21; Matthew 26.17–25; Luke 22.7–22 an expansion),

25) condemned by Caiaphas (Mark 14.53–65; Matthew 26.57–68; Luke 22.54–65), and
26) the burial (Mark 15.42–47; Matthew 27.57–61; Luke 23.50–56).

It is evident that in spite of these exceptions the overall accounts in Matthew and Luke are considerably longer than the Markan account.

The signs and wonder stories demonstrate a very different result, for the Markan accounts are invariably longer than the Matthean and Lukan accounts and longer to a considerable degree. For example, the word count for the pericope, the demoniac called "Legion," is three hundred and twenty-five words in Mark, one hundred and thirty-four in Matthew, and two hundred and ninety-two in Luke (Mark 5.1–20; Matthew 8.28–34; Luke 8.26–39). The following pericope, the daughter of Jairus and a woman with a hemorrhage, (Mark 5.21–43; Matthew 9.18–26; Luke 8.40–56), reveals a similar result. Mark uses three hundred and eighty-three words to tell the story, Matthew one hundred and thirty-seven, and Luke two hundred and eighty-one. One can argue that Mark expanded upon the stories on the premise that the tendency was and is to expand in the retelling, but it would seem more logical to reason that the authors of Matthew and Luke refined and condensed the stories in the interest of conserving space for additional materials. One must remember that there is a limit to what can be placed upon a scroll, since the unrolling and rolling in the process of reading was cumbersome and required that the scroll be manageable. The gospels of Matthew and Luke both approach the limits for length, whereas Mark's gospel is well below the limit of what can be handled comfortably. It is evident that the signs and wonder stories are of high importance to the author of Mark, since they form such a large portion of his gospel when compared to teaching tradition. It is also evident that the author has included much extraneous material that is unnecessary to the story to make the point, a consideration that will be discussed in an essay on the signs and wonder stories.

The Key to the Question of Relationships

The key to the question of relationships among the gospels lies in determining the relationship of Matthew to Mark or Mark to Matthew. The relationship of Mark to Luke or Luke to Mark is a different question, as has been suggested by our comparative word count. The word count by itself cannot resolve the problem or provide an answer to the question. We have seen that in general the Markan accounts are shorter than the Matthean accounts in three of four categories and longer in the other. Only an examination of the internal editing pericope by pericope within each gospel may provide a definitive answer to our question. It is not possible to discuss all the pericopes in this essay, since that would result in a very large volume indeed. Therefore the following will include a selection of representative examples to illustrate the problem and to set forth some tentative conclusions.

The John the Baptist Pericope

First, let us analyze the John the Baptist pericope (Mark 1.2–8; Matthew 3.1–12; Luke 3.1–18). It is apparent that the Matthean and Lukan accounts are considerably longer and include materials that are not in the Markan account. First, the former introduces John differently. After his opening statement of purpose, Mark provides the setting for the ministry of John by quoting from Isaiah, although the quotation is actually a mix of Malachi and Isaiah. Matthew and Luke agree against Mark by first introducing John and then citing the Isaiah portion of the quotation. Mark introduces the quotation very simply, "as it is written in Isaiah the prophet," whereas Matthew and Luke are both very majestic: "for this is he who was spoken of by the prophet Isaiah when he said" (Matthew 3.3) and "as it is written in the book of the words of the prophet Isaiah" (Luke 3.4).

The reference from Malachi is cited by both authors in the pericope, "John's question about the 'Coming One' and Jesus' answer" (Matthew 11.2–19; Luke 7.18–35), a pericope that is lacking in Mark. Luke alone cites an additional portion from Isaiah, "Every valley shall be filled, and every mountain and hill shall be brought low, and the crooked shall be made straight, and the rough ways shall be made smooth; and all flesh shall see the salvation of God." John is introduced as the Baptist by Matthew (a noun), as the one who baptizes by Mark (a participle or verbal adjective), and as the son of Zechariah by Luke. Luke also omits the description of John's clothing, his diet, the statement referring to all who came from Jerusalem, from Judea, and from the region about the Jordan, the latter area cited by Matthew only, and that they were baptized by John in the river Jordan, confessing their sins. Mark and Luke agree that John preached a baptism of repentance for the forgiveness of sins, whereas according to Matthew John calls on the people to repent, for the kingdom of heaven is at hand. Matthew and Luke articulate the content of John's message, both castigating the ones who come for baptism calling them vipers and warning them of the coming wrath. Luke adds specific injunctions for people in general, for tax collectors, and for soldiers.

John's characterization of himself as inferior to the coming one is set forth more vividly in Mark, "the thong of whose sandals I am not worthy to stoop down and untie." Luke omits "to stoop down" and Matthew, as is frequently the case, compresses the description into "whose sandals I am not worthy to carry," which places a quite different emphasis upon the confession of unworthiness. In Mark, it is matter of stooping at another's feet as a sign of obeisance, whereas in Matthew it is a much milder form of deference. The baptism by the coming one is with the Holy Spirit according to Mark, whereas Matthew and Luke have an additional gift, namely, a baptism with fire. The reference to fire is also strongly enunciated in the judgment that is coming upon those who do not respond appropriately to the message of the Baptist. Matthew and Luke close the pericope with a metaphor on wheat and chaff, a symbol of the separation that ultimately results from the response or lack of it by the hearers of the message from God delivered by the coming one. Fire is again used in both texts as a metaphor of the end result for those who do not respond positively to the message.

An analysis of the above information according to the view of the priority of Matthew says that Luke did the following with Matthew's text: first he specifies Matthew's indefinite "in those days" by placing the appearance of John "in the fifteenth year of the reign of Tiberius Caesar." He then identifies other ruling authorities in church and state—Pontius Pilate, Herod, Philip, Lysanias, Annas, and Caiaphas. He omits the sobriquet, Baptist, for the identification of John, simply calling him the son of Zechariah. He changes the location of John's preaching from "the wilderness of Judea" to "all the region about the Jordan," The message, "Repent, for the kingdom of heaven is at hand," becomes "a baptism of repentance for the forgiveness of sins." He changes the introduction to the citation from Isaiah as in Matthew, "for this is he who was spoken of by the prophet Isaiah when he said," to "as it is written in the book of the words of Isaiah the prophet." He adds two additional verses to the citation from Isaiah. He omits the description of John's dress, his diet, and specifics about the people who came

The Composition of the Gospels

and were baptized by him. He omits the identification of the Pharisees and Sadducees who came out to John, referring only to the multitudes.

He cites verbatim from Matthew the long passage beginning with "You brood of vipers!", a total of sixty-three words, making only three small word changes—"fruits worthy" for "fruit worthy", "presume to say" for "begin to say," and the addition of an adverb "also" (καί). He adds specific injunctions for people in general, for tax collectors, and for soldiers. He adds a comment about the expectation of the people and their question whether or not John was the Christ. He omits Matthew's reference to John's baptism as administered "for repentance." Matthew's saying that he (the Baptist) "is not worthy to carry the sandals of the coming one" becomes in Luke that he "is not worthy to untie the thong of his sandals." He adds with Matthew that the baptism of the coming one is "with fire"; and he cites the concluding admonition concerning the winnowing fork, the wheat, and the chaff, a total of twenty-six words, with only three word changes plus a change in the position of a possessive pronoun.

If, according to this theory, Mark used both Matthew and Luke as sources, the changes by the author of Mark are even more extensive. The author follows neither source in providing a setting for John's ministry, but rather introduces him by citing a composite from the prophets Malachi and Isaiah that he has taken in part from this pericope in Matthew-Luke and in part from a different pericope, "John's question about the Coming One and Jesus' answer" (Matthew 11.10; Luke 7.27). Mark prefers Matthew over Luke for the quotation from Isaiah, for he omits the two additional verses cited by Luke. He introduces the quotation simply by saying, "as it is written in Isaiah the prophet," which, of course, is in error because of the inclusion of a quote from Malachi. Thus he radically edits the more elaborate "for this is he who was spoken of by the prophet Isaiah when he said" from Matthew or "as it is written in the words of Isaiah the prophet" from Luke. He omits Matthew's specification that John preached in the wilderness of Judea and Luke's that it was in the region of the Jordan, preferring the rather vague identification "the wilderness." He prefers Luke's "preaching a baptism of repentance for the forgiveness of sins" over Matthew's "Repent, for the kingdom of heaven is at hand." Parenthetically, he never adopts Matthew's "kingdom of heaven," but always uses "kingdom of God" with Luke even where there is not a Lukan parallel. He adopts Matthew's description of John's dress and diet, but changes Matthew's "wore a garment of camel's hair" to "clothed with camel's hair." He changes Matthew's "went out to him Jerusalem and all Judea and all the region about the Jordan" to "went out to him all the country of Judea, and all the people of Jerusalem." He follows Matthew verbatim in describing how the people were baptized in the river Jordan, confessing their sins. He omits all the material in Matthew and Luke of castigation and warning and the additional material in Luke about injunctions to people, tax collectors, and soldiers.

Matthew's "I baptize you with water for repentance, but he who is coming after me is mightier than I, whose sandals I am not worthy to carry; he will baptize you with the Holy Spirit and with fire" or Luke's "I baptize you with water; but he who is mightier than I is coming, the thong of whose sandals I am not worthy to untie; he will baptize you with the Holy Spirit and with fire" is altered by the author of Mark in the following way, "After me comes he who is mightier than I, the thong of whose sandals I am not worthy to stoop down and untie. I have baptized you with water; but he will baptize you with the Holy Spirit." The different order of the phrasing is to be noted, the different ways in which John's inferiority is set forth, and the omission of the baptism with fire.

If our principle of the development of the tradition over various stages or periods of time is sound, then it is not possible for Matthew and Luke to have been Mark's exemplar for this pericope. It would be more correct to conclude that Mark did not follow either of his sources very well, if indeed they were before him. First, he has omitted all the preliminary material of the genealogy, the annunciation, the birth and childhood of Jesus; second, he has taken scripture citations out of context from his sources and commingled them without a proper identification of his sources; third, he has omitted large blocks of material and some smaller references, such as, "with fire," which clarify and give point to the prefacing of the ministry of Jesus with a narration of the ministry of John; and, finally, he has rewritten some of the crucial phrases in his sources to give them a different meaning. It could be argued that some of these changes, such as word and order changes, are possible and even probable, but there is no explanation that gives credence to all the changes and omissions found here. There are no true additions except for the citation from Malachi in Mark's account, the omission of which by Matthew and Luke is, in fact, the authentic mark of later editing. It is improbable that Mark could have lifted this addition

The Composition of the Gospels

from a distinct pericope in Matthew and Luke, inserted it at this point, and completely ignored the rest of the material in that pericope.

The logic of the priority of Mark in this pericope is defensible for the very reasons that the priority of Matthew has been rejected: the long introductory of genealogy, annunciation, birth, and childhood of Jesus; the correction of Mark's identification of scripture by the omission of the quote from Malachi and its use in another and more appropriate setting; the inclusion of traditions that clarify and give purpose to John's ministry as a preface to the ministry of Jesus; and the rewriting and rephrasing of Mark's wording. Mark alone identifies John as "he who baptizes," rather than by the more formal title, "the Baptist." Mark also uses the verbal adjective elsewhere for John (Mark 6.14, 24), although the more formal title is found in two passages (Mark 6.25; 8.28). However, it should also be stated that some early texts read "the Baptist" in 6.14, 24 and a few texts read "he who baptizes" in 6.25 and 8.28. The tendency among later scribes was to change the verbal adjective, "he who baptizes," to the formal title, "the Baptist," and the use of the formal title in every instance in Matthew and Luke confirms the conclusion that these gospels were later than Mark. A parallel to this formalization in later writings is to be seen in the identification of Jesus as "the Christ." The pre-resurrection references to Jesus as the Christ are changed to Jesus Christ, a proper name, in the post-resurrection tradition.

A peculiarity of Matthew's representation of John's message is not only that he proclaims, "Repent, for the kingdom of heaven is at hand," as compared to Mark's indirect discourse, "preaching a baptism of repentance for the forgiveness of sins," but also that he has Jesus proclaim precisely the same message when he begins his preaching ministry in Galilee (Matthew 4.17). At this point Mark announces the theme of Jesus' message to be, "The time is fulfilled, and the kingdom of God is at hand; repent, and believe in the gospel" (Mark 1.15). It is strange, if Jesus' ministry was truly unique and distinctive from every other, that he says no more and no less than that which was said by the Baptist. If Mark did use Matthew and Luke as sources for his gospel, then we would say that Mark simply preferred Luke's version over Matthew's at this point, but this is only moving the problem back a step for then it is necessary to answer the question, Why did Luke change Matthew's text and why did Mark prefer Luke's version? The problem does not seem to be nearly so difficult to resolve if we adopt the view that Mark was the earlier version, Luke preferred Mark's version, and Matthew substituted his more stereotyped formula for the message of both John and Jesus.

If Mark used Matthew as a source, he also reorganized the sequence of the material from Matthew, which is as follows:

1) the appearance of John in the wilderness,
2) the message of John,
3) the citation of the prophet,
4) the description of John,
5) the areas from which people came, and
6) their baptism and confession.

The order in Mark is:

3) the citation of the prophet,
1) the appearance of John in the wilderness,
2) the message of John,
5) the areas from which the people came,
6) their baptism and confession, and
4) the description of John.

The order in Matthew is more logical and systematic. That is to say, Mark destroys the natural flow of order as in Matthew's version. But the rule for editing is to improve, not to destroy a good natural sequence, and again the balances favor the priority of Mark.

Luke's order is:

1) the historical setting for the appearance of John in the wilderness,
2) the site for the ministry in the region of the Jordan,
3) the message of John, and
4) the citation of the prophet.

The differences in Luke's version from Mark and Matthew are very great. It is difficult to posit that there could have been any impact upon Mark's account from Luke's version with the possible exception of the content of John's message, a baptism of repentance for the forgiveness of sins. The points of similarity are few, but the comparison suggests that Luke's more

The Composition of the Gospels

sophisticated account reflects a later stage in the development of the tradition.

Again we have a change in order for the summation of John's message from Matthew to Luke to Mark. Matthew's order is as follows:

1) I baptize you with water for repentance,
2) he who is coming after me is mightier than I,
3) whose sandals I am not worthy to carry, and
4) he will baptize you with the Holy Spirit and with fire.

Mark's order is different in this way:

2) after me comes he who is mightier than I,
3) the thong of whose sandals I am not worthy to stoop down and untie,
1) I have baptized (past tense) with water, and
4) he will baptize you with the Holy Spirit (no fire).

Luke's order is as follows:

1) I baptize you with water (omit for repentance),
2) he who is mightier than I is coming,
3) the thong of whose sandals I am not worthy to untie, and
4) he will baptize you with Holy Spirit and with fire.

The order is Matthew's, but the content is closer to Mark except for the baptism with fire. It is difficult to comprehend how the author of Mark could have arrived at his order if he had Matthew and Luke before him. The order of Matthew and Luke is intrinsically an improvement over Mark's order and it is probable that the two authors could have improved upon Mark's order independently. The changes in word and phrase are more natural if we assume that the exemplar for Matthew and Luke was Mark's gospel, and that the authors also had another source before them that contained those traditions that are common to them but not to Mark. Each of the writers is not merely an editor but an author in a truly creative sense, so that the final pericopes in each of the gospels are accounts that are in general agreement and even very specific agreement at many points but that also reflect differences in emphases and interests from gospel to gospel.

The Parable of the Wicked Tenants

The example selected from the teaching material is the parable of the wicked tenants (Matthew 21.33–46; Mark 12.1–12; Luke 20.9–19). Matthew introduces the parable with the words, "Hear another parable," whereas Luke says, "And he began to tell the people this parable." Mark is closer to Luke's introduction with his wording, "And he began to speak to them in parables." It is obvious that Matthew has edited the introduction, not just because Mark and Luke are quite similar, but because he has another and unique parable immediately preceding, that is, the parable of the Two Sons. His introduction acknowledges the intrusion of this preceding parable into the context of the controversies in Jerusalem. The key role player, the "man," which is indefinite in Mark and Luke, becomes "a householder" in Matthew. It seems improbable that Luke could have changed "householder" to "man" and that Mark preferred Luke's "man" to Matthew's "householder" on the premise that Matthew is the earlier. Luke's omission of the details, "and set a hedge around it, and dug a pit for the wine press, and built a tower," is comprehensible in view of his need to abbreviate in order to conserve space for other important material, whereas Matthew basically follows Mark except for the omission of the word "pit." The "time" in Mark and Luke becomes the more specific, "the season of fruit," in Matthew. The order of the events that follow according to Matthew's narration is as follows:

1) "he sent his slaves to the tenants, to get his fruit; and
2) the tenants took his slaves and beat one, killed another, and stoned another.
3) Again he sent other slaves, more than the first; and they did the same to them."

If Luke had this text before him, he has edited it extensively:

1) "he sent a slave to the tenants, that they should give him some of the fruit of the vineyard;
2) but the tenants beat him, and sent him away empty-handed.
3) And he sent another slave; him also they beat and treated shamefully, and sent him away empty-handed.
4) And he sent yet a third; this one they wounded and cast out."

The Composition of the Gospels

And if Mark had both Matthew's and Luke's texts before him, he has also edited extensively:

1) "he sent a slave to the tenants, to get from them some of the fruit of the vineyard.
2) And they took him and beat him, and sent him away empty-handed.
3) Again he sent to them another slave, and they wounded him in the head, and treated him shamefully.
4) And he sent another, and him they killed;
5) and so with many others, some they beat and some they killed."

According to Mark, the man sent a single slave on three occasions with a progression in the severity of their reception; the first they beat, the second they wounded in the head, and the third they killed. There follows a summary of the sending of many slaves over a period of time, each ending with a similar result. Mark and Luke agree that there was a sending of individual slaves on three occasions. Matthew says that the householder sent two contingents of slaves on two occasions, but in his sequel to the first dispatch he too has a trilogy, "the tenants took his slaves and beat one, killed another, and stoned another."

This suggests that Mark and Luke are closer to the original parable in the number of sendings, although it is possible that Mark has heightened the drama of the original by adding a general sending of many slaves before the sending of the son. It is possible that Luke edited Matthew's text by expanding two general sendings of slaves into three sendings of individual slaves and that Mark then preferred Luke's version and expanded upon it further by adding a general sending. But it seems more logical to say that Matthew omitted the sending of slaves on three separate occasions and adopted Mark's sending of a group of slaves, since there is a correspondence in result. Note that Mark says, "again he sent other slaves, more than the first; and they did the same to them." Matthew says, "he sent his slaves to the tenants, ... and the tenants took his slaves and beat one, killed another, and stoned another." This is very near to what Mark says for the first three sendings, the first slave they beat, the second they wounded, and the third they killed.

The real problem to Markan primacy is the expression "the beloved son," which is not in Matthew's text. If Matthew's text is the earlier and if

Luke used Matthew as a source, the interpolation of the word "beloved" was done by this author and Mark preferred his reading. In any event the word is probably an interpolation into the text and the difficulty is, Why in Mark and Luke and not in Matthew? The word "beloved" is used in two other pericopes, the baptism of Jesus and the transfiguration, in which the voice from heaven addresses Jesus as "the beloved son." However, Luke has substituted "chosen" for "beloved" in the transfiguration pericope, a reading supported by the earliest manuscripts. It would appear to be contrary to his editing practice then to introduce "beloved" into this pericope, since he did not find the word in Matthew's text that was before him. It is more logical to suppose that he found the word in Mark, his exemplar, and uncritically copied it. The introduction of the word is usually interpreted as a transformation of the parable into a prediction of the death of Jesus and this is the basis for considering it an interpolation and not a part of the original parable. There is the possibility that it was original and that the author of Matthew omitted it. If original, it may not have had the implication that some of us have read into it, but may simply be another illustration of the inimitable way in which Jesus frequently heightens the quality of the action of a parable. If the father has a son, why should not the son be beloved? His own love for his son leads him to think erroneously that the tenants will respect him. How often do we invest our son or daughter with an aura of invincibility just because we love him or her so deeply? If this is the true interpretation, it explains why Matthew has omitted the word. It did not have the significance in the original context that we have read into it and he merely edits it out.

The next serious difference among the synoptics is the phrase that reads in Mark, "they took him (the son) and killed him and cast him out of the vineyard." Matthew reads, "they took him and cast him out of the vineyard, and killed him," whereas Luke very similarly reads, "they cast him out of the vineyard and killed him." It would be very contrary to the canons of criticism to argue that Mark has altered the reading of Matthew and/or Luke, since we would have to say he adopted the phrase, "took him," from Matthew in preference to the omission in Luke and then reversed the order, "cast him out of the vineyard, and killed him," which is the reading in both Matthew and Luke. What reason can be advanced to support such a change? But the change in Matthew and Luke follows the logic of criticism, since it follows the order for the death of Jesus as in Hebrews: "Jesus also suffered outside the gate in order to sanctify the people through his own blood" (13.12). It is reasonable to suppose that the authors of Matthew and Luke were both familiar with this tradition and altered Mark's text independently to bring it into accord with the tradition. Thus the parable indeed becomes a prediction not only of the death of Jesus, but of the very manner in which his death was carried out.

Matthew has also added glosses to the text of Mark with the additions of the phrases "to a miserable death" and "who will give him the fruits in their season." Luke has inserted the gloss, "when they heard this, they said, 'God forbid!'" The teaching of Jesus then continues with the application of the parable to the audience, a quotation from the Psalms (118.22–23). Luke omits the second verse, since apparently this verse is not relevant to the message of judgment that is the point of the parable, and inserts together with Matthew a quotation that seems to have been fashioned from the Book of Daniel (2.34–35, 44–45). The Nestle Edition places Matthew's inclusion of this verse in question, although it is found in all the early manuscripts except Codex Bezae and some of the Old Latin texts. There is, of course, the possibility that the saying found its way into Matthew's text through a scribal gloss, although thus far there is no evidence to support such a conclusion.

Matthew has an additional commentary on the quotation from the Psalms with the inclusion of the dire warning, "Therefore I tell you, the kingdom of God will be taken away from you and given to a nation producing the fruits of it." The order in Matthew appears to be secondary, since the interpolation of this commentary separates the references to "the stone" in the quotation from Psalms and the reference to the stone that breaks in pieces and crushes. Luke's order is more congenial, especially with the omission of Psalm 118.23. Those who hold to the priority of Matthew must argue that the absence of these comments in Mark were the result of editing by omission and that Luke also has edited Matthew by the omission of the saying about the kingdom of God. Incidentally, this is one of five occasions in the gospel of Matthew where the phrase "kingdom of God" occurs rather than the usual "kingdom of heaven" that is used thirty-one times. Matthew also supplies the reason why the chief priests and Pharisees were afraid of the multitudes, "they held him to be a prophet," a comment that is absent in both Mark and Luke. The consistency of Mark throughout in avoiding Christological references and the absence of the commentary upon the quotation from the Psalms supports the integrity of Mark's account at every point and leads to the conclusion that it was indeed the exemplar for the authors of Matthew and Luke.

The Prayer in Gethsemane

The example selected from the passion narrative is the prayer in Gethsemane (Matthew 26.36–46; Mark 14.32–42; Luke 22.39–46). The problem in this section, as has already been noted, is to relate the text of Luke to the texts of Matthew and Mark. The differences are so great that the conclusion seems to be correct that Luke had a second source for this period in the ministry of Jesus that he often preferred above the text of Mark. This is evident in the introduction to this pericope, since Luke omits that Jesus and the disciples sang a hymn before they left the upper room for the Mount of Olives. He adds a unique phrase, "went, *as was his custom*, to the Mount of Olives."

Does this suggest that Luke's source knew of a previous mission to Jerusalem? Can it be a confirmation of the statement early in the ministry of Jesus, "he was preaching in the synagogues of Judea" (Luke 4.44)? A reference to a ministry in Jerusalem earlier than this visit that culminates in his death is never found in Mark and Matthew. However, Jesus does indicate on more than one occasion that he has a certain familiarity with the area, the city, and certain people. For example, from the Mount of Olives he sends his disciples to an unnamed village to procure a colt (Mark, Luke) or an ass (Matthew) that had never been ridden (Mark, Luke), which the owners are willing to commit to these strangers upon their word that "the Lord has need of it." Again he sends two of his disciples into the city where they will see a man carrying a jar of water who will lead them to the house where they are to keep the Passover. This suggests long acquaintanceship, not prescience. The absence of any reference to such a ministry in Matthew and Mark therefore does not preclude its actuality.

The larger question is, Why, if there was such a ministry as is amply attested in the Fourth Gospel, do the synoptics completely omit any reference to it except for the one passing reference in Luke? A possible answer lies just in our solution to the question of the relationships among the gospels. If Mark was the earliest gospel to have been written, and if Peter was the main source for the Jesus traditions that Mark incorporates into his gospel, and if Mark is the main source upon which the authors of Matthew and Luke

The Composition of the Gospels

relied for their gospels, it could be that Jesus went to Jerusalem from time to time without his disciples; visits that were not part of Peter's recollections since he and the other disciples had remained in Galilee. Jesus' friendship with Martha and Mary (Luke 10.38–42) who are placed in Bethany near Jerusalem according to the Fourth Gospel (John 11.1) also supports a Judean ministry of a longer duration than the synoptics allow.

In addition to the differences mentioned above, Luke omits the name "Gethsemane," the injunction to the disciples to "sit here," the naming of Peter, James and John (Mark), or the sons of Zebedee (Matthew), to go farther with him, the reference to his distress; Jesus went on "about a stone's throw" (Luke) rather than "a little farther" (Mark, Matthew), he "knelt" rather than fell on the ground (Mark) or on his face (Matthew). Both Matthew and Luke omit Mark's, he prayed "that, if it were possible, the hour might pass from him" and the address in Aramaic, "Abba."

The wording of the prayer differs in both Matthew and Luke from Mark's, "Father, all things are possible to you; remove this cup from me; yet not what I desire, but what you (desire)," to Matthew's, "Father, if it be possible, let this cup pass from me; nevertheless, not as I desire, but as you (desire)," to Luke's "Father, if you are willing, remove this cup from me; nevertheless not my will, but yours be done"; Luke inserts the parenthetical expression, "when he rose from prayer," which is in character with his emphasis upon prayer. He also adds that the disciples were sleeping "for sorrow." Jesus addresses the disciples (Luke), Peter (Matthew), and Peter even more specifically, "Simon, are you asleep?" (Mark). Luke omits, "Could you not watch one hour?" and the admonitory word, "Watch," as well as the words, "the spirit indeed is willing, but the flesh is weak." Matthew specifies that he went "for the second time" and also "for the third time." Mark simply says, "he went away and prayed, saying the same words," which Luke omits and Matthew expands to, "he went away and prayed, 'My Father, if this cannot pass unless I drink it, your will be done.'" Some early texts of Luke, including a fourth century manuscript, insert, "And being in an agony he prayed more earnestly; and his sweat became like great drops of blood falling down upon the ground," Luke, in fact, except for the intrusion of this verse into some texts, omits any reference to a second and a third prayer. After the second prayer Matthew omits Mark's, "and they did not know what to answer him." Matthew then expands upon Mark's, "and he came the third time," by saying, "So, leaving them again, he went away and prayed for the third time, saying the same words." For the lengthy conclusion in Mark and Matthew, which are almost verbatim in the two accounts (three word selections differ, Matthew omits two definite articles, and a verb is positioned differently), Luke simply writes, "Why do you sleep? Rise and pray that you may not enter into temptation" (verse 46), which is repetitious when compared to verse 40.

A cursory scan of this running comparison demonstrates conclusively that Luke did not rely very heavily upon either Mark or Matthew, if at all, for his account of this event. Our concern therefore must be primarily with the relationship between the gospels of Matthew and Mark. Did Mark substitute "James and John" for "the two sons of Zebedee?" In the call of the first disciples both evangelists have "James the son of Zebedee and John his brother." In the list of disciples Mark reads, "James the son of Zebedee and John the brother of James," whereas Matthew reads, "James the son of Zebedee and John his brother." In the pericope about the positions of authority Mark writes, "James and John, the sons of Zebedee," whereas Matthew simply, "the sons of Zebedee." In a second reference in this same pericope Mark again specifies "James and John," whereas Matthew reads "the two brothers." In the transfiguration pericope Mark has "James and John" to which Matthew appends "his brother." Mark mentions James and John by name in the stories of the healing of Peter's mother-in-law, the raising of Jairus' daughter, and specifically among those who ask Jesus questions about the end of time, all of which are omitted by Matthew.

The question is, Did Mark introduce the specific names into Matthew's text or did Matthew edit them out? It is precarious to argue one way or the other for priority in many instances of differences between Matthew and Mark, and the use of proper names is one such instance. There are some discrepancies difficult to explain. For example, was the tax collector Levi, son of Alphaeus, according to Mark (2.14), or Matthew according to Matthew's gospel (9.9), or simply Levi (Luke 5.27)? Levi is not mentioned in any of the lists of disciples. The three gospels agree by including Matthew among the twelve disciples, although Matthew identifies him as "the tax collector." And all three, including Mark, list James as the son of Alphaeus. Is Mark wrong in identifying Levi as the son of Alphaeus, or did Alphaeus have two sons, one a tax collector who became a follower and another, James, who became a member of the Twelve?

The Composition of the Gospels

Mark and Luke identify the demoniac as "Legion" and the ruler of the synagogue as Jairus. In the cursing of the fig tree pericope, Mark says Peter remonstrated with Jesus, whereas in Matthew it was the disciples. Matthew alone identifies the betrayer as Judas at the last meal. In the final analysis it seems to this writer that the frequency of occurrence of the proper names in Mark and their regular omission in Matthew and the very similar exchange of personal names for sons of Zebedee in the pericope about the positions of authority precisely as in the Gethsemane pericope support the conclusion that Matthew has substituted "the two sons of Zebedee" for Mark's "James and John" and that Mark was the exemplar for Matthew. A final example that speaks perhaps more authoritatively for the priority of Mark is in the pericope of the death of John the Baptist. Mark introduces Herod as "King Herod" (6.14), which is obviously in error, an error that is corrected by both Matthew (14.1) and Luke (9.7) to "Herod the tetrarch." Mark consistently identifies Herod as king throughout the narrative, whereas Matthew is in contradiction for he uses the title king later in the account (14.9).

The address of the Aramaic *Abba* to God by Jesus in his prayer is unique to Mark who adds the translation "Father." Matthew and Luke omit Abba and read only "Father." The supposition according to the theory that Mark relied upon Matthew and Luke as sources is that Luke has followed Matthew's usage and Mark has inserted Abba into the text. However, the words of the prayer that follow are quite different in the three gospels. Matthew writes, "if it be possible, let this cup pass from me; nevertheless, not as I desire, but as you (desire)." If Luke used Matthew, he changes this wording to "if you are willing, remove this cup from me; nevertheless not my will, but yours, be done." If Mark used Matthew and Luke as sources, he changes both versions to "all things are possible to you; remove this cup from me; yet not what I desire, but what you (desire)." In the Greek text, Mark has "possible" with Matthew, although in the plural form, "remove" with Luke, "yet" for "nevertheless" against both Matthew and Luke, and "what" for "as" in Matthew. The latter phrase is quite different in Luke and cannot be related to either Matthew or Mark. It is difficult to determine who has edited the prayer words in this isolated instance, so that the conclusion must depend upon the preponderance of evidence as it is deduced from other passages. Thus the address "Abba, the Father," the translation of the Aramaic word into a Greek nominative singular in Mark, a nominative singular that also serves as the vocative in the Aramaic, is the decisive factor in the passage and must be weighed against "Father," the vocative or direct address in Matthew and Luke.

It is one of the peculiarities of Mark to use Aramaic words followed by the translation of that word(s) into Greek. All these usages are lacking in Matthew and Luke. Other occurrences are *Talitha cumi* (Mark 5.41; cf. Matthew 9.25; Luke 8.54), *Corban* (Mark 7.11; cf. Matthew 15.5), and *Ephphatha* (Mark 7.34), a passage that has no parallel in Matthew and Luke. The words of Jesus from the cross, *eloi, eloi, lama sabachthani* (Mark 15.34), are repeated in Matthew 27.46, although in the latter the name of God is hebraized to *eli, eli*. Does Mark interpolate these words into texts where he did not find them in his sources? Does he aramaize Matthew's hebraized form for the name of God? Or did Matthew and Luke omit Mark's Aramaic words from their Markan source and did Matthew hebraize the name of God that he found in the Aramaic in Mark?

A further investigation shows that Matthew and Luke use Aramaic words in other passages that are transliterated into Greek, but left untranslated. For example, *batos* (Luke 16.6), *Corbanan* (Matthew 27.6), *coros* (Luke 16.7), *raca* (Matthew 5.22), *sata* (Matthew 13.33; Luke 13.21), and *sucaminos* (Luke 17.6). Other words from the Aramaic used with some frequency by all the evangelists are *amen* and *rabbi*. Luke never uses the latter in reference to Jesus, but either omits or substitutes "Master" where he found *rabbi* in Matthew and/or Mark (cf. Luke 9.32). Matthew uses *rabbi* in three passages where there are no parallels (Matthew 23.7, 8; 26.25) and only once in agreement with Mark (Matthew 26.49; Mark 14.45). Otherwise he has *kyrios* where Mark has *rabbi* (Matthew 17.4), omits *rabbi* (Mark 11.21; cf. Matthew 21.20), or has *kyrios* for *rabbouni* (Mark 10.51; Matthew 20.33; Luke 18.41).

The real difference between Mark's usage and the usages of Matthew and Luke is that in the passages where *Abba, talitha cumi,* and *corban* are found in Mark, they are followed by a translation into Greek in Mark and are omitted in Matthew and Luke. The balance of the evidence then favors Mark as the earlier, for there does not seem to be a valid argument to support the supposition that Mark introduced these words into a Matthean context and the evidence suggests that in the parallels words of Aramaic origin and even Aramaic words are found more often in Mark than in Matthew and Luke. It is to be expected that the farther removed the writers are from the Jesus of history the fewer remnants will be found of the

The Composition of the Gospels

Aramaic origins of the Jesus tradition. And that is precisely the case as we move from Mark to Matthew and Luke.

It has been noted that in Luke's account Jesus prays only once. In Mark's account the wording for prayer one is given with the reference that Jesus prayed the same words for prayer two and then that he came "the third time" to the disciples. Matthew's account is more elaborate with the words for prayers one and two quoted and the statement that Jesus "prayed for the third time, saying the same words." If Matthew was the source for Luke, then Luke has omitted prayers two and three and has radically revised the words of prayer one. If Matthew and Luke were the sources for Mark, then Mark revises prayer one so that it is distinctly positive when compared to either Matthew or Luke, refers to prayer two without quoting the wording, and makes only an oblique reference that Jesus came a third time. If Mark is the source for Matthew and Luke, then Matthew has revised prayer one by making it more contingent, interpolated into Mark's text the words for prayer two including a phrase precisely the same as in the Lord's prayer ("your will be done" Matthew 6.10), and specifies that Jesus prayed a third time. Which of the possibilities seems to be more correct? It seems to this writer that the interpolation of phrasing from the Lord's prayer tips the scales in favor of the priority of Mark. It is a choice between expansion by Matthew or reduction by Mark and the knowledge that the tendency is for texts to grow with the passage of time suggests the priority of Mark.

In the remainder of the pericope, the account of the role of the disciples and Jesus' admonitions to them in Matthew and Mark are almost verbatim. On the basis of our conclusion that Mark's text is the earlier, we can say that a comparison of Matthew 26.40 to Mark 14.37 suggests that Matthew interpolates "to the disciples," "with me," and "thus" into Mark's text, and omits Mark's "Simon, are you asleep?" The omission is in character with what we have already found; Matthew tends to omit personal names. Matthew 26.41 and Mark 14.38 are almost verbatim; Matthew's verb "enter" is a compound verb with a prepositional prefix, whereas Mark has the verb without a prefix. In Matthew 26.42, Mark's connective conjunction is omitted and the phrase "for the second time" interpolated (Mark 14.39). In Matthew 26.43, a perfect passive participle replaces Mark's present passive participle and the prepositional prefix of the verb is omitted (Mark 14.40). In addition, Matthew omits the phrase "and they did not know what to answer him," which is replaced with, "So, leaving them again, he went away and prayed for the third time, saying the same words." In Matthew 26.45, "then," a correlative adverb of time and a favorite of the author of Matthew's gospel (ninety occurrences), replaces the connective "and" in Mark (14.41). Matthew omits Mark's "the third time" and interpolates "to the disciples." Matthew omits Mark's "it is enough" and substitutes "the hour is at hand" for Mark's "the hour has come." Finally, Matthew streamlines Mark's text by omitting two definite articles.

The pericopes that have been considered from the three categories have been picked at random and this writer is quite certain that the results would not be different if other examples had been examined in detail. Although an example from the "signs and wonder story" category is not examined in detail, the generalization can be made with some certainty that the results would be the same. However, the phenomenon is different, inasmuch as the accounts are usually much longer in Mark than in Matthew and Luke. Only in the "healing of the daughter of the Syrophoenician woman" and in the "walking on water" episodes is Matthew's account longer, in the former only by a few words and in the latter appreciably because of the addition of Peter's walk. The differences here as over against the other categories are probably due in part to the different emphases of the writers and in part to the need for the author of Matthew to stay within acceptable limits of length. Mark's Jesus is a man of action and he emphasizes the deeds of Jesus, whereas Matthew's Jesus is the teacher with a corresponding emphasis upon that feature of his ministry.

Summary of the Abridgment Argument

In summary, Mark is much the shorter gospel when compared to Matthew and Luke, but it is not an abridgment. The longer pericopes for the signs and wonder story traditions and the abbreviated accounts of important events in the life of Jesus are incomprehensible, if it is posited that the agreements among the gospels resulted from Luke's use of Matthew and Mark's use of Matthew and Luke. If this is the way it really happened, then Mark's gospel should have been as much longer than Matthew than Matthew is of Mark and as much longer than Luke than Luke is of Mark.

The Composition of the Gospels

The Order of Events for the Ministry of Jesus

It has been argued by some that the order of events for the ministry of Jesus was designed by Mark and that the authors of Matthew and Luke basically follow this order. The argument also is that whenever Luke departs from Mark's order of events Matthew is in agreement with Mark and whenever Matthew departs from Mark's order Luke is in basic agreement. This thesis must be tested to see whether or not it is viable. In order to do this it has been necessary to lay out the order of events according to Mark and then note where the differences in order fall when Matthew and Luke are compared to this outline.

After the initial statement of purpose (Mark 1.1; Matthew 1.1; Luke 1.1–4), Mark continues his "gospel of Jesus Christ" with the ministry of John the Baptist. After their initial statements of purpose, Matthew inserts a genealogy for Jesus and infancy stories, whereas Luke inserts infancy stories for both John the Baptist and Jesus as well as an excerpt from the life of Jesus at age twelve. Mark's outline is followed by Matthew through Jesus' initial proclamation of the gospel in Galilee (Mark 1.2–15), whereas Luke inserts a reference to the imprisonment of John after Mark 1.8, a genealogy for Jesus after Mark 1.11, and a ministry and rejection in his home town of Nazareth after Mark's statement of a preaching in Galilee (Mark 1.14–15). Matthew preserves Mark's order in each of these instances, since his genealogy is placed at the beginning of the infancy narratives and his accounts of the death of John the Baptist and of Jesus' rejection at his home town correspond to Mark's order.

Lukan Order Compared to the Markan Order

An examination of Luke's account of Jesus' rejection at Nazareth demonstrates that the author has knowingly removed the pericope from its proper order and inserted it into an earlier context for the ministry of Jesus. Mark reports this event after the raising of Jairus's daughter (Mark 5.21–43 and 6.1–6) and Matthew is in agreement with Mark for this location. Luke reports that in response to his critics Jesus said, "what we have heard that you did at Capernaum, do here also in your own country" (Luke 4.23). Mark reports healings at Capernaum after the call of the fishermen to be disciples (Mark 1.21). Obviously then a ministry at Capernaum has preceded a visit to Jesus' home town of Nazareth and Matthew has the events of the ministry at Capernaum and the visit to Nazareth in the same sequence as Mark.

Luke again varies Mark's order by omitting the call of the four fishermen (Mark 1.16–20) at this point and inserting an expanded version of this event (Luke 5.1–11) after Jesus' prayer in a lonely place and preaching in Galilee (Mark 1.35–39). He returns to Mark's sequence with the healing of a man with an unclean spirit (Mark 1.21–28; Luke 4.31–37) and, apart from the deviations mentioned above, follows Mark's sequence through the account of the restoration of a withered hand (Mark 3.1–6; Luke 6.6–11). His next point of departure is a small one, since his introductory words to the sermon on the plain (Luke 6.17–19) correspond in some measure to Mark's multitudes from various regions and healings by Jesus (Mark 3.7–12). Luke has simply reversed the two pericopes, since the naming of the Twelve then corresponds to Mark's order (Mark 3.13–19; Luke 6.12–16).

At this point Luke has inserted into Mark's framework a selection of non-Markan materials that is called "the little interpolation" (Luke 6.20–8.3), which includes the sermon on the plain (6.20–49), the healing of a Roman centurion's slave (7.1–10), the widow's son at Nain (7.11–17), John's question of the coming one and Jesus' answer (7.18–35), the anointing of Jesus by a sinful woman (7.36–50), which has points of similarity to Mark 14.3–9, and the women from Galilee (8.1–3).

He does not return to Mark's sequence immediately as the following comparison shows. The accusation that Jesus casts out demons by Beelzebul (Mark 3.20–27) is found in Luke 11.14–23, the blasphemy against the Spirit (Mark 3.28–30) at Luke 12.8–12, and the mother and brothers of Jesus (Mark 3.31–35) at Luke 8.19–21. Mark's sequence is again followed beginning with the teaching in parables (Mark 4.1–25; Luke 8.4–18), although he departs from the Markan sequence by omitting the parable of the seed growing spontaneously (Mark 4.26–29) and the parable of the mustard seed (Mark 4.30–32) is moved to the section known as the great interpolation (Luke 13.18–19). He also omits Mark's summary on teaching in parables (Mark 4.33–34), but returns to Mark's sequence with the account of the storm at sea (Mark 4.35; Luke 8.22) and follows Mark's order through the raising of Jairus's daughter (Mark 4.35–5.43; Luke 8.22–56). At this point he omits Jesus' rejection in his own country (Mark 6.1–6), which he has placed earlier in the ministry (Luke 4.16–30) as has been noted above. He returns to Mark's order with the pericope of the mission

The Composition of the Gospels

of the Twelve (Mark 6.6–13; Luke 9.1–6) with only a short reference to Mark's extended pericope of the death of the Baptist (Mark 6.14–29; Luke 9.7–9) since he has already told the circumstances of the imprisonment of John (Luke 3.19–20), and then follows Mark's order through the feeding of the five thousand (Mark 6.30–44; Luke 9.10–17). He omits the next section of Mark beginning with the walking on water and all the events comprising Jesus' journey north to the regions of Tyre, Sidon, and Caesarea Philippi (Mark 6.45–8.26) with only a few scattered references to materials in that section (Luke 11.37–41; 6.39; 12.1).

The confession of Peter (Mark 8.27–30; Luke 9.18–21) is placed immediately following the feeding of the five thousand and not at Caesarea Philippi, since Jesus has not made a journey northward. Thereafter Mark's sequence is again followed for a long section (Mark 8.27–9.41; Luke 9.18–50) at which point Luke makes what is entitled "the great interpolation," an extended narration of traditions (Luke 9.51–18.14) that are not in Mark, although a few parallels from Mark are relocated throughout Luke's interpolation: the great commandment (Mark 12 28–34; Luke 10.25–27), the charge that Jesus casts out demons by Beelzebul (Mark 3.22–27; Luke 11.15–22; cf. also Mark 9.40; Luke 11.23), the seeking for signs (Mark 8.11–12; Luke 11.29), the parable of the lamp (Mark 4.21; Luke 11.33), woes against Pharisees (Mark 12.38–39; Luke 11.43), the leaven of the Pharisees (Mark 8.14–15; Luke 12.1), a parable on the hidden and the revealed (Mark 4.22; Luke 12.2–3), on answering authorities (Mark 13.9, 11; Luke 12.11–12), the return of the master (Mark 13.35–37; Luke 12.38), the parable of the mustard seed (Mark 4.30–32; Luke 13.18–19), the cost of discipleship (Mark 8.34; Luke 14.26–27), a parable on salt (Mark 9.50; Luke 14.34–35), eating with sinners (Mark 2.16; Luke 15.1–2), a saying on divorce (Mark 10.11–12; Luke 16.18), a warning against causing little ones to sin (Mark 9.42; Luke 17.2), false Christs (Mark 13.21; Luke 17.21), and a warning about the end time (Mark 13.15; Luke 17.31).

We have noted that Mark's pericope of the punishment for the one who causes a little one to sin (Mark 9.42–48) is found in the great interpolation at Luke 17.1–4 and that the salt metaphor (Mark 9.49–50) is found in that same section in Luke 14.34–35. Luke omits Mark's long pericope on divorce and remarriage (Mark 10.1–12) with only a statement on that theme that is also in the great interpolation (Luke 16.18). At this point Luke returns to Mark's sequence beginning with the pericope on Jesus receiving children (Mark 10.13; Luke 18.15) and follows Mark's order through the third announcement of death and resurrection (Mark 10.13–34; Luke 18.15–34). He omits the pericope of the request of the sons of Zebedee (Mark 10.35–45) except for the teaching on greatness that issues from that request, although he places this material later in his gospel (Luke 22.24–27). He then picks up Mark's order again with the giving of sight to blind Bartimaeus (Mark 10.46–52; Luke 18.35–43), but interpolates after it the narrative of Zacchaeus and the parable of the ten pounds (Luke 19.1–27).

Mark's sequence is again followed with Jesus' entry into Jerusalem (Mark 11.1–11; Luke 19.28–40) to which he appends the weeping over Jerusalem (Luke 19.41–44). He omits both parts of the pericope on the cursing of the fig tree (Mark 11.12–14; 11.20–25), but is in sequence with the cleansing of the temple (Mark 11.15–19; Luke 19.45–46) and then adds a short pericope about teaching daily in the temple (Luke 19.47–48). His sequence again corresponds with Mark beginning Mark 11.27, the section on the controversies with religious leaders, and then follows Mark's order through the admonition to watch (Mark 11.27–13.37; Luke 20.1–21.36) with these exceptions: he omits the teaching on love for God and neighbor (Mark 12.28–34) that he has placed as a preface to the parable of the good Samaritan (Luke 10.25–28), he also omits the short saying on the gospel to all nations (Mark 13.10); and his warnings about the coming day are not precisely parallel with Mark's material (Mark 13.32–37; Luke 21.34–36). He adds a second note about teaching daily in the temple (Luke 21.37–38).

The reader must remember that, although Luke may be in sequence with Mark in the account of the Passion, the content differs strikingly, so that it has been suggested that Luke had access to another and parallel tradition to Mark that he preferred most of the time. Mark's order is followed as he narrates the plot to arrest Jesus (Mark 14.1–2, 10–25; Luke 22.1–2, 3–23), although he omits the anointing of Jesus (Mark 14.3–9) that he had placed in an earlier context (Luke 7.36–50). At this point he interpolates a dispute about greatness (Luke 22.24–30) that was found earlier in Mark (10.42–45). He again picks up Mark's thread (Mark 14.26) with the announcement of Peter's denial and follows Mark's sequence through the arrest (Mark 14.26–50; Luke 22.31–53), although he introduces sayings about a purse, a bag, and two swords (Luke 22.35–38) before the journey to the Mount of Olives. He omits the reference to the young man who fled naked (Mark 14.51–52) and then follows Mark's order in general as Jesus is led before Caiaphas and finally to Pilate (Mark 14.53–15.5; Luke 22.54–23.5). One must say "in general," because the internal order and sequence within the pericopes is quite different between Mark and Luke at many places. Luke interpolates Jesus' appearance before Herod into the appearance before Pilate and his condemnation (Luke 23.6–12). Again we return to Mark's sequence (Mark 15.6); and Mark's order is followed through the crucifixion, death, and resurrection (Mark 15.6–16.8; Luke 23.13–24.12) with the following differences: the taunting and mocking is by Herod's soldiers (Mark 15.16–20; Luke 23.11), there is an interpolation that women lament the condemnation of Jesus on the way to the cross (Luke 23.27–31), and additions are interpolated into the account of the two criminals crucified with Jesus (Luke 23.32, 39b–43).

Since Mark's gospel closes with the account of the empty tomb (Mark 16.1–8), the remaining pericopes in Luke are unique: the two disciples on the road to Emmaus (Luke 24.13–35), the appearance of the risen Jesus in Jerusalem (Luke 24.36–43), the command to wait in Jerusalem for the coming of the Spirit (Luke 24.44–49), and the blessing of the disciples and the ascension at Bethany (Luke 24.50–53).

Matthean Order Compared to the Markan Order

We now return to Matthew with a similar description of his sequence in comparison to Mark, beginning where we left off above with the preaching in Galilee (Mark 1.14–15; Matthew 4.12–17) and the calling of the four fishermen (Mark 1.16–20; Matthew 4.18–22). At this point Matthew has radically altered Mark's sequence. He omits the healing of the man with the unclean spirit (Mark 1.21–28) and skips to Mark 1.39, which is a summary of Jesus' preaching ministry throughout Galilee with additions (Matthew 4.23–25). Mark's "casting out demons" is expanded into a whole catalog of healings accompanied by fame and great crowds that come even from non-Jewish regions. At this point Matthew interpolates his sermon on the mount (chapters five through seven), although it too is out of sequence with Mark. It rightly belongs in Mark's sequence following the phrase, "he went up on the mountain and called to him those whom he desired, and they came to him" (Mark 3.13). Note the close similarity of the phraseology in Matthew, "he went up on the mountain, and when he sat down his disciples came to him" (Matthew 5.1). Thus the sermon on the mount rightly belongs in Mark's sequence before the naming of the Twelve (Mark 3.14–19). The pericopes that Matthew has skipped after Mark 1.28, the healing of Peter's mother-in-law (Mark 1.29–34), the prayer in a lonely place (Mark 1.35–38), and the cleansing of the leper (Mark 1.40–45), are placed in reverse order after the conclusion of the sermon on the mount with these differences: first, the cleansing of the leper (Matthew 8.1–4), second, the prayer in a lonely place is omitted and the healing of the centurion's slave at Capernaum that is non-Markan material substituted (Matthew 8.5–13), and, third, the healing of Peter's mother-in-law (Matthew 8.14–17). We have already noted that Luke's sermon on the plain, a parallel to Matthew's sermon on the mount in a different setting, is within the Markan sequence except for a minor alteration of order.

If it is granted that the sermon on the mount rightly belongs in Mark's sequence just before the naming of the Twelve (Mark 3.13), then Matthew has radically altered the order of the other pericopes that he has placed after the sermon on the mount and before the naming of the Twelve. He skips again to a key phrase in Mark 4.35, "On that day, when evening had come, he said to them, 'Let us go across to the other side'." He edits Mark's phraseology to introduce Jesus' movements after the healing of Peter's mother-in-law, "Now when Jesus saw great crowds around him, he gave orders to go over to the other side" (Matthew 8.18). He interpolates at this point the requirements to be a follower of Jesus (Matthew 8.19–22) and follows this with the wind and sea (Mark 4.36–41; Matthew 8.23–27) and the exorcism of the two demoniacs (Mark 5.1–20; Matthew 8.28–34), although there is only one demoniac in Mark.

Again he makes a leap backwards to Mark 2.1 "when he returned to Capernaum after some days," which becomes "getting into a boat he crossed over and came to his own city" (Matthew 9.1). Evidently Capernaum is "his own city," for Jesus heals the paralyzed man there (Mark 2.2–12; Matthew 9.2–8). He calls Matthew the tax collector (Matthew 9.9–13), not Levi as in Mark 2.13–17), and places the question of fasting and the new compared to the old according to Mark's order (Mark 2.18; Matthew 9.14–17). Now he leaps ahead to the narrative of the raising of Jairus's daughter and the woman with a hemorrhage (Mark 5.21–43; Matthew 9.18–26). He omits Mark's setting for this event, the crossing over the sea to the other

The Composition of the Gospels

side (Mark 5.21), since that crossing has already taken place in Matthew's order (Matthew 9.1) after the exorcising of the demoniacs that happened in Gentile territory. He interpolates at this point his account of opening the eyes of two blind men (Matthew 9.27–31), the exorcism of a dumb demoniac (Matthew 9.32–34), and a saying on the plentiful harvest and the need for laborers (Matthew 9.35–38).

Keeping in view that this is the proper location for the sermon on the mount (cf. Mark 3.13 "he went up on the mountain, and called to him those whom he desired; and they came to him" to Matthew 5.1 "he went up on the mountain, and when he sat down his disciples came to him"), the naming of the Twelve logically follows (Mark 3.14–19; Matthew 10.1–4) and immediately thereafter the pericope of the mission of the Twelve, which again ruptures the Markan order (Mark 6.7–13; Matthew 10.5–15). At this place he interpolates a long section of non-Markan materials, further instructions for the Twelve and the Baptist's question about the coming one and Jesus' answer (Matthew 10.16–11.30. This material is organized as follows: persecution and death predicted (10.16–23), the disciple to be like his teacher (10.24–25), admonitions against fear (10.26–31), acknowledging and denying Jesus (10.32–33), family divisions and a cross (Matthew 10.34–39), on receiving Jesus, a prophet, a righteous man, and a cup of water (Matthew 10.40–42), the instructions completed (Matthew 11.1), the Baptist's question about the coming one and Jesus' answer (Matthew 11.2–19), woes upon cities (11.20–24), truth hidden and revealed (11.25–27), and the easy yoke (11.28–30).

Following this section there is another leap backwards to pick up the Markan story with the pericope of harvesting on the Sabbath (Mark 2.23–27; Matthew 12.1–8), a withered hand restored (Mark 3.1–6; Matthew 12.9–14), and a rewritten account of the multitudes from various places including the interpolation of a quotation from Isaiah (Mark 3.7–12; Matthew 12.15–21). It is at this point that Matthew inserts his sermon on the mount (Matthew 5.1–7.29). The reasons have already been advanced for the view that this is not the logical place for this teaching material and why it should be located after Mark 3.13.

Matthew again returns to Mark's order with the Beelzebul controversy (Mark 3.20–27; Matthew 12.22–30) and blasphemy against the spirit (Mark 3.28–30; Matthew 12.31–32), after which he inserts non-Markan material—the fruits of the bad and the good trees (Matthew 12.33–37), the sign of Jonah (Matthew 12.38–42), and the unclean spirit seeking rest (Matthew 12.43–45). He resumes the Markan order with the account of the mother and the brothers of Jesus (Mark 3.31–35; Matthew 12.46–50), followed by the long section of teaching by parables (Mark 4.1–20; Matthew 13.1–23) to which he appends the non-Markan parable of the weeds among the wheat (Matthew 13.24–30). Mark's metaphors of the light under the bushel (Mark 4.21–23) and the measure (Mark 4.24–25) have been relocated at different points in the sermon on the mount (Matthew 5.15–16 and 7.1–2) and the parable of the seed growing spontaneously (Mark 4.26–29) is omitted, unless the parable of the weeds and the wheat is a substitute. The parable of the mustard seed (Mark 4.30–32; Matthew 13.31–32) with Matthew's addition of the parable of the leaven (Matthew 13.33) and the private explanation of the parables (Mark 4.33–34; Matthew 13.34–35) follow in Mark's sequence. Matthew then interpolates additional parables beginning with an explanation of the weeds and wheat (Matthew 13.36–43), the hidden treasure (Matthew 13.44), the pearl (Matthew 13.45–46), the net (Matthew13.47–50), the householder (Matthew 13.51–52), and the reference to the completion of this teaching (Matthew 13.53a).

The next long section of Markan material (Mark 4.35–5.43) has been relocated to earlier points in the ministry of Jesus, so that the Markan sequence is resumed after the parables section with the rejection of Jesus in his own country (Mark 6.1–6; Matthew 13.53b–58). Thereafter he omits the mission of the Twelve (Mark 6.7–13), which has also been moved to an earlier location, and continues Mark's order with the death of the Baptist (Mark 6.14–29; Matthew 14.1–2), the feeding of the five thousand (Mark 6.30–44; Matthew 14.13–21), the walking on water (Mark 6.45–52; Matthew 14.22–33), healings by the touch of his garment (Mark 6.53–56; Matthew 14.34–36), a controversy about tradition and defilement (Mark 7.1–23; Matthew 15.1–20), the daughter of the Syrophoenician woman (Mark 7.24–30; a Canaanite woman Matthew 15.21–28), the substitution of healings on the mountain (Matthew 15.29–31) for Mark's healing of a deaf mute (Mark 7.31–37), the feeding of the four thousand (Mark 8.1–10; Matthew 15.32–39), Pharisees seek a sign (Mark 8.11–13; Matthew 16.1–4), the leaven of the Pharisees (Mark 8.14–21; Matthew 16.5–12), the omission of Mark's giving sight to the blind man at Bethsaida (Mark 8.22–26), the confession of Peter (Mark 8.27–30; Matthew 16.13–20), including the interpolation of the announcement, "You are Peter" (Matthew

16.17–19), the first announcement of death (Mark 8.31–33; Matthew 16.21–23), the charge to take up the cross (Mark 8.34–9.1; Matthew 16.24–28), the transfiguration (Mark 9.2–8; Matthew 17.1–8), Elijah comes first (Mark 9.9–13; Matthew 17.9–13), the epileptic son (Mark 9.14–29; Matthew 17.14–20), second announcement of death (Mark 9.30–32; Matthew 17.22–23), the interpolation of the shekel in the fish's mouth (Matthew 17.24–27), and a teaching on receiving children (Mark 9.33–37; Matthew 18.1–5).

After this long section in agreement, Matthew omits casting out demons in Jesus' name (Mark 9.38–41), although reminiscences are found (Matthew 12.30; 10.42). Again the Markan order is resumed with the punishment for causing a little one to sin (Mark 9.42–48; Matthew 18.6–9), but at this point there is the interpolation of another section of teaching material that includes the parable of the lost sheep (Matthew 18.10–14), forgiveness and the power to bind and loose (Matthew 18.15–22), the parable of the unmerciful slave (Matthew 18.23–35), and the completion of this teaching (Matthew 19.1a). He omits Mark's metaphor on salt (Mark 9.49–50), which has already been used with some adaptations earlier in the sermon on the mount (Matthew 5.13).

Again Mark's order is resumed for an extended section of material with interpolations at various places. This begins with pronouncements on divorce and remarriage (Mark 10.1–12; Matthew 19.1–12), blessing children (Mark 10.13–15; Matthew 19.13–15), the rich young man and the peril of riches (Mark 10.17–31; Matthew 19.16–30), after which there is the interpolation of the parable of the laborers in the vineyard (Matthew 20.1–16). Thereafter there is agreement in order with Mark for the third announcement of death (Mark 10.32–34; Matthew 20.17–19), the request of the sons of Zebedee (Mark 10.35–45; Matthew 20.20–28), although the mother of the sons of Zebedee is the requester according to Matthew, the restoring of sight to Bartimaeus (Mark 10.46–52; Matthew 20.29–34), although Matthew has two blind men, and the entry into Jerusalem (Mark 11.1–11; Matthew 21.1–11). The withering of the fig tree in two parts in Mark (11.12–14, 20–25 (the cleansing of the temple being sandwiched between Mark 11.15–19), is brought together in Matthew in the following order: the cleansing of the temple (Matthew 21.12–13), an interpolation of an account of the children in the temple (Matthew 21.14–17), and then the account of the withered fig tree (Matthew 21.18–22).

There follows another extended section of Mark, the controversies in Jerusalem with religious leaders, which is followed in order by Matthew with some interpolations: the authority of Jesus (Mark 11.27–33; Matthew 21.23–27), the interpolation of the parable of the two sons (Matthew 21.28–32), the parable of the wicked tenants (Mark 12.1–12; Matthew 21.33–45), the interpolation of the parable of the wedding feast (Matthew 22.1–14), the question of taxes to Caesar (Mark 12.13–17; Matthew 22.15–22), the question of resurrection (Mark 12.18–27; Matthew 22.23–33), the commandment to love God and neighbor (Mark 12.28–34; Matthew 22.34–40), the son of David question (Mark 12.35–37; Matthew 22.41–46), and the warnings against the scribes (Mark 12.38–40; Matthew 23.1–7). This very brief pronouncement by Jesus according to Mark is extended into a lengthy indictment of the scribes and Pharisees (Matthew 23.8–36), concluding with a lament over Jerusalem (Matthew 23.37–39).

Matthew omits the account of the gift of the widow to the temple (Mark 12.41–44), but follows the order for the so-called "Little Apolypse in Mark, concluding with the admonition to watch (Mark 13.1–37; Matthew 24.1–44), except for the transposition of the saying about the gospel to all nations that is moved from Mark's position following the saying about testimony before authorities (Mark 13.9) to a position after the sayings about betrayal by family members (Mark 13.12–13). Following the "Little Apocalypse" Matthew has introduced a number of parables: the faithful and wise slave (Matthew 24.45–51), the ten maidens (Matthew 25.1–13), the talents (Matthew 25.14–30), and the coming of son of man in glory as judge (Matthew 15.31–46). The section of teaching material concludes with a summary statement that the teachings of Jesus are finished (Matthew 26.1–2).

For the remainder of the account of the passion and of the resurrection, Matthew is in agreement with Mark's sequence except for the following omissions and interpolations: the omission of the young man who fled naked (Mark 14.51–52), the interpolation of the pericope about the repentance of Judas and his death (Matthew 27.3–10) following Mark's account that Jesus was delivered to Pilate (Mark 15.1), the interpolation of the account of the guard at the tomb (Matthew 27.62–66) after the burial of Jesus (Mark 15.42–47), and the additions to the account of the empty tomb (Mark 16.1–8). These additions include the bribery of the guards

The Composition of the Gospels

(Matthew 28.11–15), the appearance to the eleven, and the command to make disciples (Matthew 28.16–20).

Summary of the Results of the Comparison of Order

A summary of the results of this comparison of order suggests that Luke in general has been more closely bound to Mark's sequence and that the introduction of his non-Markan material does not result in such massive relocations of pericopes as we have found for Matthew. There is no single instance of agreement of order between Matthew and Luke against Mark when there has been transposition of material. For example, Luke relocates the imprisonment of the Baptist and the visit of Jesus to Nazareth to an earlier position in Mark's outline; Matthew is in agreement with Mark's order. Luke relocates the call to the four fishermen to a later time sequel in Mark; Matthew agrees with Mark's order. Matthew omits the cleansing of the unclean spirit at Capernaum; Luke includes the event in Mark's order. Matthew has relocated the accounts of the healing of Peter's mother-in-law, the cleansing of a leper, the healing of the paralyzed man, the call of Levi, the question of fasting, harvesting on the Sabbath, and a withered hand; Luke is in agreement with Mark's order. Matthew locates the non-Markan account of the healing of the Roman centurion's servant after the cleansing of the leper; Luke places this pericope at the conclusion of the sermon on the plain. In Luke, the choosing of the Twelve and the sermon on the plain approximate Mark's order very closely, whereas the interpolation of the sermon on the mount by Matthew has led to numerous relocations of Markan pericopes.

Matthew places the charge of exorcising demons by the power of Beelzebul and the blasphemy against the spirit after the healing of the withered hand; Luke locates this material in his great interpolation, both departing from the Markan order. Matthew places the mother and brothers of Jesus episode with Mark just before the section on teaching in parables; Luke locates this pericope after that series of parables. With this exception Luke follows the Markan order for the teaching in parables and the succeeding pericopes, whereas Matthew does not. That is, the storm at sea, the exorcism of the demoniac of the Gerasenes, the daughter of Jairus and the woman with a hemorrhage are in the Markan sequence in Luke; they are all out of the Markan order in Matthew. In addition the metaphors of the light and of the measure are transposed to the sermon on the mount by Matthew; they are in Mark's sequence in Luke. On the other hand, the parable of the mustard seed is located in the great interpolation in Luke; it is in Mark's sequence in Matthew, although we have noted that the entire section of teaching material is out of sequence in Matthew when compared to Mark.

The sending forth of the Twelve two by two in Luke is placed after Jesus' rejection in his own country in the Markan account. This same pericope follows a selection of non-Markan material in Matthew, the nearest Markan parallel being the raising of Jairus's daughter. But Matthew has relocated the narrative of Jesus' rejection in his own country to a place after the teaching in parables, so that the proximity of the sending of the Twelve to the raising of Jairus's daughter is unnatural. Luke places the sending of the Twelve immediately after the raising of Jairus's daughter, so that it might seem at first glance that there is an agreement in order between Matthew and Luke against Mark. But again this is not the case, since Luke has relocated the rejection in his own country to a much earlier position in his gospel as we have seen. It is the only relocation of pericopes that results in an apparent agreement between Matthew and Luke.

After the sending forth of the twelve, the death of the Baptist, and the feeding of the five thousand, Luke omits the long account of Jesus' journey north to Tyre, Sidon, and Caesarea Philippi. It is striking that Matthew is in sequence with Mark throughout this section. Luke returns to the Markan sequence with the confession of Peter. From this point and on Matthew and Luke are in agreement with Mark's sequence of events up to Jesus' teaching on the commandment to love God and neighbor, the setting for this precept being Jerusalem. It is to be noted, however, that there are numerous interpolations into the Markan framework, including Luke's great interpolation. Luke has placed Jesus' teaching on love into that interpolation, so that Matthew continues in agreement with Mark against Luke. Luke has also taken the sayings on false Christs out of Mark's context of the "Little Apocalypse" and placed this also in his great interpolation. Another major difference in order is Luke's assignment of the anointing of Jesus to his little interpolation during Jesus' Galilean ministry. From this point and on the order of events is essentially the same through the account of the death and resurrection of Jesus in the three gospels.

The Sequence of Events in the Three Gospels is Basically Markan

It seems clear from this analysis that the framework for the account of the events of the life and ministry of Jesus was formulated by Mark and that the authors of Matthew and Luke basically follow that framework. There remains one final check for order, however, in order to demonstrate the conclusion conclusively; that is, a comparison of order between Matthew and Luke to determine whether or not there is any logical sequence for their two accounts of the life and ministry of Jesus. The purpose is to test the validity of the argument that Luke used Matthew as a source and that Mark used both Matthew and Luke.

Comparison of the Sequence of Events in Matthew and Luke

Matthew's opening statement of purpose has a fleeting similarity to Mark's and is biblical in orientation, whereas Luke's is formulated in the classic Greek style. There is a similarity in approach, since both continue with infancy narratives. However, their content is very different, as has been pointed out in another essay. The ministry of Jesus is preceded in each with an account of the ministry of the Baptist. If Luke used Matthew as his source, he changes the indefinite "in those days" to a more definite historical setting. He alters radically the message of John, adds to the quotation from Isaiah, omits the description of John's dress, diet, and baptisms in the Jordan, adds a section on John's charge to the people, to tax collectors and soldiers, and appends a brief account of John's imprisonment that Matthew gives in great detail after Jesus' rejection in his own country (Matthew 14.1–12; Luke 3.19–20). Luke omits the account of John's hesitation to baptize Jesus and changes the words addressed to Jesus from "this is my beloved son" to "you are my beloved son." Luke than places a quite different genealogy for Jesus after the baptism pericope rather than at the beginning of the gospel as in Matthew (Matthew 1.2–17; Luke 3.23–38). The temptation account is similar, except Luke reverses temptations two and three from Matthew's order.

Luke follows Matthew in giving a general statement of the opening of Jesus' ministry, although his ministry is teaching rather than preaching as in Matthew (Matthew 4.12–17; Luke 4.14–15). Luke then departs radically from Matthew's order by skipping the call of the four fishermen, a general preaching and healing in Galilee, and the sermon on the mount to insert at this point the account of Jesus' rejection at Nazareth, an event that Matthew relates at a much later time; in fact, the rejection is placed after the choosing and mission of the Twelve and after the long section on teaching in parables (Matthew 13.53–58; Luke 4.16–30). The sermon on the mount, which corresponds to Luke's sermon on the plain, is moved by Luke to a position after the naming of the Twelve. Luke then interpolates an account of cleansing a man of an unclean spirit, a pericope lacking in Matthew, relocates Matthew's account of the healing of Peter's mother-in-law, which Matthew has located after the sermon on the mount (Matthew 8.14–17; Luke 4.38–41), and substitutes prayer in a lonely place and preaching in Judea for Matthew's preaching and healing in Galilee (Matthew 4.23–25; Luke 4.42–44).

At this point Luke places the story of the call of the fisherman, which Matthew reports immediately after Jesus' initial preaching in Galilee (Matthew 4.18–22; Luke 5.1–11), and moves the pericope of the cleansing of a leper from Matthew's location after the sermon on the mountain to follow the calling of the fishermen (Matthew 8.1–4; Luke 5.12–16). The pericope of the healing of the centurion's slave follows immediately after the sermon on the plain in Luke, so that he is in partial agreement with Matthew whose order is as follows: sermon on the mount, cleansing of a leper, and healing of the centurion's servant. Luke removes the demands of discipleship from its location after the healing of Peter's mother-in-law in Matthew and relocates this material to the beginning of Jesus' journey to Jerusalem (Matthew 8.18–22; Luke 9.57–62). The storm at sea and the demoniacs of the Gadarenes are in tandem in Luke as in Matthew but relocated after the section on teaching in parables. The healing of the paralytic that follows these events in Matthew is moved forward by Luke to a new location immediately after the cleansing of the leper (Matthew 9.1–8; Luke 5.17–26).

This analysis could continue, but let us turn back to examine the order of traditions that Matthew has incorporated into the sermon on the mount and their location into different contexts by Luke. Both open with beatitudes, although Matthew cites nine and Luke four plus four woes. These must be different formulations and not dependent one upon the other. A comparison of beatitude one illustrates their differences in a striking fashion. Whereas Matthew writes, "Blessed are the poor in spirit, for theirs is the kingdom of heaven," Luke states, "Blessed are you poor, for yours is the kingdom of God" (Matthew 5.3; Luke 6.20).

There are three essential differences and if we hold that Luke has used Matthew as a source then he has changed indirect to direct address, omitted "in spirit," and changed "kingdom of heaven" to "kingdom of God." But, in fact, Luke's direct address has the ring of authenticity just because this is the way Jesus taught. How could he have made the impact he did as teacher if he had addressed the people out there instead of confronting his disciples directly? Is "in spirit" an omission by Luke, or is it an addition by Matthew? Again Luke's version seems to be more authentic because the beatitude without "in spirit" is an attack upon the prevailing notion that poverty is a mark of God's disfavor. The inclusion of "in spirit" removes the radical nature of the saying and reduces it to a religious cliché. Jesus' teaching was anything but trite and provincial. However Luke's version may differ from the original, it retains the radical challenge of Jesus to the status quo.

This is also true of the expression "kingdom of heaven" as compared to "kingdom of God." Jesus did overturn the conventions by using the name of God, as we have seen in the Markan address "*Abba*." The use of "heaven" is a typical Jewish circumlocution for the divine name, which was characteristic in the Jewish community. Jesus challenged many of the Jewish ways of religious speaking and practice as subterfuges, and Luke's version is an example of his forthrightness in the use of the divine name. There can be no question but that we have different versions of Jesus' saying in Matthew and Luke and the burden of proof is upon those who argue that Luke used Matthew as a source to demonstrate how Luke's version of the beatitude could have been derived from Matthew's.

The salt metaphor (Matthew 5.13) is located in a completely different teaching context in Luke (14.34–35) and seems to have as many affinities to Mark as it does to Matthew. The light metaphor is unique to Matthew, but the lamp under the bushel is located in two places in Luke: first, after the explanation of the parable of the sower (Luke 8.16) and again after the sign of Jonah pericope (Luke 11.33). Luke omits the comparison of the old to the new (Matthew 5.17–24), although there are some similarities between the saying on the law and the prophets (Matthew 5.17–18; Luke 16.16–17). The "making friends with the accuser" saying (Matthew 5.25–26) is located in an entirely different context in Luke (12.58–59).

The saying on adultery is omitted by Luke and the saying on divorce and remarriage without Matthew's excepting clause (Matthew 5.31–31) is located after the saying on entering the kingdom of God violently (Luke 16.18). The saying on oaths is omitted, but the saying on retaliation is found in Luke's sermon on the plain (Luke 6.29–30) as is also the saying, "Love your enemy" (Matthew 5.43–48; Luke 6.27–36).

Luke omits the sayings on piety, on alms, and on empty prayers (Matthew 6.1–8) and his much briefer version of the Lord's prayer is located in the context of Jesus' praying following his visit to the home of Martha and Mary (Luke 11.1–4). The sayings about forgiving and receiving forgiveness and about fasting are omitted by Luke and a somewhat different version of the saying about treasure in heaven (Matthew 6.19–21) is located in yet another teaching context (Luke 12.33.34). The metaphor of the eye as a lamp with additions by Luke follows the metaphor of the lamp under a bushel (Luke 11.34–35; cf. Matthew 6.22–23 and 5.15–16). The saying on two masters is located by Luke in the great interpolation in the context of teaching on honesty and faithfulness (Matthew 6.24; Luke 16.13) and the admonitions against anxiety in another teaching context in the great interpolation (Matthew 6.25–34; Luke 12.22–31). The sayings on judging, on the measure, and on the speck in the brother's eye are in the sermon on the plain. The parable about the blind leading the blind, which Matthew places in the context of a controversy about observing tradition (Matthew 15.14), is interpolated at this point by Luke (Luke 6.39), as well as the saying that the disciple is not above his teacher (Luke 6.40). Matthew places this saying in the context of the instruction of the Twelve for mission (Matthew 10.24).

The saying of pearls before swine is omitted by Luke; and Matthew's trilogy on asking, seeking, and knocking and the saying on gifts to children (Matthew 7.7–11) are located in the teaching on prayer in Luke (11.9–13). The saying on doing to others (Matthew 7.12) is in Luke's sermon on the plain, but after the sayings on retaliation (Luke 6.31). The narrow gate saying (Matthew 7.13–14) is relocated by Luke into a section of teaching material as Jesus is on his way to Jerusalem (Luke 13.23–24). Luke omits the warning against false prophets, but includes the saying on the fruits of grapes and figs with variations and additions (Matthew 7.16; Luke 6.44–45). Matthew's saying on the sound and bad trees is relocated by Luke to the sermon on the plain, but after the saying on fruits and grapes rather than before it as in Matthew's order. Luke has only an abbreviated form of Matthew's teaching about those who say, "Lord, Lord," (Matthew 7.21–23; Luke 6.46), although the saying is in the same position in the two sermons, for it immediately precedes the parable of the two houses, the conclusion to both sermons.

Matthew's Gospel not the Exemplar for Luke

This running comparison of Luke's gospel to the first seven chapters of Matthew demonstrates that it is highly improbable, if not impossible, for Luke to have had Matthew's text before him when he composed. There is no rationale that explains the wide-ranging variation in arrangement of the gospel materials, either for the narrative or for the teaching tradition. The second part of the theory, that Mark had the texts of both Matthew and Luke before him when he composed, is simply incomprehensible from the point of view of order and in no way explains the omissions of great masses of tradition in Mark. There are unsolved problems for the thesis that Mark was the primary source for Matthew and Luke, since some of the rearrangements of tradition, especially by Matthew, defy explanation, but our analysis has demonstrated that there is a logic to the overall plan and framework when the sequence of materials for Matthew and Luke is compared to Mark.

A Comparison of the Internal Evidence

A final section of this essay will be devoted to a close comparison of the internal evidence, that is, the variations in word choice and phraseology, which may throw light upon the question of priority. Although this study should be based upon the Greek text since translations do not always give us a true picture of the differences, this essay is intended for readers who do not have this capability and therefore will be confined mostly to those examples that are readily visible in translation form. It is evident that Mark does not write in a literary form of the *koine* Greek when compared to either Matthew or Luke. One reason for this is that his phraseology and word order are Aramaic dressed up in Greek vocabulary. An example to illustrate this point is Mark's "the stars will be falling from heaven" (13.25) compared to Matthew's "the stars will fall from heaven" (24.29). Luke avoids the Aramaism by either rewriting Mark in another way or by preferring an alternate tradition for this saying (21.25).

An example of the repetition of an idea by the use of a subordinate clause, which is a Semitic form of expression, is noted in Mark 7.13: "making void the word of God through your tradition *that you hand on.*" Perhaps a clearer example for the English reader is the expression in Mark 13.19: "from the beginning of the creation *which God created.*" The phrasing is improved in accord with the standards for Greek grammar by the omission of the italicized clauses (Matthew 15.6; 24.21). Another Semitic form of expression is the use of a coordinate parallel sentence; for example, in Mark 2.19: "Can the wedding guests fast while the bridegroom is with them? *As long as they have the bridegroom with them, they cannot fast.*" Both Matthew and Luke remove the redundancy by omitting the latter phrase (Matthew 9.15; Luke 5.34).

A second illustration is found in Mark 4.30: "With what can we compare the kingdom of God, or what parable shall we use for it?" Matthew 13.31 reads simply, "The kingdom of heaven is like . . ." Luke (13.18) corrects the phrasing in a different way: "What is the kingdom of God like? And to what shall I compare it?" The reader is also referred to the additional expression, "to do them," in Mark 11.28, which is omitted in Matthew 21.23 and Luke 20.2. There are many other Semitic types of expression found in our gospels, too many to list and illustrate here, but the above are given to demonstrate that either Mark purposely transformed Greek literary phrases into Semitic expressions or the authors of Matthew and Luke corrected Mark's vernacular language into a more literary style. It should be made clear that Matthew and Luke are not void of Semitic or Aramaic expressions, but the point is that in the preponderance of cases listed by grammarians the text of Mark has been corrected or improved to a more literary style by Matthew and Luke rather than vice versa.

An example of a more literary word used in the place of the vernacular is the substitution of "bed" (Matthew 9.2; Luke 5.19) for Mark's "pallet" upon which the paralyzed man was carried to Jesus (Mark 2.4). This minor agreement between Matthew and Luke against Mark should not be interpreted to suggest that Luke borrowed this word from Matthew, for then one would have to explain why it is that Mark, finding the more literary word in his texts, substituted the vernacular. That is to say, one would have to argue that the more literary becomes more vernacular in the later writing, an argument that is against all the conventions for serious literature.

In the temptation pericope, was Jesus "driven out by the Spirit into the desert" (Mark 1.12), or was he "led into the desert by the Spirit" (Matthew 4.1), or was he led in the Spirit in the desert" (Luke 4.2)? The word used by Mark for this experience is the same word used by all the evangelists for the driving out of the money changers from the temple, a word that means literally to throw out more or less forcibly. It seems reasonable to suppose that the harshness of Mark's expression is toned down to a more acceptable understanding of the Spirit's mediation by both Matthew and Luke, although each has created a new phraseology. It is difficult to explain how either Matthew's or Luke's phraseology could have been converted into Mark's if theirs was already the established norm. The primitive description at the conclusion of this event in Mark, "he was with the wild beasts," is edited out by both Matthew and Luke that, when seen against the background of other improvements upon Mark's text, confirms that these writers tend towards a higher sophistication.

A similar example is in the calling of the four fishermen where Mark simply uses a verb that means literally "to throw about" without any mention of the net to describe the actions of the fishermen (Mark 1.16), whereas Matthew uses both the verb "to cast" and the noun "net" (Matthew 4.18), an improvement over Mark's vernacular expression. All we need to do to demonstrate the correctness of this interpretation is to check the textual variants; we find that Mark's reading is supported by only three early manuscripts and the great majority of scribes have corrected Mark's reading by adding the noun, whereas there is not a single instance where scribes have corrected Matthew's text by omitting the noun. That is to say that scribes who were specialists in the Greek language and who made copies of Mark's gospel for use in the church were inclined to correct Mark's text precisely as the author of Matthew had done.

The expansion of Mark 1.39, the reference to a peripatetic ministry by Jesus throughout Galilee in which he preaches and casts out demons, into a preaching and a healing of every disease and infirmity of people from as far away as Syria, Decapolis, Jerusalem, and beyond the Jordan is an instructive illustration of the kind of pious growth of tradition with the passage of time. If this is a description of reality, one wonders how it could be that the adulation and awe of the people could have been transformed in such a short period of time into an enmity and hatred that resulted in Jesus' death. It does not seem possible that the people would dispose of one who had such power over physical disease and who had brought such relief from suffering to so many so lightly, much as we would dispose of a soiled napkin. It also seems improbable that Mark could have reduced such an extravaganza to his almost innocuous description of a Jesus' mission throughout Galilee.

In the pericope of the cleansing of a leper, Mark relates that the afflicted man came "beseeching and kneeling" before Jesus (Mark 1.40), whereas Matthew says that he "worshipped" him (Matthew 8.2). Unfortunately, the translation to English does not bring out this striking difference in this passage and in others. It is, however, properly translated in the temptation account where Jesus is invited to "worship" Satan and he responds that it is proper to worship God only (Matthew 4.9–10). The question is, Did Mark change Matthew's highly reverent and worshipful expression to the more ordinary way of showing respect? The evidence that he did not is to be seen in Matthew's use of Mark's word for "kneeling" in his account of the passion: the soldiers knelt, the same word Mark uses in the leper story, and mocked Jesus (Matthew 27.29). Thus there is a sharp distinction in meaning for this word in the gospels, as Matthew himself attests.

This same variation is found in the pericopes of the healing of Jairus's daughter and the Canaanite woman who beseeches Jesus in behalf of her daughter. The ruler of the synagogue, Jairus, fell at Jesus' feet (Mark 5.22; Luke 8.41), whereas he "worshipped" him (Matthew 9.18; compare Mark 7.26 to Matthew 15.25). The word is introduced into the walking on water pericope by the author of Matthew where it does not occur in Mark. According to Mark the disciples were utterly astounded when he stepped into the boat and the wind ceased(Mark 6.51–52), whereas according to Matthew they worshipped him, saying, "Truly you are the Son of God" (Matthew 14.33). Matthew's usage here corresponds to his usage in the temptation story and also to the response of the women and of the disciples to the risen Jesus (Matthew 28.9, 17); it is the worship of a divine being and illustrates the differences in the estimates or attitudes toward Jesus during his ministry that are apparent between the two gospels.

There are additional illustrations of the growing reverence for Jesus that point up the differences in more oblique ways. For example, in the pericope of the restoring of the withered hand, the question is raised about

The Composition of the Gospels

the lawfulness of healing on the Sabbath. Jesus responds by pointing up the hypocrisy of the questioners; a sheep is more valuable to them than a human being, since they would lift out a sheep fallen into a well on a Sabbath day but would not respond to human need. Mark writes that Jesus "looked around on them with anger" (Mark 3.5). Both Matthew and Luke omit this statement (Matthew 12.13; Luke 6.10), since anger is not an appropriate response or attitude for Jesus or for one of his followers. Does not Matthew quote Jesus as saying, "Every one who is angry with his brother shall be liable to judgment" (Matthew 5.22)? A similar change in text that reflects an enhanced appreciation of Jesus is found in the account of Jesus' rejection by his own people in his own country. Mark concludes, "he could do no mighty work there," that is edited by the author of Matthew to read, "he did not do many mighty works there" (Mark 6.5; Matthew 13.58). Mark's phrasing suggests incapability, which is not an appropriate image for the one whom Christians proclaim to be Lord of all and Savior of mankind. Matthew has corrected such an impression by rephrasing in such a way as to remove all doubt as to Jesus' capability. He was able to heal, but he chose not to because of their unbelief.

Matthew describes the storm at sea with a word that means literally "shaking" or earthquake (Matthew 8.24), whereas the word in Luke and Mark is "a great gust of wind" (Luke 8.23; Mark 4.27). The question is, Did Luke change Matthew's very strong word for a weaker one and did Mark prefer Luke's word substitution over what he found in Matthew? The evidence is that the word can be used for the shaking of a storm at sea, but the word is used almost exclusively for "earthquake" and this is the meaning of the word as it is used on two other occasions by Matthew. This author alone introduces the word "earthquake" into the accounts of the death and of the resurrection of Jesus, which suggests that he has a certain affinity for the word. It is probable then that Matthew has substituted the word "shaking" or "earthquake" for Mark's "wind" or "whirlwind," just as he has introduced the word into the accounts of the death and resurrection. It has already been noted that he heightens the powers of Jesus in this same narrative with the address, "Lord, save."

The narrative of the exorcism of the demoniac provides another example of editing. Were there two demoniacs (Matthew 8.28), or only one (Luke 8.27; Mark 5.2)? Matthew has an affinity for the number two, as is evident from a comparison of the gospels. There are two sets of two brothers fishing (Matthew 4.18, 21); Mark gives the names and Luke has two boats in a partially parallel passage (Mark 1.16; Luke 5.2). There are two miles (Matthew 5.41) and two blind men (Matthew 9.27) in passages unique to Matthew. There are two sparrows sold for a penny (Matthew 10.29) where Luke has five sparrows sold for two pennies (Luke 12.6). There are two witnesses (Matthew 18.16), two who agree (Matthew 18.19), and two or three gathered together (Matthew 18.20) in passages unique to Matthew. There are two sons of Zebedee (Matthew 20.21, 24) where Mark again gives names (Mark 10.37, 42). There are two blind men (Matthew 20.30) where Mark has the son of Timaeus (Mark 10.46); Luke agrees with Mark, although the blind man is nameless (Luke 18.35). There are an ass and a colt in Matthew's account of the entry into Jerusalem (Matthew 21.2), but only a colt in Mark and Luke (Mark 11.2; Luke 19.30). There are two sons (Matthew 21.28, 31) in a parable unique to Matthew, unless the parable of the prodigal and elder brother is a parallel (Luke 15.11). There are two great commands (Matthew 22.40); the number is not used in Mark (12.32). There are two talents (Matthew 25.15, 17, 22) where Luke has ten pounds, one to each of ten slaves (Luke 19.14). Again there are two sons of Zebedee (Matthew 26.37) where Mark gives the names (Mark 14.33). There are two false witnesses in Matthew (Matthew 26.60), but not so specified in Mark. The Jews are given the option of choosing between the two, Barabbas or Jesus (Matthew 27.21); again the number is not cited in Mark or Luke.

A comparison to Mark indicates that Matthew uses the number two much more frequently. Mark alone has the number two in only two passages that parallel Matthew and Luke: Jesus sends out the disciples two by two (Mark 6.7) and he sends two disciples to prepare the Passover (Mark 14.13). Matthew omits the specific number in these passages, whereas Luke uses the two by two formula for the sending of the seventy (Luke 10.1) and gives the names, Peter and John, as those who go to prepare the Passover (Luke 22.8). The information above only indicates that there is a tendency in Matthew to use the number two in passages where Luke and Mark are either less precise or give the proper names for persons.

The critical passages in the decision making process are three: the exorcism of the demoniac (Mark 5.2; Matthew 8.28; Luke 8.27), the blind man Timaeus (Mark 10.46; Matthew 20.30; Luke 18.35), and the entry into Jerusalem on a colt (Mark 11.2; Matthew 21.2; Luke 19.30). In each of these instances, Luke has either changed Matthew's two to a one and Mark has preferred Luke's number or Matthew has changed Mark's one to a two. It would seem that the burden of proof is upon those who elect the first option in view of the tendency of the author of Matthew to use the number two with high frequency. The entry into Jerusalem suggests that the change was made by the author of Matthew, since in his version of the event the disciples place their garments upon the two beasts and Jesus rides upon them. If this was the original version, then Luke has corrected a nonsensical text and Mark has agreed with this change. But there is greater possibility that the author of Matthew has changed Mark's version to make the description of the event conform to the scripture, since one of his principal interests is to demonstrate that Jesus is always and everywhere the fulfillment of the scriptures.

One of the most interesting passages from the point of view of differences is the saying on divorce and remarriage that is found in all three evangelists. The question of the lawfulness of divorce is raised by Pharisees to test Jesus. After pointing out that the basis for marriage is found in creation and that God has intended this covenant between a man and a woman to be indissoluble, Jesus acknowledged that divorce resulted from human sin and was granted in the Mosaic law because of the hardness of human hearts. He concludes, according to Mark, "Whoever divorces his wife and marries another commits adultery against her; and if she divorces her husband and marries another, she commits adultery" (Mark 10.11–12). Matthew writes, "Whoever divorces his wife, except for unchastity, and marries another, commits adultery" (Matthew 19.9; cf. 5.32 where the author also incorporates the saying into his sermon on the mount). Luke does not provide the background for the pronouncement, but only cites it in a section of teaching material as an illustration of the principle that the law and the prophets will stand forever. His version reads, "Every one who divorces his wife and marries another commits adultery, and whoever marries a divorced woman commits adultery" (Luke 16.18).

There are three major differences in these three versions: first, Matthew's excepting clause found in both his citations of the saying; second, Mark's addition that a woman may divorce her husband; and, third, Luke's addition that to marry a divorced woman is to commit adultery. It is not difficult to find in the midst of this variety what may have been the original pronouncement by Jesus, since there is unanimous agreement that whoever divorces his wife and marries another commits adultery. How then to explain the variants in the additions, especially in Mark, if his is the earliest written version of the saying? The second clause, "if she divorces her husband," cannot have been spoken by Jesus. He was a member of a community in which women had limited rights and where divorce was the prerogative of the male only. Such a saying would have been nonsensical in this setting, but fits very well into a setting in which Roman culture and law are predominant. Women did have the right to institute divorce proceedings in Roman society. If Mark's gospel were composed in Rome, as has been suggested, it would have been very appropriate to adapt a saying of Jesus to the conditions of that society.

If Mark were a principal source for the authors of Matthew and Luke, the omission of this new interpretation and application by Matthew is appropriate, since it is generally acknowledged that his gospel was written within and for a Jewish Christian community in which the Mosaic law prevailed. The author of Luke has edited Mark's addition not by omission, but by reinterpreting it so that it becomes a prohibition of remarriage by a divorced person. Thus the absolute quality of Jesus' pronouncement against divorce and remarriage is preserved by Mark and Luke. The excepting clause in Matthew is clearly a late intrusion into the saying by the author or by the community that he represents as leader. This is confirmed by a reference to the earliest pronouncements upon the subject in the writings of the Apostle Paul. He writes in First Corinthians, "To the married I give charge, not I but the Lord, that the wife should not separate from her husband (but if she does, let her remain single or else be reconciled to her husband)—and that the husband should not divorce his wife" (7.10–11). Here is the same absolute that we have found to be basic in the divorce saying in all the evangelists and also the support for Mark's reference to a wife divorcing her husband. The letter to the Corinthians was written to a city that was governed by Roman law and custom and this is recognized by the apostle. But there are no exceptions about remarriage for the believer! This suggests above all that Matthew's version is later than either Paul's or Mark's and that the believing community has had to come to grips with the problem of divorce and remarriage within its own membership. Divorce is still a manifestation of human weakness and sinfulness, but a compromise has had to be forged much as in the Mosaic community of old as acknowledged by Jesus, "for the hardness of heart Moses allowed you to divorce your wives" (Matthew 19.8). Human nature has turned out to be human nature even within the new community and concessions have had to be made to the realities of life. Is this to fault the author of Matthew? Not at all! The absolute clearly applies to all who are able to receive it and live by it, but the author clearly indicates that absolutes and realities are not always possible in life. He concludes this section of teaching with the admission, "He who is able to receive this, let him receive it" (Matthew 19.12). The words of Jesus must be applied to human beings and to society in creative ways that do not stultify or even destroy. After all, there is only one unpardonable sin and that is neither divorce nor remarriage of the divorced.

The Argument of Minor Agreements

There remains only one argument to consider that is used to support the priority of Matthew by its defenders: the argument of the minor agreements between Matthew and Luke against Mark. Approximately two hundred and thirty such agreements have been identified by previous investigators, although it is probable that a complete and careful analysis would uncover a considerably larger number. Taking the John the Baptist pericope as an example, this writer has identified thirteen agreements of one kind or another between Matthew and Luke when compared to Mark.

Listing them in their order of occurrence they are as follows:

1) Matthew and Luke agree against Mark in introducing John first and following with the quotation from Isaiah, whereas Mark opens with a quotation;
2) Matthew and Luke agree against Mark in placing the event in a time frame, although Matthew's is the indefinite "in those days," whereas Luke is more specific, "in the fifteenth year of the reign of Tiberius Caesar";
3) Matthew and Luke agree in omitting the quotation from Malachi that, however, is located in another pericope that relates to John (Matthew 11.10; Luke 7.27);
4) Matthew and Luke agree against Mark in including an indictment of those who come for baptism (Matthew 3.7–10; Luke 3.7–9);

5) Matthew and Luke agree against Mark in the general organization or order in which the announcement concerning the coming one is worded (Matthew 3.11; Luke 3.16; cf. Mark 1.7–8);
6) Matthew and Luke agree against Mark in using the particles meaning "on the one hand," and "on the other hand" in that announcement to sharpen the contrast;
7) Matthew and Luke agree against Mark in omitting the word "to stoop down";
8) Matthew and Luke agree against Mark in using the present tense, "I baptize," in the announcement where Mark uses the aorist (past) tense, "I have baptized";
9) Matthew and Luke agree against Mark in omitting the particle "but," saying simply, "he will baptize," for Mark's "but he will baptize";
10) Matthew and Luke agree against Mark in the word order "he you will baptize" where Mark reads "but he will baptize you";
11) Matthew and Luke agree against Mark in using the pronoun "in" in the phrase "in the Holy Spirit," whereas it is omitted, although understood, in Mark;
12) Matthew and Luke agree against Mark in adding that the baptism is also "in fire," a phrase not in the text of Mark; and
13) Matthew and Luke agree against Mark in adding the saying about the winnowing fork, the wheat, and the chaff to conclude the pericope.

It is necessary to make a few comments upon these agreements between Matthew and Luke against Mark to determine the validity of the argument that they demonstrate and support the thesis that Matthew was the earliest gospel written, that Luke used Matthew as a source, and that subsequently Mark used both Matthew and Luke as his sources. The first two agreements, the different order for opening and placing the events in a time frame, can be discussed together. The very abruptness of Mark's opening with a quotation rather than with a person and the lack of a time frame in Mark at this point could have resulted in two authors using Mark independently as a source to have reorganized Mark's materials into an approximate agreement for the beginnings of the ministry of John. The beginnings in the two gospels have only an evanescent similarity, however, as is attested by the striking differences in their time references; Matthew's vague reference to time and Luke's elaborate listing of the political and religious authorities who held power in that approximate period. On the one hand, one could argue that Luke simply expanded upon and made more specific Matthew's vague reference and that their agreement, such as it is, confirms that Luke used Matthew as his source. But on the other hand, if this thesis is maintained, then one would have to substantiate logically why Mark completely ignored their order and their time references to begin as he does. The very abruptness of his beginning suggests to this writer a more primitive gospel that is consciously improved upon by those who came after.

Again it is far more logical to view the agreement of Matthew and Luke in omitting the quotation from Malachi, wrongly identified by Mark as Isaianic, at this point, especially since they found the same quotation in another piece of Baptist tradition in another source that they also both used independently. It is a much more difficult argument to demonstrate that Mark ignored that piece of Baptist tradition in Matthew and Luke, if they were his sources, except for this quotation from Malachi that he then transferred to his initial introduction of the baptizer. It is also difficult to support logically Mark's omissions of the warnings and strong indictments leveled against those who came to be baptized and the saying about the winnowing fork, the wheat, and the chaff that are in the texts of Matthew and Luke. A reading of Mark's narrative of the death of the baptizer (Mark 6.14–29) demonstrates that he could include a lengthy and verbose account of a rather pointless event, especially when this narrative is compared to other Jesus' traditions that he ignored if he really used Matthew and Luke. What explanation can be given for his omitting the baptizer's teaching material from his Matthean and Lukan sources in his initial introduction of the forerunner, teaching material that is much more relevant to the gospel than a beheading?

The change in order for the wording of the announcement of the coming one in Matthew and Luke is a literary improvement over the rather garbled form in which it appears in Mark. Mark's order is to begin with the announcement of the exalted status of the coming one. This is followed by a reference to the comparative lowliness of the baptizer, and a comparison of the baptism by the baptizer to the more exalted baptism by the exalted coming one. Matthew and Luke begin with the statement about the baptism by the speaker, followed by the announcement of the exalted status of the coming one, the comparative lowliness of the "voice" when compared to the coming one, and the final statement about the more exalted baptism by the coming one. This is an improvement over Mark's statement as the internal agreements between Matthew and Luke verify.

It should be evident that Matthew's and Luke's improvements are not verbatim, as if the one were copied from the other, but rather are in character with how two authors writing independently might have improved similarly but not exactly upon a text that was before them. For example, the more literary "on the one hand" and "on the other hand" in Matthew and Luke, number five on our list (page 188), is simply the completion of what is only partly present in Mark who has only the second part of the two, number nine on our list (page 188), although in a different location. The omission of the participle translated "to stoop down" appears to be one of those accidental agreements, since Matthew has really compressed the Markan text, "the thong of whose sandals I am not worthy to stoop down and untie," into "whose sandals I am not worthy to carry," whereas Luke repeats the Markan text without "to stoop down." But this compression by Matthew in reality weakens the strong emphasis in Mark upon the qualitative difference between the speaker and the coming one and again tends to support the priority of the former.

The more primitive expressions in Mark often call for improvement and the resultant changes by Matthew and Luke do not always achieve that goal. The change of Mark's "I have baptized" in past (aorist) tense to Matthew's and Luke's "I baptize" in the present tense is also an instance of the lessening of the dramatic, much as the change of the verb used by Mark in the baptism pericope, "the heavens were torn asunder," to the less dramatic "the heavens were opened" in Matthew and Luke (Mark 1.10; Matthew 3.16; Luke 3.21). The past tense, "I have baptized," refers to an action completed in a moment, or "the aorist of the action just happened." The change of order in the Greek from "but he will baptize you" in Mark to "he will you baptize" in Matthew and Luke signifies the authors' purpose or emphasis. Mark places the emphasis upon "*he* will baptize," whereas Matthew and Luke stress that it is *you* he will baptize. This is a matter of preference by authors and no great significance should be attached to this small difference in order, since it is very possible for two authors to make such a change in their exemplar independently. The absence of the preposition "in" or its presence is another matter of preference, since either usage is proper. It should be noted here that the preposition is omitted by Mark in the text of Codex Vaticanus, the Greek text being used as the background for all comparisons throughout this essay.

A more significant agreement between Matthew and Luke against Mark is the baptism "in fire." This has long been identified as an addition from the second source used independently by the authors of Matthew and Luke. This appears to be verified when a study is made of the content of the Baptist's teaching material in Matthew and Luke but not in Mark. Matthew's word total for this additional material is one hundred and Luke's ninety-five. We can discount from this total thirteen words from Matthew and eight from Luke that consist of the introductory words or connective tissue and in which there is not a single word agreement between the two: "But when he saw many of the Pharisees and Sadducees coming for baptism he said to them" (Matthew 3.7) and "He said therefore to the multitudes who came out to be baptized by him" (Luke 3.7). This leaves eighty-seven words in each of the two gospels. It is astonishing to discover that eighty-one of the eighty-seven words are exactly the same in the two, both in sequence and in order. The possibilities are these: either Luke copied Matthew, Matthew copied Luke, or each used a second source independently. That their introductory words to the sayings are altogether different and that the sayings themselves are almost verbatim strongly suggests that they used a second source and created their own connective tissue as a bridge between the sayings and the previous material. But the point to be made here is that in these sayings of the Baptist tradition used by Matthew and Luke the word "fire" occurs twice: "the tree that does not bear good fruit is cut down and thrown into the fire" (Matthew 3.10; Luke 3.9) and "the chaff will be burned with unquenchable fire" (Matthew 3.12; Luke 3.17). Mark uses neither of these references.

This strongly supports the conclusion that the previous saying, "After me comes he who is mightier than I, the thong of whose sandals I am not worthy to stoop down and untie. I have baptized you with water; but he will baptize you with the Holy Spirit" (Mark 1.7–8), was also in this second source and that the authors of Matthew and Luke had the saying before them in two forms when they composed their gospels, the Markan form and the second source form. This then could account at least in part for some of the agreements between Matthew and Luke against Mark throughout this pericope, since we do not know, or we know only in part by a comparison of the non-Markan material in both Matthew and Luke, what that second source contained. And this could account for the agreement between Matthew and Luke against Mark in the addition of the baptism "in fire."

Minor Agreements of Mark and Matthew against Luke and Vice Versa

But there is another dimension to the problem that to my knowledge has never been examined or discussed; that is, the minor agreements between Mark and Matthew against Luke and the minor agreements of Mark and Luke against Matthew. In our pericope for discussion, there are five minor agreements between Mark—Matthew against Luke as follows:

1) the omission of the additional words from the Isaianic quotation;
2) John appeared or came in the wilderness, whereas the word of God came to John in the wilderness;
3) the description of the dress and diet of John in Matthew and Mark but lacking in Luke;
4) the lack in Mark and Matthew of the injunctions against the people, the tax collectors, and soldiers; and
5) the lack in Mark and Matthew of Luke's addition that John continued to "preach good news" and of his subsequent imprisonment by Herod (Luke 3.18–20).

One could argue that in each of these instances Mark preferred the Matthean version to the Lukan, but what rationale is there for preferring the shorter Isaianic quote from Matthew over Luke's longer citation and then prefacing the quote with words from Malachi and identifying them as Isaianic? It is clear that Luke's different manner of introducing John, "the word of God came to John the son of Zechariah," is in accord with the infancy narratives in that gospel and that Mark, if he used both Matthew and Luke, has totally ignored these narratives in both gospels. But it is not so clear why he would do so.

The very title, "John the baptizer," in Mark is a more primitive form of address than either Matthew's, "John the Baptist," or Luke's, "John the son of Zechariah." Matthew uses the title, "John the Baptist," in seven passages (Matthew 3.1; 11.11, 12; 14.2, 8; 16.14; 17.13). Mark uses "the baptizer"

The Composition of the Gospels

in another Matthean parallel (Mark 6.14), omits the reference in the parallel to Matthew 17.13, but agrees with Matthew's "the Baptist" in two other parallel passages (Mark 6.25; 8.28), although Codex L retains "the baptizer" at Mark 6.25 and two cursives, 28 and 565, retain it at Mark 8.28.

This raises the question, Did the process of harmonization influence Mark 6.25 and 8.28 at an early time in the copying of the text, since the title "the Baptist" was the more accepted norm? The first usage, Mark 6.25, is in the account of the beheading of John where "the baptizer" has already been used (Mark 6.14) and the second (8.28) in the well-known and probably oft quoted passage, the response to Jesus' question, "Who do men say that I am?" It is interesting to note that the usage in Mark 6.14 has also been changed to "the Baptist" in a number of manuscripts, including the fifth century Codex W, the sixth century Codex D, the ninth century Codex Theta, and several cursive manuscripts, although no manuscript changes the reading in the initial occurrence of that title (Mark 1.4). Luke prefers to read only the proper name "John" in three passages parallel to Matthew (Matthew 11.11–Luke 7.28; Matthew 11.12–Luke 16.16; Matthew 14.2–Luke 9.7; note that Mark has "the baptizer" 6.14 for this parallel). Luke has no parallel passage for Matthew 14.8 or 17.13, although he uses the title in agreement with Matthew (Matthew 16.14–Luke 9.19), and again where there is no parallel in Matthew (Luke 7.20), and again at 7.33 where Matthew has only the proper name (Matthew 11.18). If the title, "the baptizer," is the more primitive, which seems to be a reasonable assumption on the basis of the evidence that Mark alone uses this title and that "the Baptist" is never edited in any of our manuscripts to read "the baptizer," then this supports the view that Mark is the earlier of the gospels, although not necessarily the conclusion that Matthew and Luke used Mark as a source. But it is prima facie evidence supporting the latter proposition, if we can demonstrate successfully on the basis of the cumulative evidence that this proposition is also true.

The agreement of Mark and Matthew against Luke by including a description of the dress and diet of John can be explained in the light of Luke's general abbreviation of the role of John and of his need to focus upon the truly significant traditions rather than the adiaphorous. Luke does have references to the expected appearance of the prophet Elijah (Luke 9.8, 19), but he does not equate the person of John with the Elijah who is to appear in the manner of Matthew and Mark. Matthew makes this equation specifically in his commentary upon the transfiguration: "The disciples asked him, 'Then why do the scribes say that first Elijah must come?' He replied, 'Elijah does come, and he is to restore all things; but I tell you that Elijah has already come, and they did not know him, but did to him whatever they pleased So also the son of man will suffer at their hands.' Then the disciples understood that he was speaking to them of John the Baptist" (Matthew 17.10–13). Mark says all of the above without the final specific equation (Mark 9.11–13). Therefore it is appropriate for these two writers to include the description of dress and diet, since these are in the pattern of the Elijah who appeared in history in the time of King Ahab of Israel (1 Kings 17–21; 2 Kings 1–2). We note especially that he dwelt in the wilderness (1 Kings 17.3; 19.4) and his dress was "a garment of haircloth, with a girdle of leather about his loins" (2 Kings 1.8). Luke does not need this description, since he does not make this specific identification. The analysis of the descriptive material in Matthew and Mark suggests again that Matthew has improved upon Mark's earlier and more primitive account in a number of ways: first, by replacing Mark's repetitive "and" throughout with a more literary particle as a connector between clauses or with "then," a correlative adverb of time, and by reformulating Mark's "was clothed with camel's hair" to "wore a garment of camel's hair" and Mark's "ate locusts" to "his food was locusts."

The lack of the injunctions to people, tax collectors, and soldiers in Matthew is readily explained, if his were the earliest gospel and the source for Luke and Mark. It is not so readily evident, if Mark used both Matthew and Luke as sources. In fact, as we have seen above, Mark has omitted most of the teaching material of John according to the theory that he used the other two evangelists as sources. The same would apply to the omission of the information that John continued to "preach good news" as in Luke 3.18 and the position of the imprisonment of John at this place in the gospel account (Luke 3.19–20). This is one of those variations in order where the most defensible conclusion is that Luke has moved the imprisonment pericope to an earlier position in his account for theological reasons and Matthew has followed Mark's order.

Minor Agreements of Mark and Luke against Matthew

The agreements between Mark and Luke against Matthew are more numerous:

1) Mark—Luke's second aorist indicative (past time) form of the verb "to become, come to be" for Matthew's compound form of the verb with a prepositional prefix in the present indicative meaning "to come, arrive, be present" (Mark 1.4; Luke 3.2; Matthew 3.1);
2) Mark—Luke's "baptism of repentance for the forgiveness of sins" versus Matthew's, "Repent, for the kingdom of heaven is at hand" (Mark 1.4; Luke 3.3; Matthew 3.2);
3) Mark—Luke's "it is written" for Matthew's "who was spoken of" (Mark 1.2; Luke 3.4; Matthew 3.3);
4) Mark—Luke lack Matthew's "when he said" before the Isaianic quotation (Matthew 3.3);
5) Mark—Luke's present indicative active "he comes" for Matthew's present participle of the same verb and the present indicative of the verb "to be" (Mark 1.7; Luke 3.16; Matthew 3.11);
6) Mark—Luke's use of the definite article before the comparative form of the adjective, "mightier" (Mark 1.7; Luke 3.16; Matthew 3.11);
7) Mark—Luke's "the thong of whose sandals I am not worthy to untie" against Matthew's "whose sandals I am not worthy to carry"; and
8) the lack in Mark—Luke of Matthew's "for repentance" (Mark 1.8; Luke 3.16; Matthew 3.11).

A number of these differences are only semantic. The first one, however, reflects the choice of a compound form of the verb that more aptly describes the event of John's coming than the simple form of the verb in Mark. Luke saw no need to change, whereas Matthew came up with a better idea. Would both Luke and Mark opt for the less expressive word if they had found it in their exemplar? The second represents a difference of some magnitude: Mark—Luke's "a baptism of repentance for the forgiveness of sins" against Matthew's "Repent, for the kingdom of heaven is at hand." Matthew's reading at this point is suspect because he has Jesus announce precisely the same theme for the opening of his ministry (Matthew 4.17) and for the disciples who are sent out to proclaim the same message without the "repent" (Matthew 10.7). Mark does report that Jesus' initial message is, "The time is fulfilled, and the kingdom of God is at hand; repent, and believe in the gospel" (Mark 1.15), which Matthew has abbreviated and stereotyped for the messages of John, Jesus, and the disciples. And Mark actually concludes Jesus' instructions to the twelve by summarizing their ministry in the words, "they went out and preached that men should repent" (Mark 6.12). So Mark alone has consistently maintained that repentance was the theme of the three ministries, but each in a different form of expression. The question is, Did Mark edit Matthew in two of these contexts and prefer Luke's version for the third, or did Matthew edit Mark for all three?

The expression, "kingdom of heaven," is also vintage Matthew, a phrasing never found in Mark and Luke. The latter always read "kingdom of God," whereas the author of Matthew consistently used "kingdom of heaven" with only one exception in all those passages where there are parallels in the three gospels (Matthew 19.24) and always with only one exception where there are parallels in Matthew and Luke (Matthew 12.28). In addition, there are two passages unique to Matthew where "kingdom of God" is used (Matthew 21.31, 34). It should be noted that the cursive family of manuscripts, family one, reads "kingdom of heaven" at Matthew 19.24, which possibly suggests a careless scribe who was so accustomed to copying "kingdom of heaven" that he did not note the exception in this passage and the error was perpetuated by those who copied from his manuscript. In addition, there are two other cursive manuscripts that have made this same error in transcription. It is difficult to explain why Luke would have changed Matthew's phrase so radically and why Mark would have preferred Luke's version over Matthew's. And, since Luke does not cite the words of the theme for Jesus' initial mission, Mark would have been responsible for changing Matthew's "kingdom of heaven" to "kingdom of God" (Mark 1.15; Matthew 4.17). But the consistent use of "kingdom of God" by Mark and Luke's consistent agreement suggests strongly that neither writer was using Matthew as his exemplar and that Matthew has changed the expression to accord with the Jewish practice of using a circumlocution for the divine name. The occasional lapses in Matthew, the four passages cited above, are consistent with the view that the expression "kingdom of God" was in his exemplar or in the oral tradition that he used as source material and that he simply overlooked making the change in these four passages.

The agreement between Mark and Luke against Matthew in the use of the definite article before "mightier" is only apparent, since Matthew has already used the definite article with the present participle of the verb "to come," the entire phrase "he who is coming after me" being the subject of the verb "to be" and the phrase, "mightier than I," being a predicate nominative. Mark and Luke, in fact, use the definite article before "mightier" because they have the finite form of the verb, the subject of which is "he who is mightier than I." The other agreements in the saying pertaining to the coming one have been discussed sufficiently in the previous section on the minor agreements between Matthew and Luke against Mark, so there remains only the phrase, "for repentance," (Matthew 3.11) that is lacking in Mark 1.8 and Luke 3.16. Initially, this looks very much like an example of the author of Matthew, who having inserted a form statement for the message of John with the imperative, "Repent", now transfers Mark's "baptism for repentance" from this location in the pericope to the message of the Baptist pertaining to the coming one, "I baptize for repentance, but he." This in all probability is the solution to the problem.

The case for the minor agreements as a support for the thesis that Luke used Matthew as a source and that Mark subsequently used both Matthew and Luke as sources in composing his gospel is certainly ambiguous and at most a very fragile reed upon which to lean so great a weight. The very intensive examination of the Mark—Matthew agreements against Luke and the Mark—Luke agreements against Matthew demonstrate that these are equally valid areas of consideration in the formulation of a conclusion as to which gospel was the exemplar for the others.

Conclusions

The examination and discussion have laid bare in a new way how complicated is the problem and how difficult to arrive at a decisive solution. The decision will not rest upon one aspect of a many-faceted problem, such as the minor agreements of Matthew and Luke against Mark, but only upon the cumulative evidence as it is amassed from an investigation of every aspect of the problem. This should include a comparative study of the historical development of religions and what light this information sheds upon the development of the Jesus' tradition as reflected in our gospels, the sequence of pericopes, the agreement and disagreement of subject materials, the grammatical and literary differences, and especially the examination of individual passages to determine, if possible, which represents an earlier version and which a revision.

The conclusion of this writer based upon the cumulative evidence assembled in this investigation is that there are only two possibilities to explain the order for the composition of the gospels: Mark was the exemplar for the authors of Matthew and Luke or each of the gospels is an independent composition formulated by the authors out of oral traditions and early written sources that have since disappeared. Though there are unsolved problems for either of these possibilities, there are fewer problems for the first alternative than for the second. The conclusion of this writer is that the priority of Mark and its use by the authors of Matthew and Luke in the composition of their gospels is the most viable thesis. The weight of the evidence set forth as objectively as possible in this essay favors Markan priority. This is not to say that the authors of Matthew and Luke were not creative. The differences that have been pointed up in the very minute comparison of every word and phrase attest the high quality of their creativity.

Each writer came to his task with an agenda and with presuppositions and these are reflected in every word difference, in every inflection of meaning represented by such a simple change as the reversal in order of two or three words, in the omission of a word or a whole section of words, in the addition of a word or of many words, and in the positioning of materials at different locations in the whole. Each writer wrote at a different time and place and at a different stage of development in the community's faith and life. Each of these has made its impact upon the final result and account in many instances for the differences that are found from gospel to gospel. The conclusion that Mark was the earliest gospel and that the authors of Matthew and Luke used Mark as a source is a working hypothesis that perhaps can never be conclusively proved. As a working hypothesis, however, it goes far to explain many of the differences that have been identified and can only be superseded with the finding of new information that is not presently available.

The value of this investigation by and for the author is that the very close comparative study of even the most minute differences among the three gospels has proven to be of the highest importance. Too often we are guilty of the harmonization of the three accounts of the life and ministry of Jesus, his deeds and his words, because we have ignored what seem to be very minor differences. In essence, the acute and careful consideration of these seemingly minor differences is crucial for our understanding of the text and for our exegesis of it. To ignore these small differences results in eisegesis, our reading into the text(s) what we want to find there. For each one of us brings a great load of baggage to our reading and interpretation of the text. It is most difficult to be objective, to let the text(s) speak to us. It is so easy for us to speak to the text, to read into it what we want it to say. This is the fundamental consequence of Biblical illiteracy—to depend upon our security blanket rather than upon the hard work, the perspiration that can alone lead to inspiration. In my experience, inspiration has never come apart from the heavy lifting that stretches and expands the muscles of our mind and of our spirit. God breathes into a lump of clay and that clod comes to life, a living being. This is the beginning, for the Lord God would have that living being grow in mind and spirit inch by inch and day by day through a lifetime of devoted effort to become a fully grown man or a fully grown woman in Christ. This does not come about by chance, but only through diligent and tireless effort under the guidance and tutelage of Word and Spirit. These words are intended as a challenge, for only as we probe the depths of the Word will the treasures of its thought and of its deep meaning be grafted into our being, so that we become transparent, more like Christ our Lord in thought, word, and deed, more a fulfillment of the intention of God who created each one of us in his image.

www.ingramcontent.com/pod-product-compliance
Lightning Source LLC
Chambersburg PA
CBHW051738230426
43670CB00012B/2068